CRIME WAVE

Crime Wave

The American Homicide Epidemic

James Tuttle

NEW YORK UNIVERSITY PRESS
New York

NEW YORK UNIVERSITY PRESS
New York
www.nyupress.org

© 2025 by New York University
All rights reserved

References to Internet websites (URLs) were accurate at the time of writing. Neither the author nor New York University Press is responsible for URLs that may have expired or changed since the manuscript was prepared.

Please contact the Library of Congress for Cataloging-in-Publication data.

ISBN: 9781479831111 (hardback)
ISBN: 9781479831159 (paperback)
ISBN: 9781479831173 (library ebook)
ISBN: 9781479831166 (consumer ebook)

New York University Press books are printed on acid-free paper, and their binding materials are chosen for strength and durability. We strive to use environmentally responsible suppliers and materials to the greatest extent possible in publishing our books.

The manufacturer's authorized representative in the EU for product safety is Mare Nostrum Group B.V., Mauritskade 21D, 1091 GC Amsterdam, The Netherlands. Email: gpsr@mare-nostrum.co.uk.

Manufactured in the United States of America

10 9 8 7 6 5 4 3 2 1

Also available as an ebook

To Abigail, in hope for a better future

CONTENTS

Preface: The Homicide Epidemic	ix
1. Crime Wave: Contextualizing the Alarming 2015–2021 Homicide Increase	1
2. The Limited Impact of "De-policing": An Examination of the Evidence	21
3. Getting Drunk: American Malaise, Part I	44
4. Using Drugs: American Malaise, Part II	60
5. Buying a Gun: The Legitimacy Crisis, Part I	78
6. Protesting the Police: The Legitimacy Crisis, Part II	99
7. Alcohol, Drugs, and Guns: An Analysis of State-Level Crime Trends, 2010–2021	119
8. Protests, Policing, and Crime: A City-Level Examination of 2020	135
Conclusion: Attempting to Predict Future Crime Trends	157
Acknowledgments	173
Notes	175
References	183
Index	203
About the Author	209

PREFACE

The Homicide Epidemic

The subject of this book is the unexpected and unprecedented homicide rate increase spanning from 2015 to 2021. The recent increase in the homicide rate was unexpected because of the declining trend prior to 2015. Since the "Great American Crime Decline" of the 1990s (Zimring 2007), the rate of violent crime in the United States had been low, steady, and falling. The homicide spike in 2015 and especially in 2020 upended this pattern. The increase in homicide is also unprecedented, as it was *not* accompanied by a general increase in criminal offending, contrary to previous historical periods when homicide rates increased. The overall crime rate, as reported to the Federal Bureau of Investigation (FBI), has actually declined since 2015, and yet the homicide rate of 2021 was the highest in more than two decades.

This increase in homicide, or the "homicide epidemic" as I call it, presumes a baseline. From 2010 through 2014, the homicide rate was near historical lows; for five consecutive years, there were 4.8 homicides per 100,000 population or fewer in the United States. This is not impressive compared to our western European counterparts but historically rare in the US context. Prior to the early 2010s, the last time the homicide rate was 4.8 per 100,000 or less for five consecutive years was between 1954 and 1958; homicide victimization was briefly at its lowest point in nearly sixty years prior to the recent trend reversal. However, by 2020 and 2021, homicide rates in several cities and states more closely resembled those of the mid-1990s than the mid-1950s.

As I argue this in this book, the reason for this historical reversal in the homicide trend is due to different manifestations of American decline.

American decline is twofold, involving both the decline in psychosocial well-being *and* the deteriorating strength of and trust in its institutions. There are numerous indicators of this decline, but the most important in the discussion of trends in the homicide rate are the increasing use of drugs and alcohol, an increasing number of firearm purchases, and distrust/protests of the police. As outlined in the middle portion of this book (chapters 3 through 6), each of these markers of decline has contributed to an unprecedented spike in homicide.

One underlying premise of this book is that the pandemic year of 2020, while abnormal, did not represent a departure from prevailing trends in the United States. In 2020, firearm purchases spiked; yet the increase in firearm purchases spans at least a decade, partially as a response to the long-term decline in trust of the government and major social institutions. In 2020, a record number of Americans (to that point) lost their lives to drug abuse and addiction; yet the opioid epidemic spans back to at least the early 2000s and had previously featured a troubling increase in overdoses caused by illicit drugs (fentanyl) prior to the pandemic. Alcohol consumption spiked in 2020; yet alcohol consumption has been trending upward for more than a decade. Protests against police brutality in 2020 reflected the largest such movement since the civil rights era of the 1960s; yet Black Lives Matter had formed as a response to police brutality nearly a decade earlier. Increases in the prevalence of guns, drugs, alcohol, and distrust in the police and government all accelerated in 2020, but these trends were not a departure from an ongoing twenty-first-century American decline.

To be clear, I am not predicting that homicide trends will continue to increase in lockstep with American decline. The years 2015–2021 mark a period of great tumult, punctuated by a pandemic that accelerated several disturbing trends in mental health, substance abuse, and distrust of institutions. Some of the most criminogenic manifestations of societal decline have already shown signs of decelerating, at least for now. Additionally, there are various countervailing forces, such as declines in property-motivated offenses and youthful offending, which make a sustained increase in the homicide rate less likely. It is very possible that American decline will continue into the near future, but homicide trends will not continue to rise.

The initial 2022 crime data provide evidence that that homicide rate peaked in 2021. This, along with the limited data availability for more recent years, motivated me to feature 2021 as the final year within the analyses (chapter 7). However, by the definition of "epidemic" that I outline in chapter 1, 2021 does not mark the end of the homicide epidemic. For that to happen, we would need to return to our baseline rate of homicide offending established during the early 2010s. In all likelihood, although with less certainty, the homicide rate will decline in the near future. An unanswered question, however, is whether we will return to the 2010–2014 baseline in homicide victimization. It is only then that we could claim that the homicide epidemic has ended.

1

Crime Wave

Contextualizing the Alarming 2015–2021 Homicide Increase

But perhaps some problems would have been easier to address had not the social structure appeared to collapse.
—James Q. Wilson, discussing the 1960s crime increase in *Thinking about Crime*

During the past few years, the United States has experienced a crime wave. There is a growing perception that crime has spread across the country and is worse than at any time in recent memory. This perception of increasing crime is akin to that generated by a natural disaster, like a tidal wave flooding across the country. The popular imagination of the crime wave has not been that of individual offenses committed by specific perpetrators with idiosyncratic motivations but a collective experience of crime victimization wreaking havoc on society. Recent news headlines have been filled with stories of violence, disorder, and wanton disregard of the law. Shoplifting is rumored to be so severe in some cities that retail chains have closed in frequently targeted areas. There is a general perception that criminals have been emboldened due to police reticence to enforce the law, prevented from doing so by out-of-touch politicians and overzealous activists. Crime victimization is once again a major concern of Americans; there is an intense apprehension that crime is "out of control" and could possibly even make its way into a neighborhood near you.

As the fear of crime enters our collective consciousness, objective crime trends become a secondary consideration. Although the term "crime wave" is sometimes used to denote an increase in the rate of crime, the mere perception of a crime increase makes it "real" in its effect. As Mark Fishman (1978, 531) writes of a media-perpetuated crime wave against the elderly in New York City during the 1970s, "When we speak of a crime wave, we are talking about a kind of social awareness of crime, crime brought to public consciousness. It is something to be remarked upon at the corner grocery store, complained about in a community meeting, and denounced at the mayor's press conference. One cannot be mugged by a crime wave, but one can be scared." There is no objective standard to determine whether crime rates are too high (they always are) or have increased by too much (they always have). The collective experience of crime being "out of control" is sufficient to define any increase in crime as a "crime wave," no matter how little crime rates have actually increased, if at all (Sacco 2005).

However, there is some "real" substance to the recent crime wave: beginning in 2015, there was an abrupt increase in the rate of violent and deadly assaults. After hitting the lowest rate of homicide in more than fifty years in 2014 (4.4 homicides per 100,000 population), the homicide rate had increased by nearly 55 percent by the end of 2021 (6.8 per 100,000), according to FBI (2022) estimates. In some cities, this increase has produced record-setting statistics. St. Louis became the "murder capital" of the United States in 2020, posting a total number of homicides (263) not experienced in the city since the early 1990s and the highest homicide rate ever recorded, given the city's population decline over recent decades. Milwaukee and Memphis experienced more homicides in 2020 and 2021 than during any previous year on record, even exceeding marks set during the crime-plagued 1980s and 1990s (FBI 2022). News reports suggest that more than a dozen cities have set new records for homicide victimization, including Albuquerque, Austin, Baton Rouge, Columbus, Indianapolis, Louisville, Philadelphia, Portland, Rochester, St. Paul, Toledo, and Tucson (Hutchinson 2021).

The collective perception of a crime wave seems to have been partially spurred on by a very real *homicide epidemic*. Borrowing the term from epidemiology, an "epidemic" refers to a growing incidence of infectious disease, increasing above its expected or baseline rate. In retrospect, the baseline rate of homicide victimization established in 2013 and 2014 has been exceeded during every subsequent year, spanning to at least 2021. Accordingly, I use the term "homicide epidemic" to refer to the elevated rates of homicide from 2015 to 2021, which have exceeded the 2014 baseline. Initially, there was some disagreement about whether the increase in homicide in 2015 and 2016 was "abnormal," in the sense that homicide trends fluctuate within a certain range each year (McDowall 2019; Yim, Riddell, and Wheeler 2020). However, by 2021, it was clear that the national homicide rate had reversed its previous declining trend and that we were in the midst of an epidemic of violent assault.

The increase in homicide constitutes a homicide epidemic; this epidemic, alongside sensationalized media reports of retail theft, has provided the substance for public perception of a crime wave. Therefore, there has been both a *crime wave*, existing in the collective consciousness of the public, and also a *homicide epidemic*, represented in homicide offending and mortality statistics. This book focuses on the latter, as I attempt to explain the sudden and unexpected increase in the homicide rate.

The Homicide Epidemic

To date, the 2015 and 2016 increase in the homicide rate has been examined separately from that of 2020 and 2021. The 2015 and 2016 crime patterns were extensively covered by the media, discussed during the 2016 presidential debates, and studied by researchers as an anomaly given the general decline in crime since the early 1990s (Rosenfeld and Fox 2019). The homicide trend in 2017 and 2018 subsequently lost the public's attention, despite the fact that both years posted a higher rate of homicide than 2015. Homicide trends were then thrust back into the public consciousness due to their rapid incline in 2020 and 2021, with record-breaking rates recorded in several cities across the country. Yet very few (e.g., Wade 2023) have connected these time periods; there is currently no comprehensive explanation of the overall increase in homicide from 2015 onward.

As I outline in this chapter, there is continuity between these two periods (2015–2016 and 2020–2021); these were not two completely separate or distinct eras of increasing violence but part of a singular crime trend. The continuities linking 2015 through 2021 include the divergence of violent and property-motivated crime patterns, a shifting geography of homicide toward the interior of the country/Midwest, and an initial attribution of crime trends to police brutality, protests, and a subsequent lack of proactive policing.

Divergence of Homicide from Other Crime Trends

The first continuity linking the two eras of rapid increase in homicide rates (2015–2016 and 2020–2021) is the continued divergence of violent and property-motivated offending trends. Recent crime patterns are unique in that the reversal in the homicide trend is almost exclusively limited to violent offenses and, specifically, homicide and aggravated assault. Figure 1.1 depicts the percentage change in the homicide, aggravated assault, robbery, and burglary rates from 2010 to 2021 (centered at 0 percent in 2014) using national crime data derived from the FBI's (2022) Crime Data Explorer. From 2010 to 2014, all four types of criminal offenses were declining. From 2015 through 2021, the homicide trend began to diverge from other criminal offenses. The homicide rate increased by nearly 55 percent from 2014 to 2021, and aggravated assault also increased during this period (18.8 percent). Conversely, the burglary rate continued to decline and was significantly lower in 2021 (49.6 percent) than in 2014. Robbery, although a violent offense, is a property-motivated crime that also declined dramatically during this period (35.3 percent), although not to the same degree as burglary.

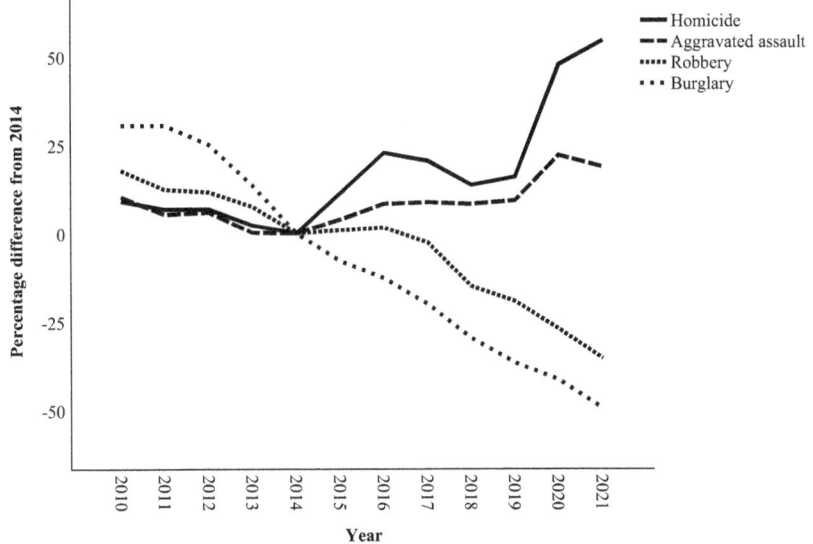

FIGURE 1.1. Percentage change in crime rates, 2010–2021

The divergence in these crime trends suggests that the United States has become much more violent and specifically more homicidal in recent years, but overall crime rates have either remained stable or even declined. This pattern is contrary to historical crime trends. In general, the contours of trends in burglary and homicide tend to mirror each other (Baumer, Vélez, and Rosenfeld 2018). During the largest crime wave of the twentieth century, which took place in the 1960s and 1970s, all types of criminal offenses increased almost simultaneously (Cohen and Felson 1979; J. Wilson 1975). Then, during the homicide decline of the 1990s, there was also a nearly simultaneous decline of all types of criminal offenses (Zimring 2007). Unlike these historical crime patterns, the recent trends in burglary and homicide could not have been more different.

In addition to suggesting that these periods (2015–2016 and 2020–2021) are a continuation of the same crime trend, the diverging patterns in violent and property-based crime imply an offense-specific origin of the homicide epidemic. Perspectives that hypothesize that the increase in homicide is indicative of a general increase in criminality are, at the very least, partially incorrect, as the overall crime rate has declined since 2014. The violent assaults represented by homicide and aggravated assault statistics seem to be driven a different set of factors than trends in robbery and burglary. Accordingly, attempts to explain recent crime trends should focus on why people are suddenly more prone to perpetrating violent assaults but not more likely to commit property-based offenses.

The Shifting Geography of Homicide Offending

A second source of continuity between 2015–2016 and 2020–2021 is that homicide victimization shifted toward the interior of the country. In the aggregate, it is true that the homicide rate has not returned to its early-1990s peak. The overall homicide rate in 2021 (6.8 per 100,000) would have needed to increase by an additional 44 percent to match that of 1991 (9.8 per 100,000). However, the aggregate picture obscures trajectories within specific regions of the country. For many cities and states, the homicide rate in 2020 and 2021 was higher than it was during the 1990s; for some, the recorded homicide rate had never been higher. Additionally, many of the same locations that experienced the most pronounced homicide increase during the 2015–2016 era also experienced the largest in 2020–2021.

Over the past decade, the most dramatic increase in violent crime has taken place in the nation's heartland. Despite the increase in homicide impacting most of the country, the surge in violence has been relatively modest in many major cities and populous states that were among the most violent in the nation during the 1990s. For example, the 468 homicides recorded in New York City in 2020 are 79 percent fewer than the highest number of homicides (2,245) recorded in the city in a single year (1990), despite a larger population size (FBI 2022). Unlike New York City (and New York State, for that matter), some parts of the country have experienced a level of violence not seen in decades, if ever before. Table 1.1 ranks US states by the degree to which they exceed their highest

TABLE 1.1. States with a 2020–2021 Homicide Rate as High as during the 1990s

State	Highest 1990s homicide rate	Homicide rate in 2020–2021	% difference
North Dakota	2.2 (1996)	4.2 (2020)	+91
Delaware	5.4 (1991)	9.7 (2021)	+80
Iowa	2.3 (1993)	3.5 (2020)	+52
South Dakota	3.4 (1993)	4.5 (2020)	+32
Pennsylvania	6.8 (1993)	8.4 (2021)	+24
Wisconsin	4.8 (1991)	5.6 (2021)	+17
Kentucky	7.2 (1995)	8.3 (2021)	+15
New Mexico	11.5 (1996)	12.9 (2021)	+12
Missouri	11.3 (1993)	11.8 (2020)	+4
Ohio	7.2 (1991)	7.5 (2021)	+4
Montana	4.9 (1990)	5.0 (2020)	+2
South Carolina	11.3 (1991)	11.4 (2021)	+1
Colorado	6.2 (1992)	6.2 (2021)	Same

1990s homicide rate. As depicted in table 1.1, the homicide rate (per one hundred thousand population) recorded in 2020 or 2021 in twelve states exceeded all annual homicide rates recorded during the 1990s (North Dakota, Delaware, Iowa, South Dakota, Pennsylvania, Wisconsin, Kentucky, New Mexico, Missouri, Ohio, Montana, and South Carolina). In one additional state, Colorado, the 2021 homicide rate matched the previous 1990s high, last recorded in 1992.

The shift in violence toward the Midwest is also apparent in overall regional statistics. Figure 1.2 depicts homicide deaths rates (per one hundred thousand population) reported by the Centers for Disease Control (CDC Wonder 2023), split by region to compare the Midwest to the rest of the country. As illustrated in figure 1.2, the Midwest has transformed from the least homicidal region in the country during the early 1990s to exceeding the mean homicide rate for the rest of the United States during the late 2010s. The beginning of the homicide epidemic (2015) was the first year in which the midwestern homicide rate exceeded the average for the non-Midwest. What is also remarkable is that the 2021

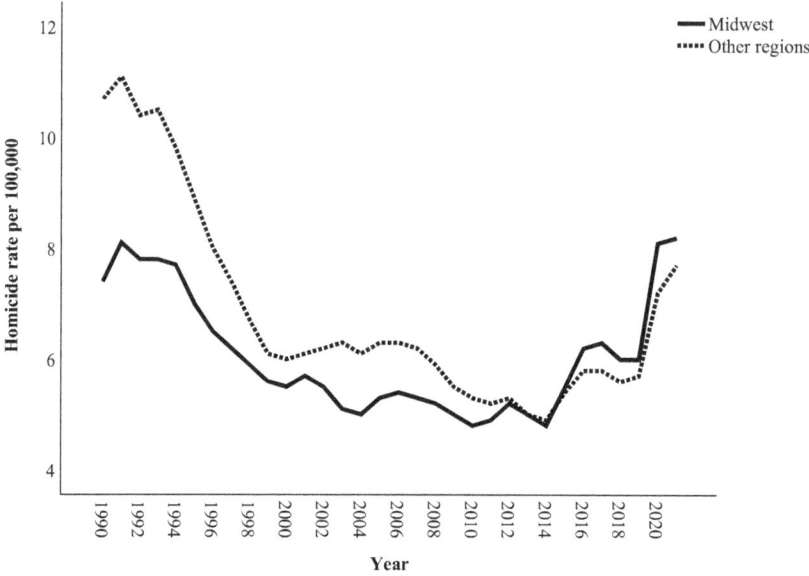

FIGURE 1.2. Regional trends in the homicide rate, 1990–2021

homicide rate in the Midwest (8.2 per 100,000) exceeds all homicide rates recorded in the region during the 1990s, second only to its rate in 1980 (8.3 per 100,000). It should be noted that the South still had a higher homicide rate than the Midwest in 2021 (9.9 homicides per 100,000), but this figure is nowhere near the highest rates recorded in the South during the 1990s (13.1 per 100,000 in 1991).

Overall, it is apparent that homicide offending has shifted geographically. While most of the United States has experienced an increase in homicide since 2014, the proportional increase in the Midwest was nearly 24 percent greater than the rest of the country, including a larger increase from 2014 to 2016 (29.2 percent versus 18.4 percent) and from 2019 to 2021 (36.7 percent versus 35.1 percent), according to CDC Wonder (2023) homicide mortality data. The geographical shift in homicide toward the interior of the country broadly and the Midwest specifically provides some insight into the origins of the homicide epidemic. Trends that have been more pronounced in the Midwest, including the increase in alcohol abuse and drug overdose deaths (see chapters 3 and 4), are a potential clue for understanding the dramatic increase in violence within this region.

Attribution of Crime to Protests and Policing

The third continuity between the two periods of rapidly increasing homicide rates (2015–2016 and 2020–2021) is their concurrence with high-profile acts of alleged police brutality that energized a protest movement. On August 9, 2014, Michael Brown, a teenager living in a suburb of St. Louis called Ferguson, was shot and killed by a police officer. The exact timeline of events that led to Brown's tragic death is still somewhat in dispute, but the general narrative is that Brown was confronted by police officer Darren Wilson as Brown was walking in the street. This confrontation escalated to a brief struggle for Wilson's gun, an attempt to flee, and then a second confrontation in which Brown was eventually shot and killed by Wilson in what the officer claimed to be an act of self-defense. A grand jury would later validate this claim, as it declined to indict Wilson for killing Brown (US Department of Justice 2015). The public reaction to the failure to indict the officer was swift and severe. Nationwide protests indicted the entire criminal justice system as racially biased due to the implications of a White police officer shooting and killing an unarmed Black teenager and not facing any legal consequences.

Some observers, particularly those who were critical of the protests against police brutality, quickly attributed the increase in homicide in 2015 to a "war on cops." This perspective, popularized by Heather Mac Donald (2016), advances the argument that the protests against police brutality in the wake of the killing of Michael Brown made police officers reticent to proactively patrol US cities. Instead of conducting stops, searching suspects, making arrests, and showing a strong presence to deter crime, the police retreated in the fear that citizens would protest their actions. Mac Donald's framing suggested that if people would stop protesting police and just let the police enforce the law, everyone would be safer.

Similarly, protests erupted in 2020 after the murder of an unarmed Black man by a White police officer in a midwestern city. On May 25, 2020, George Floyd purchased a pack of cigarettes at a convenience store in Minneapolis with what appeared to be a counterfeit twenty-dollar bill. An employee at the store called the police, who later arrived on the scene and attempted to take Floyd into custody. After Floyd was handcuffed, he resisted being placed in the back of a patrol car, claiming to be claustrophobic. Derek Chauvin, one of the four officers making the arrest, proceeded to kneel on the back of Floyd's neck for nearly nine minutes. Despite Floyd's pleas that he could not breathe, Chauvin continued to kneel on Floyd until he was unresponsive. Floyd was later pronounced dead, murdered by Chauvin in broad daylight and caught on cell-phone video. The excruciating video quickly spread around the world. Protests in Minneapolis began the next day, when the video was shared online. By the time Chauvin was charged with Floyd's murder four days later, protests were taking place nationwide (Hill et al. 2020). The 2020 protests were even more widespread and sustained than those of 2014 and 2015, with several protests escalating to riots that sometimes featured violent clashes between demonstrators and police.

In 2020, widespread protests also corresponded with a sudden decline in arrests made by the police. In this case, the protesters went beyond demanding reform, often calling for "defunding the police." Some commentators, often aligned against the goals of the protestors, have attempted to link the 2020 and 2021 homicide patterns with the protest movement and the call for defunding of the police. However, very few cities actually enacted any version of a "defunding" policy (Friedman and Youngblood 2022). What is true is that there was a pattern of reduced arrests that occurred immediately after the protests began in 2020, repeating the pattern noted in 2014–2015. This apparent correlation has caused some observers to attribute the increase in homicide rates to a lack of policing (Cassell 2020). In both 2015 and 2020, much of the broader public attributed the increase in violent crime to a decrease in police proactivity, or "de-policing."

As we will see in chapter 2, the actual timeline of the increase in homicide in 2020 may not have comported with the onset of protests or decline in police proactivity. There is probably some role that discontent with the police and witnessing police brutality played, which I discuss more extensively in chapters 6 and 8. However, the popular narrative that a "lack" of policing is the primary cause of the homicide epidemic is false; de-policing has played a secondary role in shaping recent crime trends (see chapter 2). Put another way, a lack of trust in the police and de-policing both possibly contributed to recent homicide trends, but they have played an outsized role in the public's imagination of the crime wave.

Each of these similarities and continuities between 2015–2016 and 2020–2021 suggest that this entire period is part of the same crime trend. Trends in property-motivated offenses and violent offenses continued to diverge; the geography of homicide continued to shift toward the Midwest; alleged incidents of police brutality and protests have contributed to an intense preoccupation with the role of policing on crime trends. While it is potentially valuable to examine the unique characteristics of these two periods (2015–2016 and 2020–2021) separately, it also obscures the broader trends in crime. Accordingly, throughout this book, I refer to and analyze this period as a singular "homicide epidemic" and not two distinctive periods in which homicide trends were increasing. Before attempting to explain the contributing factors of the homicide epidemic in further detail, I must first address some of the difficulties in making definitive predictions (and conclusions) about the direction of recent crime trends.

Defying Criminological Gravity

Crime trends are difficult, if not impossible, to predict with much precision. Unlike economic trends, in which businesses and customers alike will make most of their intentions known, criminals tend to keep their plans concerning upcoming crimes a secret; criminals rarely share their projections for crimes committed during the next fiscal quarter. Additionally, even if criminals were willing to provide a list of their upcoming offenses, this only helps us to predict the crimes that they plan ahead of time. Criminals are often impulsive (Gottfredson and Hirschi 1990) and may not be able to anticipate their future offenses. Some criminal offenses occur in the "heat of the moment," which no one planned. Crime is also shaped by opportunity (Felson and Clark 1998), which causes the intention to commit a crime to be somewhat decoupled from actually having the ability to perpetrate an offense. This leaves the criminologist at a considerable disadvantage to the economist in projecting trends in their respective fields.

To compensate for these limitations, the study of crime trends must use past events and prior research to inform predictions about the future. Richard Rosenfeld (2018) labels this as the "normal science" approach to crime trends research: using accumulated knowledge about the social conditions that correspond with variation in crime trends to understand increases (or decreases) in the crime rate. Typically, crime trends change relatively slowly over time. Since the 1990s, much of the research on crime trends had outlined why crime rates are low and falling. There are several factors that probably caused crime rates to decline during the past few decades, including the waning of the crack cocaine epidemic, improving economic conditions, more security measures in homes/cars, and an aging population (Farrell, Tilley, and Tseloni 2014; Zimring 2007). Over time, researchers can trace different factors and examine whether they correspond with trends in crime.

However, recent homicide trends have defied many of their previously established predictors. Some factors that usually serve as a harbinger of a crime wave did not assist in predicting the current one. One such factor is economics. Economic trends, such as those capturing consumer inflation (Rosenfeld, Vogel, and McCuddy 2019) or consumer sentiment (Rosenfeld and Fornango 2007), are predictive of property-based offenses. When prices suddenly rise or economic conditions deteriorate for the average person, more people are expected to be motivated to illegally supplement their income or purchase items from underground markets. Economically motivated offenses, sometimes referred to as "acquisitive crimes" (Rosenfeld 2009), do not usually involve a murder, but a subset of robberies, burglaries, and motor-vehicle thefts contribute to homicides. Therefore, you can usually predict the general direction of homicide trends by examining economic conditions or, at the very least, trends in economically motivated criminal offenses (Rosenfeld 2009; Baumer, Vélez, and Rosenfeld 2018).

Yet there is little indication that these economic factors have played a direct role in shaping recent homicide trends. Consumer sentiment had remained fairly high throughout the late 2010s, until dropping precipitously in 2020 (Federal Reserve Bank of St. Louis 2024). While we might be tempted to see this as a major contributor to the historic increase in homicide during that year, it is doubtful given the corresponding decline in robbery, burglary, and larceny. Additionally, inflation remained near historical lows until mid-2021 (US Bureau of Labor Statistics 2024). Just as inflation began to rise in the United States, it appeared that the worst of the homicide epidemic had subsided, with FBI (2022) estimates depicting a decline in the homicide rate in 2022.

To illustrate the decoupling of these economic conditions and homicide trends, figure 1.3 examines the relative change in the homicide rate and the rate of acquisitive crime from 1990 to 2021. This graph is similar to figure 1.1 but on a longer time scale to illustrate this historical anomaly. To measure the acquisitive crime trend, I combine robbery, burglary, and motor-vehicle theft rates; these are the felony property-motivated offenses that are the most likely to contribute to a homicide according to the FBI's Supplementary Homicide Reports. The statistics presented in figure 1.3 are derived from the FBI's (2022) crime data explorer online tool. The lines in this figure represent the percentage of the 1990 crime rate for acquisitive crimes and homicide. The 1990 crime rate is set at 100 percent, with numbers less than 100 percent representing a lower crime rate throughout the proceeding years.

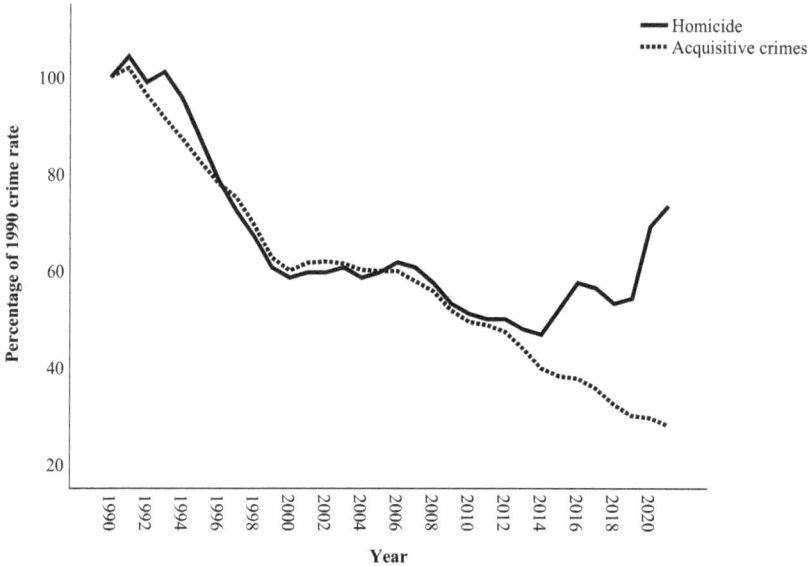

FIGURE 1.3. Crime rates as a percentage of the 1990 rate, 1990–2021

As is apparent in the comparison of these trends, the association between rates of acquisitive crime and homicide is typically extremely close. From 1990 to 2010, the trends in homicide and acquisitive crime are nearly identical. This is to be expected, as not only are a significant proportion of homicides the (usually unintended) result of theft, but criminal offending is believed to be multifaceted rather than offense-specific. Put another way, criminal offenders tend not to limit themselves to one type of crime but are versatile in the types of offenses they commit (Gottfredson and Hirschi 1990). A person who had previously burglarized houses is also more prone to commit a violent assault than is a person who has never committed a crime in the past. Therefore, when there are fewer criminal offenders in general, we should expect a decline in all types of crime, not a specific decline in property-based offenses. In the aggregate, this is why we refer to the 1990s as a period of "crime decline," not just a "homicide decline."

However, from about 2012 onward, the homicide trend begins to diverge from the trend in these "acquisitive" offenses. This divergence grew slowly at first, resulting only in a slightly slower descent of homicide in comparison to acquisitive crimes from 2012 to 2014. The spike in the homicide rate from 2014 to 2015 marked a distinct trajectory change and made the divergence even more apparent. Since 2014, the forces that seem to be pulling overall crime rates downward have not been sufficient to cause a decline in the homicide rate as well. If the homicide trend had not defied its historical pattern of following acquisitive crime trends, it would have been the lowest in recorded US history in 2021. Instead, it was the highest homicide rate recorded since 1997.

This defiance of historical precedents, especially those established during the 1990s, can be seen in other patterns. Notably, the spike in homicide occurred despite a general decline in youth offending. While simple demographic trends, such as those tracing the proportion of the population in peak offending ages (fifteen to twenty-four), do not always produce accurate forecasts of crime trends (e.g., Fox 1996), the rate of youth offending is usually important in understanding crime trends. This was especially true during the 1990s, in which youth offending and victimization were one of the apparent causes of both the overall increase and then the subsequent decline in violent crime rates (Fox and Zawitz 2007; O'Brien and Stockard 2009). Not only has youth offending declined dramatically since the early 1990s, but it has also continued to decline (Baumer, Cundiff, and Luo 2021). In fact, the burglary arrest rate among seventeen-year-old males has declined by 90 percent from 1985 to 2019 (Tuttle 2024). The low rate of youth offending today could not be more different from that of the 1990s, which would suggest that homicide rates should be declining under "normal" circumstances.

Other prominent 1990s crime explanations would predict homicide rates to continue to decline. The reduction of environmental lead exposure was hypothesized to produce fewer children with brain damage who would grow up to commit criminal offenses (i.e., Nevin 2000). Environmental lead exposure is now (historically) low and has been decreasing since the 1970s (Environmental Protection Agency 2023). The 1990s crime decline was also prominently attributed to putting "more police on the streets" (Levitt 2004). The number of police per capita has remained steady from 2010 onward (2.4 officers per 1,000 people), at roughly the same rate as during the late 1990s, according to FBI (2022) police data. Even the more disputed hypotheses, such as the idea that fewer firearm restrictions caused crime rates to decline during the 1990s (Lott 2010), are not plausible explanations of the recent homicide trend. States have increasingly adopted permitless ("constitutional") carry provisions, enacting fewer restrictions on firearms since the 1990s (Brownlee 2023). While it is possible that these factors had some impact on 1990s crime trends, it is clear that none of these explanations could plausibly account for the recent increase in homicide. If anything, some of these trends would have even suggested a further homicide decline.

If not these 1990s-inspired explanations, what can account for the increase in homicide? The initial reaction has been to attribute the homicide trend to some sort of change in policing due to an "exogenous shock" (Rosenfeld 2018). The "Ferguson Effect" of 2014–2015 (Mac Donald 2016) and the "Minneapolis Effect" of 2020 (Cassell 2020) are both attempts to highlight the abnormality of policing and crime after widespread anti-police-brutality protests. While there is some potential contribution of these "shocks," the nearly decade-long upward trajectory in violent assaults would not be easily explained by these temporary changes in police practices.

Instead, we will turn to factors that played a role in previous crime trends but have often been neglected in both academic and media coverage. Specifically, there has been an increase in alcohol consumption, the resurgence of illicit drug abuse, and the proliferation of firearms, which have caused the homicide rate trend to defy its typical demographic and economic predictors. These factors, in combination with the discontent with the police and publicized acts of police brutality, caused the homicide epidemic.

American Decline as the Cause of the Homicide Epidemic

The argument advanced in this book is that the homicide epidemic is due to the (often) counterproductive ways in which Americans have coped with their nation's decline. There are two distinctive parts to this decline. One part is marked by a deterioration of Americans' psychosocial well-being. Americans are more depressed, anxious, prone to substance abuse, and suicidal, living shorter lives in 2021 than they did during the late 1990s. Two particular ways that Americans have coped with this decline in well-being, using illicit drugs and drinking alcohol, have contributed to the increase in violent assaults.

The second portion of American decline is institutional. Americans report less trust in their government and major institutions than during decades past. The distrust of government and its officials has manifested in the high-profile outbreaks of protest against the police but also in an increase in firearm purchases. Figure 1.4 provides an outline of the connection between the two main manifestations of American decline, the intervening mechanisms, and the homicide epidemic. Four of the subsequent chapters (chapter 3 through 6) are devoted to explaining each of these facets of societal decline and their connection to homicide trends in greater detail. I briefly outline this argument here.

The decline of Americans' psychosocial well-being, or *malaise*, is evident through several negative health trends. Over the past two decades, the increase in life expectancy has stalled. Life expectancy for Americans even declined from 2015 through 2017 (Kochanek, Anderson, and Arias 2020) and then again in 2020 and 2021 (Arias et al. 2022). Although the recent drop in life expectancy is largely due to the COVID-19 pandemic, the high rates of "deaths of despair" have cut Americans' lives short due to higher rates of suicide, drug overdose, and alcohol-related death (Case and Deaton 2020). These self-inflicted deaths are indicative of several negative societal trends, including increased loneliness and social isolation (Kannan and Veazie 2023) as well as the declining economic prospects of the working class (Case and Deaton 2020).

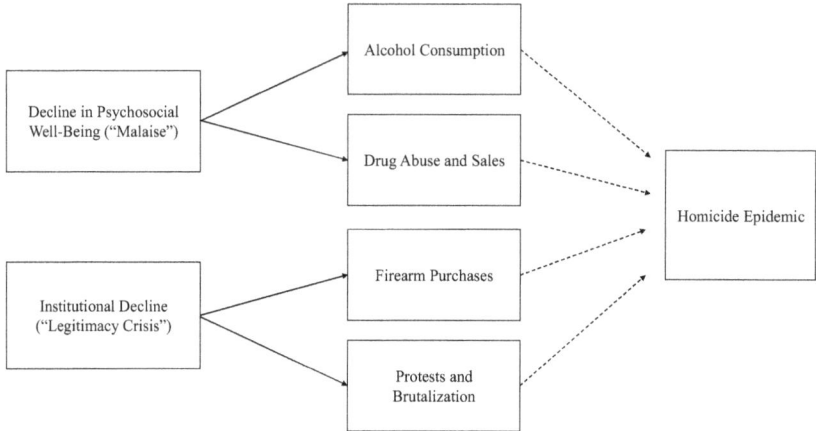

FIGURE 1.4. Model of American decline and the homicide epidemic

As more Americans use drugs and alcohol to self-medicate and numb the pain of the decline in their standard of living, it has provided the context for a rapid increase in violence. Not only do the altered psychological states associated with drug and alcohol abuse make people more prone to erratic and (sometimes) violent behavior, but the proliferation of profitable illicit drug markets enables an expansion of drug trafficking and organized crime, with "business" transactions often enforced through the threat of violent retribution (Goldstein 1985). As the opioid crisis shifted from prescription medications to illicit drugs circa 2012 (McGranahan and Parker 2021), the homicide epidemic was not far behind. As outlined in chapters 3 and 4, the increase in the homicide rate corresponded with America's increasing issues with substance abuse.

American institutions have also suffered from an acute decline or legitimacy crisis. Polling indicates that Americans are deeply cynical about their leaders and the federal government (Brenan 2021). Partisan distrust of government even contributed to an attempted coup d'état in 2021. Less well documented is how the distrust in the federal government has contributed to a gun-buying spree. Even prior to the COVID-19 pandemic, firearm sales had been elevated. The twin crises of 2020 (pandemic and protests) provided further motivation to purchase firearms, as the events of that year continued to spiral out of control. One of the notable features of the recent homicide epidemic is that nearly the entire increase is attributable to assaults committed with a firearm. High rates of firearm possession do not always lead to higher rates of homicide, but in the case of the recent homicide epidemic, guns have been the weapon of choice (see chapter 5).

This general decline of institutional trust has been coupled with a legitimacy crisis for police departments across the country. While overall public opinion concerning support for the police is relatively split, the size and scale of protests against police brutality in 2020 rivaled those of the civil rights movement of the 1960s. Accordingly, this crisis in police legitimacy is readily apparent, with a protest movement indicating a deep distrust of the police and the criminal justice system. The protest movement has drawn the public's attention to specific instances of alleged police brutality, which have periodically caused a sharp rise in violent assaults, mirroring a "brutalization effect" (see chapter 6). In all, Americans are increasingly under the influence of drugs and alcohol, armed, and distrustful of each other, the police, and their government. Each of these social conditions has predisposed the United States to an epidemic of violent assault. In fact, it would be surprising if these societal conditions *did not* contribute to an increase in violent crime.

Conclusion

The homicide rate and, to a lesser degree, the rate of aggravated assault have increased dramatically since 2014. Many of the typical explanations used to explain the crime trends of the 1990s are either irrelevant to this increase or would have actually predicted a decline in homicide. Yet, as US institutions eroded and Americans' well-being deteriorated, the causes of a homicide epidemic lurked just beneath the surface. As more Americans coped with their declining well-being through the use of drugs and alcohol, purchased firearms in response to greater distrust of the government, and protested against police brutality, the rate of violent assaults soared. In the subsequent chapters of this book, I develop each of these arguments in greater detail.

However, before addressing each symptom of American decline and the causes of the homicide epidemic, I must first assess the role of de-policing. Policing is by far the most widely discussed issue in reference to the increase in homicide. In fact, a majority of the criminological research about the crime trends in 2015 and 2016 was devoted to addressing whether a decline in arrests contributed to the uptick in violence. By pursuing the red herring of the "Ferguson Effect," we now have several studies that demonstrate that de-policing, or a decline in police proactivity, had little to no impact on homicide rates in 2015 and 2016. In chapter 2, I discuss why a lack of policing is a poor candidate to explain the ultimate origin of the recent homicide epidemic.

2

The Limited Impact of "De-policing"

An Examination of the Evidence

The Victimization Survey found no statistically significant differences in crime in any of the 69 comparisons between reactive, control and proactive beats.
—excerpt from *The Kansas City Preventative Patrol Experiment: A Summary Report*

By far, the most popular explanation of the homicide rate increase among the general public is that the police have been prevented from proactively patrolling communities, thereby reducing deterrence. In 2015, the purported "Ferguson Effect" suggested that protests against police brutality were preventing proactive patrols, thereby causing crime rates to increase (Mac Donald 2016). In 2020, the connection between the protests of police brutality and the increase in homicide rates returned to the public consciousness. Part of this connection was (again) attributed to a lack of arrests made by the police in the wake of the protest movement (Cassell 2020). Additionally, in the case of the 2020 homicide spike, there was also an amorphous sense that police departments around the country had been "defunded" as a response to the protests. A 2022 *Politico* poll found that fully 75 percent of Americans sampled attributed the recent increase in violent crime, at least in part, to the "defunding" of police departments.

However, there are several reasons to doubt that a "lack" of policing is the ultimate origin of the homicide epidemic. First, a decline in deterrence would not explain the divergence in crime trends after 2014. If an increase in the homicide rate is attributed to a lack of police presence and proactivity, why would rates of robbery, burglary, and larceny decline throughout the same period? The divergent trends in property-based offenses and homicide suggest that, at the very least, there must be another factor added to the de-policing hypothesis. Otherwise, we would have to believe that the police had simultaneously improved at deterring robbery, burglary, and larceny while their ability to deter aggravated assault and homicide deteriorated.

A second reason to doubt a police-centric narrative is due to the accumulated evidence on policing and crime rates. Why would policing exert such a strong effect during a crime wave but have an otherwise modest impact on crime? This modest impact has been documented since at least the Kansas City Preventative Patrol Experiment, which was conducted during the early 1970s. In this experiment, Kansas City police were assigned to three conditions in their neighborhood patrols: a control group that was assigned to its normal level of police activity, a reactive condition in which police only answered calls for service and did not actively patrol the neighborhood, and a proactive condition in which patrols were increased by two to three times their normal amount. After a year of subjecting neighborhoods to these three policing conditions, the experimenters found no statistically significant differences in crime victimization, citizen satisfaction, or any other important metric (Kelling et al. 1974). Recently, a reanalysis of this data suggests that neighborhoods assigned to proactive policing had less crime than neighborhoods in the control group, but there was no difference between the reactive and the control beats for crimes other than burglary (Weisburd et al. 2023). In short, mirroring allusions to the claims about policing in 2015 and 2020, *reactive* policing (similar to de-policing) produced no discernable impact on violent crime in this experiment. As I discuss shortly, the relatively modest impact of variation in policing practices on crime is a common theme in previous research, contradicting the notion that changes in police proactivity would explain a significant amount of the increase in the homicide rate.

The third reason to doubt a police-centric narrative is the accumulated evidence on de-policing in 2015 and the overall timeline in 2020. Although it is certainly true that arrest rates declined in the wake of protests in 2014–2015 (Shjarback et al. 2017) and 2020 (Cheng and Long 2022), the link between declining arrests and increases in crime during these years is often missing, especially in 2015 (Pyrooz et al. 2016; Rosenfeld and Wallman 2019; Shjarback et al. 2017). There have been some recent studies examining variation in arrests in 2020 in New York City (Kim 2024) and Denver (Nix et al. 2024), which found an effect of the police pullback on crime rates. But some of the decline in arrests occurred *before* the George Floyd protests, suggesting that this increase in violent crime may have been due to the exogenous shock of the pandemic as much as the protest movement. As I summarize shortly, de-policing in 2015 had no consistent impact on crime trends, and the spike in homicide in 2020 occurred prior to the murder of George Floyd, contradicting the de-policing-due-to-protests narrative.

While this chapter is critical of the argument that changes in police proactivity are central to explaining the homicide epidemic, I must make it clear that the police can and do prevent crime. In fact, as we will see in chapter 8, it is likely that police reticence to make firearms-related arrests exacerbated the homicide increase in 2020 across US cities. Additionally, recent evidence shows that in cases where there is virtually no possibility that the police will respond to a crime, there is a higher rate of offending. This was evident in the Capitol Hill Occupation Protest (CHOP) Zone of Seattle in 2020, where police were prevented from responding to offenses; crime rates were significantly higher in the CHOP Zone as a result (Piza and Connealy 2022).

However, de-policing in 2015 and 2020 was more akin to a change of policing strategies, such as the reactive condition in the Kansas City Preventative Patrol Experiment, than a disbanding of the police, more similar to the CHOP Zone. As long as the police could conceivably apprehend suspects and intervene in ongoing offenses, most of their deterrent impact remains intact. Accordingly, it would be unlikely that a lack of proactive policing during specific years of the homicide epidemic was among the most important factors shaping recent patterns in criminal offending.

When You Buy a Police Force . . .

There is one really good reason to focus on policing during a crime wave: the police are the people we pay to prevent crime. There is a considerable amount of tax revenue wrapped up in funding police departments across the country. At the same time that spending on social welfare programs has remained stagnant, spending on policing and prisons continues to increase (Ingraham 2020). Data compiled by the Vera Group Institute of Justice (2020) show that cities across the United States spend billions of dollars on their respective police departments each year. In Los Angeles and Chicago, annual police department budgets are close to $2 billion, while New York City spends more than $5 billion annually. In some cities, such as Billings (Montana) and Milwaukee, more than half of the city's entire budget is devoted to the police department. Even the "defunded" policing budget of Seattle was nearly $400 million in 2022 (Thompson 2021).

When you buy a police force, every crime looks like a lack of deterrence. Because our primary resource allocation intended to prevent crime is to fund a threat of punishment, it creates the illusion that crime varies in strict accordance with the degree of deterrence. And, if crime is perceived to be simply a question of deterrence, then the only conceivable short-term solution is for there to be police on the streets, making more arrests, and politicians enacting more stringent penalties for criminal offending. This makes the discussion about policing strategies seemingly unavoidable, as they can (hypothetically) change quickly in response to an increasing crime rate.

The implicit assumption that crime is due to a lack of deterrence, coupled with a positive perception of police officers by about half of

Americans, creates the odd dynamic of crediting the police for crime declines and blaming others for crime rate increases. In the 1990s, the police wanted to take credit for causing the crime rate to fall in New York City. By following the policies of "Zero Tolerance" and "Broken Windows" policing (Kelling and Wilson 1982), New York City achieved the unthinkable: a sudden decline in crime after decades of elevated rates of violence (Kelling and Bratton 1998). Yet the "unthinkable" occurred nearly everywhere: crime rates fell in cities across the United States during this same period, regardless of whether they instituted similar policies to New York City (Baumer and Wolff 2014). Overall, research suggests that changes in police strategies implemented in New York had a relatively modest impact on crime trends (Rosenfeld, Fornango, and Rengifo 2007), but many people still want to credit police for making it one of the safest big cities in the country.

Conversely, when the homicide rate began to increase in both 2015 and 2020, few people blamed the police, nor were the police issuing apologies for their failure to deter violent crime. Instead, everyone else but the police were supposedly to blame for the crime wave. A portion of the public blamed overzealous activists, "Democrat-run" cities, progressive prosecutors, "Antifa," and Black Lives Matter protesters for preventing the police from "fighting crime." At the same time that crime was perceived to be out of control, many people perceived the police to be victims of a smear campaign (Mac Donald 2016) rather than inept and responsible for a failure to produce public safety.

Oddly, a portion of the American public perceives the failure of the police to prevent or stop an increase in violent crime as the failure of the public to respect the police enough, fund them sufficiently, or provide them a proper amount of support. A significant segment of Americans also seems to implicitly agree that the police are only responsible for crime rate trends when they are declining, not when they are increasing. This dynamic creates yet another peculiar element of the discussion around American crime and policing: when the police fail to produce a sense of safety, they are often rewarded with even more tax dollars.

Funding and "Defunding" the Police

Given the oddities of the perception of American policing, police reform efforts in the wake of the murder of George Floyd by a Minneapolis police officer, often referred to as "defund the police," were quickly blamed for the increase in homicide in 2020, 2021, and beyond. The phrase "defund the police" originated from demands by anti-police-brutality protestors who used this phrase to represent various desired policy changes. Opinions among activists ranged from outright abolishment of policing in general to more moderate calls to reallocate some of the billions of dollars spent on police departments each year to social services. There were a few cities that complied with the latter demand in the wake of the 2020 protest movement, with as many as thirteen cities enacting some conscious reallocation of portions of the police department budget to other government services (McEnvoy 2020). As homicide rates continued to increase into 2021, most cities reversed their initial plans to reduce police funding, and many increased police department budgets instead (Elinson, Frosch, and Jamerson 2021).

Although the increase in homicide occurred (to varying degrees) throughout the country in 2020 and 2021, this did not stop people from blaming a decline in police department funding, which only occurred in a few cities. The popular belief that defunding the police is the cause of high rates of homicide does not withstand much critical scrutiny. First, the largest increase in the homicide rate occurred in 2020. Because annual city budgets are (usually) prospective, set in place in the year or years prior to being spent, police department funding was not reduced in 2020. That is, if defunding police departments was a major cause of the homicide epidemic, why would it have occurred *after* the period when homicide increased most rapidly? Second, why did much of the country experience an increase in homicide in 2021, despite the fact that only a few cities actually "defunded" police departments? If defunding was central to the explanation of recent homicide trends, we would expect to see homicide rates increase only in cities where budgets had been reallocated ("defunded"). Instead, an increase in homicide in 2021 occurred in both cities that increased and those that decreased police department funding.

To more systematically assess the impact of changes in police budgets on city homicide rates, I examined the association between police department funding per capita and the homicide rate across 168 US cities with at least one hundred thousand residents. Unfortunately, due to issues related to switching to a new data-collection system (NIBRS), FBI (2022) data are missing or incomplete for many cities in 2021. There are other cases in which data are reported for 2021, but I deemed them to be unreliable or incomplete after comparing them with other sources. Because of some of the issues associated with the change to the new reporting system and the associated missing data, the results presented here should be interpreted with some caution.

To assess changes in police department funding, I draw on data collected by Andy Friedman and Mason Youngblood (2022) for their article on defunding the police. They compiled data on more than four hundred cities, finding that very few departments actually experienced substantial budget cuts in 2021. Some departments experienced small cuts as part of a larger budget reduction for the city overall, but only a handful of cities made major cuts to police budgets that were not reflective of COVID-19-related retrenchment. The police funding and homicide data are standardized per one hundred thousand population using US Census data. City population data for 2021 are imputed using 2020 population data. A list of all of the cities included in this analysis is included in the note to this chapter.[1]

This sample includes both cities that made substantial police department cuts in 2021 and also cities that *increased* their police department budgets. Cities that made notable cuts in this sample are Austin, Minneapolis, and Seattle. In 2021, both Austin and Minneapolis experienced an increase in homicide. Ironically, one of the cities that most infamously "defunded" the police (Seattle) actually experienced a decline in homicide from 2020 to 2021. Overall, the mean police budget per capita across the cities in the sample increased by 4.8 percent from 2019 to 2020 and 0.6 percent from 2020 to 2021. The mean increase in the homicide rate across the cities in the sample was 38.1 percent from 2019 to 2020 and 9.2 percent from 2020 to 2021. At first glance, the year in which police budgets grew the most was also the year in which homicide increased by the largest proportional margin, suggesting a relatively modest (or even positive) association between police funding and homicide rates.

In table 2.1, I present fixed-effects regression models examining the impact of the total amount of dollars (per capita) devoted to the city's police department on the homicide rate. The panel analyses capture change in police budgets and homicides from 2019 to 2021 while simultaneously holding stable differences between cities constant. Before adding any controls, there was actually a *positive* association between police department funding per capita and homicide, implying that homicide rates *increase* when police departments receive a larger budget. However, because 2020 and 2021 had higher homicide rates in general than 2019 did, probably for reasons other than police funding, an additional control for "period effects" was added in the subsequent models.

In Model 2 of table 2.1, I include period effects in the model, which account for the degree to which city homicide rates were higher in 2020 and 2021 than in 2019. After including these controls, there is a negative association between changes in police funding per capita and annual variation in the homicide rate. However, this effect does not meet the conventional cutoff point for "statistical significance" (p-value < .05). This finding implies that had this been a random sample of cities, we could not confidently attribute any effect of changes to city homicide rates to variation in police department funding. Finally, Model 3 includes the lagged impact of the homicide rate within each city from the previous year, attempting to account for issues related to reverse causality, namely, an increase in crime contributing to more police funding. The results are substantively the same as Model 2, as there was no statistically significant effect of police funding on changes in city homicide rates.[2]

TABLE 2.1. Annual Police Funding and the Homicide Rate across 168 Cities, 2019–2021

Variable	Model 1: No controls	Model 2: With period effects	Model 3: With period effects and lagged homicide
Police funding per 100,000	.04** (.01)	−.01 (.01)	−.01 (.01)
P-value	.00	.44	.49
R-squared (within)	.05	.29	.31

* = $p < .05$; ** = $p < .01$

Overall, these results suggest that decreases in the police budget had little to no impact on annual variation in city homicide rates across the United States. It is true that after adding controls for period effects, police funding was negatively associated with the homicide rate. This suggests that when police budgets declined, homicide rates increased. However, this association was weak, as most of the explained variance in city homicide rates was due to the addition of period effects, and not statistically significant. Accordingly, we can tentatively conclude that "defunding the police," at least to the degree it was practiced during 2020 and 2021, was not the primary cause of the increase in homicide.

Of course, if police budgets were reduced to zero, there would probably be an impact on the homicide rate; but within the restricted range that budgets are allocated in the real world, there was no discernable impact. Potentially, more sophisticated analyses that account for how police department budgets are allocated, include a more robust set of control variables, or more adequately account for reverse causality (or simultaneity bias) could find some impact of changes to police budgets. However, as we attempt to locate the major determinants of recent homicide trends, these results suggest that the attribution of the homicide increase to defunding the police is simply a popular myth.

The Mixed Results of Policing Research

The null finding regarding defunding the police provides a great segue into a broader discussion of the effect of policing on crime. Similar to this analysis, research on the effect of policing on crime is often mixed, usually documenting a relatively modest impact. Some studies find a sizable impact of policing on crime, while others find little to no impact. Taken together, the research literature suggests that variation in policing practices can affect crime rates on the margins but has a modest impact on overall crime rates or crime trends.

For much of the twentieth century, criminologists questioned whether policing and punishment impacted crime *at all*. During the era that the Kansas City Preventative Patrol Experiment was conducted (the 1970s), there was still an active debate regarding whether criminal sanctions did anything to reduce crime. The frequency of recidivism among individuals convicted of criminal offenses inspired the creation of "labeling theory" (H. Becker 1963; Tannenbaum 1938), which argues that the labeling of offenders by the criminal justice system through trial and conviction actually contributes to *more* crime, not less. In fact, prior to prominent theoretical statements by Jack Gibbs (1966) and Gary Becker (1968), the concept of "deterrence" had been largely abandoned by criminologists trying to understand variation in crime rates.

One of the possible reasons that mid-twentieth-century criminologists overlooked the impact of deterrence is the relatively weak and contradictory association between punishment and crime. At any given point in time, cities, states, and countries that impose more punishment usually have higher, rather than lower, rates of crime. A significant subset of studies have documented that a larger police force is often correlated with more crime rather than less (Pratt and Cullen 2005). A similar dynamic is present in states and countries with higher rates of incarceration; violent crime rates are higher in nations where more people are imprisoned (Stemen and Rengifo 2011). Additionally, in 2019, the homicide rate was about 25 percent higher in US states that had retained the death penalty than in those that had abolished it (Death Penalty Information Center 2020). Overall, if you simply examine the amount (or severity) of punishment at any one given point in time, you would conclude that more punishment is associated with higher rates of crime.

Size of Police Force

As you may have surmised, the cross-sectional correlation between punishment and crime is more complicated than it first appears. Because fear of crime seems to motivate "tough on crime" policies, higher crime rates usually result in more punishment (Garland 2001). Accordingly, crime rates often influence the number of police hired within a city, causing the cross-sectional correlation between police and crime to be positive, rather than negative. This situation, in which police force size both influences crime rates and is partially the consequence of crime rates is referred to as "simultaneity bias" (Levitt 2002). This bias often requires more fine-tuned and sophisticated research to trace the elusive impact of policing on crime.

One such methodological innovation that provides evidence of a crime-preventing impact of police force size uses an "instrumental variable" approach. This approach sidesteps the issue of reverse causality (more crime leading to more police being hired) by identifying a variable that is only associated with the causal variable but not hypothesized to be related to the outcome variable in any way. In this case, the instrumental variable should have no conceivable relationship to the crime rate but should be associated with changes in police force size. Steven Levitt (2002) uses variation in the number of firefighters per capita as a proxy measure of city budget expenditures that are unrelated to the amount of crime. Using this strategy, Levitt (2002) finds a significant impact of police force size/expenditures (indicated by spending on firefighters) on crime rates. Subsequent research using a similar approach has confirmed that more police officers will contribute to less crime (Lin 2009).

Despite these findings, the overall evidence suggests that the impact of police force size is relatively modest. For example, some researchers have argued that the instrumental variables used by Levitt are "weak" by the standards of econometrics and do not allow us to make as strong of claims of a causal relationship between police force size and crime rates as Levitt implies (Kovandzic et al. 2016). More damning for the association between police force size and crime was a systematic review of all available research conducted on the topic between 1968 and 2013, by YounJei Lee, John Eck, and Nicholas Corsaro (2016). The authors found that the overall impact of police force size on crime rates is relatively small, and when assessed as a whole, it is not "statistically significant." This review also considered whether prior research had effectively addressed the simultaneity bias issue, finding that even the more sophisticated methods were no more likely to document a robust impact of changes in police force size on crime rates. In the discussion of the results, the authors conclude "that merely increasing police force size does nothing to reduce crime" (Lee, Eck, and Corsaro 2016, 446).

Adding to these doubts are key questions about whether there is any direct effect of the size of the police force on general deterrence. Notably, Gary Kleck and J. C. Barnes (2014) found that there is no association between the number of police officers assigned to a city (per capita) and the perceived risk of arrest. This finding challenges the general deterrence argument, as deterrence depends on the perception of potential punishment, not (necessarily) on its actual likelihood; the perception of police presence continues to be the missing link in this proposed causal chain. Overall, it would be accurate to say that the research literature on the impact of police force size on crime is quite mixed, with a handful of studies suggesting that more police can deter crime (Levitt 2002; Lin 2009), but a majority of the research finds little to no impact (Lee, Eck, and Corsaro 2016).

Policing Strategies

Directly related to the de-policing argument, researchers have developed more sophisticated methods and approaches since the Kansas City Preventative Patrol Experiment (Weisburd et al. 2023). One methodological breakthrough used to uncover the impact of policing strategies was to examine crime "hot spots." This type of research does not address the total number of police officers patrolling a city but engages in a strategy by which police are deployed to maximize their potential impact on criminal offending. By using information about past offending patterns across a neighborhood or city to discover when and where crime is most likely to occur, police can be positioned to arrest/deter offenders in frequently targeted areas, maximizing their crime-reducing impact.

In one of the initial studies using this innovative strategy, police were deployed strategically to areas of the city where crime rates were the highest. This intervention reduced crime rates by between 6 and 13 percent (Sherman and Weisburd 1995). Unlike the Kansas City Preventative Patrol Experiment's focus on entire patrol areas, the microtargeting of locations where crime is most likely to occur does appear to reduce the rate of crime. Reviews of this literature have described the crime-reduction effect of hot-spot policing as "small but noteworthy" (Braga, Papachristos, and Hureau 2012).

There are clear reductions in crime associated with the specific hot spots targeted by police, but the overall effect on crime within the city is a bit more modest. The reason for this modest overall impact is that when police are assigned to a specific area, there is a "displacement" effect, in which crime patterns move away from police presence. That is, potential offenders go elsewhere to commit offenses and avoid police detection. There is still an overall crime-reduction effect even after accounting for displacement, but it is relatively small (Braga et al. 2019).

The overall pattern of finding significant but relatively modest effects of different policing strategies on crime is a consistent theme in the research literature. For example, during the much-heralded success of policing during the 1990s crime decline (Kelling and Bratton 1998), research on the impact of order-maintenance policing strategies found "small crime-reduction effects" (Rosenfeld, Fornango, and Rengifo 2007, 356). Similarly, research on the impact of New York City's "stop-and-frisk" policy suggests that there is some impact of more aggressive policing techniques, but again, the impact is relatively modest (Rosenfeld and Fornango 2017). In fact, one study even found that once New York

City ended its stop-and-frisk policy, rates of several criminal offenses *declined* (Sullivan and O'Keeffe 2017).

An exception to the "modest effects" of policing is the emerging evidence on focused-deterrence strategies. These policing strategies, exemplified by Boston's "Operation Ceasefire" initiative of the 1990s, involve directly communicating with (potential) offenders about incentives or disincentives (Braga and Weisburd 2012). In the case of youth gang violence, the focused-deterrence approach may include multiple strategies, including the involvement of community members, tracing firearm sales, and directly communicating about harsh punishment for violence to the gang members themselves (Braga et al. 2001). There are fewer examples of this strategy, but the effects could be described as "moderate" rather than "modest" (Braga and Weisburd 2012). However, this example does not directly apply to the de-policing argument of 2015 and 2020, which hinges on "normal" police operations becoming "reactive" in the wake of a protest movement, more akin to a naturally occurring Kansas City Preventative Patrol Experiment.

Overall, the research literature is supportive of the idea that proactive and strategic policing techniques can reduce crime but that the amount of crime reduction is usually somewhat small. In the case of the recent homicide epidemic, changes in policing would not plausibly account for the size of the increase in the homicide rate in recent years, nor would they account for an offense-specific increase in violent assaults and a decline in property-based offenses. In the next section, I summarize research that specifically examined the de-policing argument directly in 2015 and 2020.

De-policing and the "Ferguson Effect"

On the surface, the de-policing argument is plausible as the timing of the decline in police activity (arrests, stops, etc.) roughly aligns with the timing of increases in homicide in both 2015 and 2020. Police morale and proactive policing declined in the wake of widespread anti-police-brutality protests in 2015 (Deuchar, Fallik, and Crichlow 2019). This decline in morale and reticence to proactively patrol impacted the number of arrests. One study examining jurisdictions in the state of Missouri found that police made fewer stops and were less likely to find contraband in the aftermath of the anti-police-brutality protests in Ferguson. The effect of de-policing was especially pronounced in areas with larger African American populations, which were subject to significantly fewer stops, searches, and arrests in 2015 than in 2014 (Shjarback et al. 2017). Similarly, the Ferguson Effect seemed to contribute to de-policing (fewer arrests) in New York City as well (Capellan, Lautenschlager, and Silva 2020).

Despite evidence of a decline in proactive policing, de-policing has been an inconsistent predictor of an increase in crime rates. Crime rates were unrelated to de-policing in jurisdictions across Missouri in 2015 (Shjarback et al. 2017). Throughout the United States, there were a few cities whose crime patterns fit a Ferguson Effect pattern, but there was no systematic effect on homicide rates (Pyrooz et al. 2016). Despite New York City also experiencing de-policing, changes in crime rates there from 2014 to 2015 were seemingly unrelated to a decline in arrests made by police (Capellan, Lautenschlager, and Silva 2020). Similarly, in a study examining fifty-three cities from 2010 to 2015, Rosenfeld and Wallman (2019) found no impact of arrest rates on crime rates, including during the 2015 increase in homicide. Overall, the balance of the research evidence during the 2015–2016 spike in homicide suggests that there was no effect of de-policing on crime.

The results of research examining the impact of de-policing in 2020 are more mixed. Ironically, a study of Minneapolis suggests that there was no impact of de-policing on shootings and homicide patterns (Larson, Santaularia, and Uggen 2023), providing direct evidence against a "Minneapolis Effect" (e.g., Cassell 2020). Another study examining changes in police behavior after the protest movement in 2020 in Seattle found a decline in police proactivity but also found that de-policing was unrelated to the increase in crime rates (Roman et al. 2023). Conversely, in analyses of New York City (Kim 2024) and Denver (Nix et al. 2024), researchers documented a significant impact of the decline in arrests on crime. However, in both of these studies, the researchers noted that the decline in arrests corresponded with COVID-19 restrictions *in addition to* the anti-police-brutality protests. Accordingly, it is somewhat difficult to isolate the impact of the protests that caused de-policing and their impact on crime rates.

There are reasons to doubt policing's central role in the 2020 homicide increase. Specifically, the homicide trend was elevated *prior* to the George Floyd protests. Although an initial study of city-level changes in crime suggests that the homicide rate increased during the onset of the national protest movement in June (Lopez and Rosenfeld 2021), national monthly homicide victimization data do not support a narrative that focuses specifically on protests and policing. Figure 2.1 depicts the monthly homicide victimization rate in the United States (standardized by one million) for each individual year from 2010 to 2020, compiled using CDC Wonder (2023) mortality data. The monthly homicide victimization rate in 2020 is depicted with the solid line, while the homicide victimization rates during years of the prior decade (2010–2019) are depicted with dotted lines. A vertical line is inserted at May to separate the pre- and post–George Floyd protest eras.

Instead of a spike in homicide only after the protests, we see an abnormally high rate of homicide in 2020 even before George Floyd was murdered. In fact, the homicide rate was somewhat elevated even before the implementation of COVID-19-related restrictions in March 2020. The mean monthly homicide rate from December 2019 to February 2020 was higher than any such period during the previous decade (4.9 homicides per 1,000,000). This three-month-average was 2.6 standard deviations greater than the mean of all December–February periods between 2010 and 2019 (4.2 per 1,000,000). February 2020 was already the most homicidal February in more than a decade, which was *prior to* when COVID-19 restrictions were put in place in the United States.

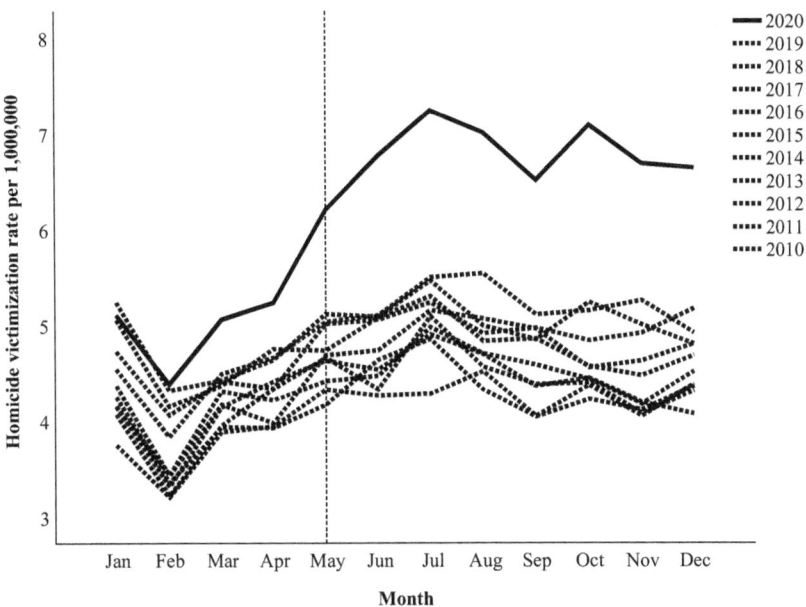

FIGURE 2.1. Monthly homicide victimization by year, 2010–2020

Then, during the initial months of the COVID-19 pandemic national emergency, the homicide rate increased abruptly. By the end of March, the annual climb in the homicide rate during the spring months had noticeably outpaced every year of the previous decade. In April, the monthly homicide rate had already surpassed all monthly homicide rates recorded during the initial year of the homicide epidemic (2015). By May 2020, there were more homicides per capita than in any month in the previous two decades.

While it is true that George Floyd was murdered on May 25, 2020, the nationwide protest movement did not begin until June (Cassell 2020). Accordingly, we would not expect to see the homicide rate for the entire country be significantly impacted by the protests during the end of May, primarily taking place in Minneapolis. By June, the increase in the homicide rate was already decelerating from the previous month, increasing by only 9 percent from May, which is proportionally less than the

19 percent increase from April to May. Given the fact that homicide rates tend to climb each year from February to July, it is unclear what impact, if any, protest-related de-policing had on changing this upward trajectory. While this timeline does not rule out the role of protests and de-policing, it suggests that 2020 was going to be a violent year regardless.

If the spike in homicide did not begin with the protests, we would have to examine the increase in homicide as a result of other factors. The police "pullback" that corresponded with the beginning of COVID-19 restrictions has been suggested as an alternative explanation to a protest-centric explanation (e.g., Kim 2024; Nix et al. 2024). Yet it was not just policing that changed during March 2020. Everything changed. Schools closed or went online. "Nonessential" businesses in many states were required to shut their doors, putting millions of Americans out of work. People began to panic-buy items from the few stores that remained open, at one point producing a national shortage of toilet paper.

These disturbances probably had little impact on the rate of homicide, but there were others that could have been more directly related to violence. For example, given the documented impact of antiviolence nonprofit organizations (Sharkey, Torrats-Espinosa, and Takyar 2017; Sharkey 2018), the social-distancing orders may have thwarted community control efforts that have proven to be effective in reducing interpersonal violence. Also, panic about the pandemic led to a record number of attempted firearm sales in March 2020 (see chapter 5). With more guns on hand and fewer people working to deescalate community conflict, COVID-19 restrictions may have produced more violence for reasons that had nothing to do with policing.

Relatedly, during the height of despair and isolation in the wake of the COVID-19 pandemic, Americans died in record numbers due to drug overdose and alcohol-related deaths. As we will discuss in subsequent chapters, alcohol and drug abuse are frequent contributors to violent crime. As depicted in figure 2.2, the increase in the monthly homicide victimization rate is closely aligned with patterns in drug

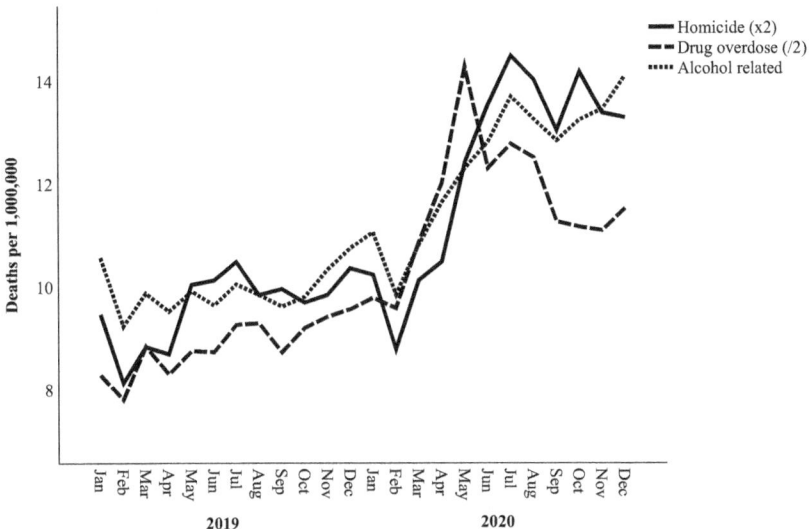

FIGURE 2.2. Monthly homicide, drug overdose, and alcohol-related deaths per million, 2019–2020

overdose and alcohol-related deaths in 2019 and 2020. These data are derived from the CDC Wonder (2023) mortality database. In this figure, the homicide rate (per one million) is multiplied by two and the drug overdose death rate (per one million) is divided by two to bring these trends closer for visual comparison. The monthly homicide rate is strongly correlated with the monthly drug overdose rate ($r = .82$) and alcohol-related death rate ($r = .95$) during this period.

These trends, as proxies for excessive alcohol consumption and illicit drug sales, provide an alternative explanation to the police pullback as to why the COVID-19 pandemic emergency was associated with a spike in homicide. As more people consumed drugs and alcohol and bought illicit drugs from street dealers, violent assaults increased. Similar to the homicide trend, drug overdose deaths increased rapidly from February to May, and alcohol-related deaths increased from February to July, remaining elevated throughout the rest of the year. Additionally, the increase in drug overdose and alcohol-related deaths in late 2019 may help explain why December 2019 and January–February 2020 had abnormally high rates of homicide predating the COVID-19 national emergency.

Overall, without accounting for the myriad of changes that occurred during the exogenous shock of the pandemic, the evidence linking a decline in arrests in March to a spike in homicide is incomplete at best. To be clear, this comparison of aggregate trends is more suggestive than definitive. However, the combined implication of figures 2.1 and 2.2 is that policing played a secondary role in shaping the homicide trend in 2020. The homicide rate was elevated before the beginning of pandemic-related restrictions in the US and increased rapidly prior to the nationwide George Floyd protests. Additionally, the homicide rate remained elevated well into 2021, presumably after policing practices had stabilized. In fact, the monthly homicide rate in June 2021 (6.82 per 1,000,000) was even higher than that of June 2020 (6.77 per 1,000,000). These overarching trends suggest that the 2020 protest-related de-policing happened in the middle of an already rapidly escalating homicide trend.

Policing, Not De-policing, as a Cause of the Homicide Epidemic

As much as there has been an effort to attribute the homicide epidemic to de-policing, fewer people have recognized the role that policing has played in exacerbating the homicide epidemic. Specifically, an approach to policing that does not adequately foster trust, uses brutality and violence, and still perpetuates discrimination provides the context for elevated rates of crime. As long as the police are perceived to be biased against racial/ethnic minorities, and specifically Black men, police use of excessive and/or deadly force will inspire antipolice sentiment and, sporadically, antisystemic protests. Some of these protest movements, like those of 2014–2015 and 2020, will garner enough support to become nationwide referendums on policing.

In the popular narrative about crime trends, the de-policing discussion mostly serves as a red herring, refocusing attention on protestors rather than the police. The focus on de-policing sanctifies the police brutality that spurred the protests by focusing on the *reaction* to government-sponsored murder rather than the murder itself. It suggests that the ongoing legitimacy crisis suffered by the police within some segments of the Black community is the fault of citizens, not the government agents who have provided little reason for trust and cooperation. The de-policing narrative provides no solutions to solving the homicide epidemic, suggesting that we simply return to the same type of policing that spawned the protest movement in the first place, maybe even getting a little bit "tougher" on crime.

The recasting of police as innocent bystanders not only fails to understand the causes of the homicide epidemic but provides the context for further distrust of the police and a chronically elevated rate of violent crime. One salient example of this dynamic is the murder of Tyre Nichols. After setting a record for the most homicides recorded in the city in 2021, Memphis officials attempted to increase deterrence by forming a special unit designed to patrol high-crime areas and apprehend felony offenders. This unit, labeled the SCORPION unit, was initially credited for reducing the violent crime rate in 2022 (Pereira and Deliso 2023). In early 2023, however, the aggressive approach of this unit led to the tragic death of Tyre Nichols, who was beaten to death by four officers after he ran away from a traffic stop. Not only was his death the result of the overemphasis on "getting tough," but it further undercut trust in the police and spurred protests in cities around the country (Franklin and Bowman 2023). While this murder lacks the racialized element of previous incidents (both the victim and the officers were Black), these types of incidents illustrate that it is police brutality, not the protests of that brutality, that helps to maintain American exceptionalism in the rate of homicide offending.

To be fair to the police, public distrust and crime rates are somewhat out of their control. The stratification of US society along racial and economic lines inspires distrust of social systems and institutions in general (Warren 2011). Trust in the police tends to be lower in societies with a greater degree of ethnic/racial heterogeneity (Morris 2015). The higher rates of distrust of the police by ethnic/racial minorities are not just a problem in the United States but one that other multiethnic and multiracial democracies have struggled to resolve as well. However, blaming protestors for pressuring for police reform continues to be a distraction from resolving both policing and societal issues that contribute to elevated rates of violent crime.

Conclusion

In conclusion, "defunding" the police and "de-policing" have had a minimal impact on the overarching homicide trend. As documented in this chapter, variation in police budget allocation explained so little variation in homicide in 2020 and 2021 that it cannot be confidently distinguished from no impact at all. Similarly, previous research examining a lack of deterrence during the homicide epidemic has been mixed and incomplete in relation to the broader increase in homicide both before and after June 2020. The current evidence is more supportive of the idea that de-policing occurred *during* the homicide epidemic but had little to no impact on the overarching homicide trend; de-policing may have exacerbated the homicide epidemic but was not its ultimate cause. We will return to this issue in chapter 8.

It is at this point that the discussion on recent crime trends has usually stopped. The vast majority of research on crime trends from 2015 onward has either implicitly or explicitly been motivated by an attempt to support or contradict the de-policing narrative. I have concluded, like others before (e.g., Rosenfeld 2020), that de-policing is a poor candidate to explain the recent increase in the homicide rate. Yet no alternative explanation has filled this void in understanding. If it was not de-policing, then what caused homicide rates to increase?

In the next few chapters, I argue that the context that enabled the homicide epidemic has been hiding in plain sight. Specifically, it can be attributed to the decline of American society. There are multiple indicators of this decline, but the most impactful are the outgrowth of US institutional deterioration and the decline in Americans' psychosocial well-being. It is fairly obvious to even the most casual observer that US society is in decline or at the very least on the "wrong track." Yet few have made the connection between American decline and its increased proclivity for violence. In chapter 3, I examine the decline of Americans' psychosocial well-being and a resulting increase in alcohol consumption, which has contributed to a greater number of violent assaults and homicides.

3

Getting Drunk

American Malaise, Part I

Sadly, the American Dream is dead.
—Donald J. Trump

The United States is experiencing a slow, yet steady, decline. The confident, self-assured vision of the future that once inspired Francis Fukuyama (1989) to see the triumph of liberal democracy and capitalism as the "end of history" during the twentieth century has been replaced in the twenty-first century with apocalyptic visions of the end of the world. Fukuyama's sentiments reflected an optimism that many people felt during that time. Technological innovation, economic prosperity, and a belief in American exceptionalism inspired the idea that each generation would live more prosperous lives than the last. A terrorist attack, a failed military venture, a financial collapse, and a pandemic later, America's vision of the future has dimmed a bit. These societal calamities have been coupled with the increasingly unaffordable price of health care, higher education, housing, and child care, which have made the lives of working- and middle-class Americans more precarious with each passing year. The decline of American prestige, frequent "once-in-a-century" societal and environmental disasters, and precarious economic conditions for working people have contributed to a vague sense, or even hopefulness, that we are living near the end of the United States as we know it.

Most Americans have at least some awareness of their nation's decline, but few have made the connection between our current societal malaise and the recent homicide rate increase. This lack of awareness is understandable, as American decline has happened little by little over the past few decades, with no particular event appearing to correspond with an increase in crime rates. Even during the largest financial collapse since the Great Depression, known as the "Great Recession" of 2008, crime rates remained stable and even continued to decline (Rosenfeld 2014). For decades, it seemed that there was no connection between criminality and the stagnant wages, rising prices, and the abandonment of hope that characterized working-class life. Why is it only recently that American decline has caused a homicide epidemic?

In this chapter, I argue that American decline has caused people across the country to cope with their negative emotions through the use of drugs and alcohol. The increase in drug and alcohol abuse has been well-documented in the discussion of "deaths of despair" (Case and Deaton 2020). Beginning with this premise, this chapter addresses the role of a neglected topic: the impact of increasing alcohol consumption on violent assaults and, particularly, homicides. Drunken disinhibition and impulsivity contribute to fights, assaults, and even murders that would not have otherwise occurred had everyone been sober. However, before addressing the specific role of alcohol consumption on the homicide epidemic, I contextualize the increase in alcohol-related deaths, and other deaths of despair, as a symptom of American malaise.

American Malaise

The term "malaise" implies an ailment of no definitively determined origin that contributes to a general feeling of unwellness or unease. In the case of the United States, the apparent decline in psychosocial well-being fits this description. There are several potential contributing factors, but there is no definitive conclusion about the precise cause of increasing rates of mental illness, substance abuse, and premature death.

One potential culprit is the high and rising rate of income inequality. Income inequality has increased during recent decades in the United States (Saez and Zucman 2020). More unequal nations tend to have a myriad of problems related to social dysfunction, mental illness, and a shorter life expectancy (Wilkinson and Pickett 2011). However, it is ultimately unclear if the recent trends in illness, disease, and death are solely attributable to US economic inequity.

One reason that we cannot definitively attribute American malaise (solely) to income inequality is due to the respective trends in inequality and malaise. Income inequality has been increasing in the United States since at least the mid-1970s, and wage stagnation for middle-income earners has long been a consistent feature of the US economy (Saez and Zucman 2020). That is, the apparent economic and social contributors of malaise have been a part of American life predating the apparent despair of the twenty-first century. It is possible that income inequality has reached a threshold that has triggered a lack of hope for the future, but this is still unclear.

What is clear are the characteristics of those who are most likely to die of deaths of despair: members of the working class. Anne Case and Angus Deaton (2020) attribute increasing deaths of despair to the deteriorating economic conditions for working-class people. For example, wages for the tenth percentile in income earners actually declined from 1979 to 2013 after accounting for inflation (Mishel, Gould, and Bivens 2015). Even for middle-income earners, the modest increase in wages has not kept pace with the exploding cost of many of the markers or middle-class life, such as housing and higher education (N. Wilson 2021). In the shadow of hollowed-out rust-belt cities, abandoned farmhouses, and the empty storefronts of once-thriving downtown areas, the experience of working-class America is one of declining hope that the future will bring prosperity.

However, the hollowing out of rust-belt cities also predates the increase in deaths of despair, suggesting that there must be another contextual factor to explain increasing mortality rates. To resolve this conundrum, Case and Deaton (2020) also point to a breakdown of community life. There has been greater social atomization, evident in the steep decline in community participation, including less church attendance, fewer people joining community organizations, and a general decline of time spent with others (see also Putnam 2000). Without the family and community support of previous generations, declining economic prospects are faced in isolation. With people bereft of nonmarket support provided by family and friends, their economic struggles are not cushioned by community assistance. Instead, many feel socially isolated (Kannan and Veazie 2023), left to face their dwindling prospects alone.

The atomization of social life is especially pernicious in the United States, as there are few comprehensive social programs to care for the sick, needy, and desperate. Unlike many other wealthy democracies, where there are universal programs that provide some mixture of health care, housing assistance, subsidized child care, and education to all citizens, the threadbare social safety net in the United States leads many people to the conclusion that you are on your own. Social programs in the United States are heavily means-tested, which causes recipients to lose support if their income increases. Accordingly, upward mobility for the most impoverished could result in the loss of health care, child care, and housing, even if you are fortunate enough to live in a state that provides this assistance in the first place.

Political deadlock has curtailed hope for collective uplift, leaving Americans to compete with their neighbors for the scraps left from "trickle-down" economic policies. Instead of perceiving themselves as taking part in a collective class struggle, Americans are often looking to profit off the next crisis and, ostensibly, off the desperation of their neighbors. Whether it is hoarding hand sanitizer at the beginning of the pandemic in an attempt to sell it at an inflated price or buying water futures to profit from a worldwide shortage, American culture has turned increasingly nasty and brutish. Americans are more than willing to milk profit from the desperation of others so as not to end up on the wrong side of the poverty line. Not surprisingly, given the stagnation of wages coupled with this "dog-eat-dog" culture, an increasing number of Americans are depressed, are overwhelmed by stress, and see little hope for the next generation (Villaume, Chen, and Adam 2023).

This stress has contributed to Americans living sicker, shorter, more desperate lives than they were at the beginning of the century. Life expectancy at birth plummeted to 76.1 years in 2021, a level not experienced in the United States since 1996 (Arias et al. 2022). Many other countries have experienced a rebound in life expectancy since the initial phase of COVID-19 (Schöley et al. 2022), leaving the United States to fall even farther behind during the second year of the pandemic. In 2021, life expectancy at birth in the wealthiest country in the history of the world was tied with Panama, closer to Cuba, Nicaragua, and Vietnam (74 years) than the United Kingdom (81), Germany (81), and Canada (83) (World Bank 2022). The open secret is that this decline in life expectancy was not merely attributable to the pandemic, or even resistance to COVID-19 vaccines, but the underlying hopelessness, sickness, and despair that caused Americans to die prematurely and be less resilient during the pandemic.

Even before the pandemic, life expectancy gains had stalled and reversed. From 2014 to 2017, Americans' life expectancy unexpectedly declined (Kochanek, Anderson, and Arias 2020). This drop in life expectancy was slight but was unprecedented outside of periods in which a significant number of deaths were caused by war or a health epidemic. For some demographic groups, this decline was more dramatic. Between 1999 and 2013, middle-aged (non-Hispanic) White Americans experienced a decline in life expectancy at the same time that nearly all other demographic groups were experiencing increased longevity. This increase in early mortality was especially concentrated in less-educated groups: specifically, middle-aged non-Hispanic Whites lacking a college degree. Much of this apparent reversal in the life expectancy trend appeared to be due to higher rates of suicide, drug poisoning, and cirrhosis of the liver (Case and Deaton 2015).

Coping with Decline

As economic prospects and a sense of community declined, an increasing number of Americans have coped in a self-destructive manner. A prominent criminological theory that examines the impact of coping with negative emotions on substance abuse is known as "general strain theory." This theory predicts that the experience of "strain," which refers to a negative experience ranging from having a cherished goal blocked by circumstance to having an item of value stolen from you, evokes a negative emotion. The desire for revenge and feelings of anger or frustration in the lack of ability to acquire that which is desired pressures individuals who have experienced "strain" to sometimes cope by committing a criminal offense (Agnew 1992, 2006).

In the specific case of our current cultural malaise, the strains that Americans are experiencing include a perceived decline in the standard of living, community and societal deterioration, and a general lack of a hope for a prosperous future. These strains evoke negative emotions, such as the depression, anxiety, and stress, which have seemingly become more common with each passing year. And, increasingly, people have chosen to cope with these negative emotions through substance abuse.

Of course, strain does not automatically contribute to substance abuse. The manner in which someone copes with strain depends on the situation, their personal attributes, and the resources at their disposal (Agnew 2006). Some individuals may cope with the ever-looming sense of falling behind financially by attending college or starting a small business. Others may buy Bitcoin or join a multilevel marketing "opportunity" in an attempt to supplement their income. Some may pay a therapist to help them talk through their looming sense of dread and hopelessness.

But for many, there are limited options to cope with the negative emotions surrounding an economic and political system that feels impersonal and immune to attempts to reform it. As Robert Agnew (2006, 15) writes of coping with negative emotions: "Individuals may not be able to reduce or escape their strains, and they may not be able to obtain revenge against those who have wronged them. . . . Individuals often drink excessively or use illegal drugs in an effort to seek relief from the strains they are experiencing." The real or perceived inability to cope with strain in a prosocial way contributes to an attempt to escape through alcohol, drugs, or even suicide.

The ways in which Americans have coped with societal decline is alarming; rates of drug overdose, alcohol-related deaths, and suicide have dramatically increased. Supercharged by fentanyl overdoses (National Institute on Drug Abuse 2022), the drug overdose rate increased by an astounding 463 percent from 1999 to 2021, according to CDC mortality statistics (CDC Wonder 2023). Alcohol-related deaths have increased by 133 percent during this same period. In 2018, the suicide rate increased to 14.8 deaths per 100,000, the highest rate of suicide recorded in the United States since World War II (Ducharme 2019). The increase in the suicide rate (38 percent) has been modest compared to the increases in the other types of deaths of despair but is still alarming.[1]

These deaths of despair, particularly drug overdose and alcohol-related causes, accelerated during the homicide epidemic (2015–2021). In chapter 4, I discuss the role that drug abuse has played in causing the spike in homicide. In the remainder of this chapter, I outline how the accelerating trend in alcohol consumption during the past decade has contributed to an increase in violent assaults. Before doing so, I must first provide some theoretical and historical background for the association between alcohol consumption patterns and homicide trends.

Background: Alcohol Consumption and Homicide Trends

The connection between alcohol consumption and violent assault is believed to be due to alcohol's disinhibitory effects. Robert Nash Parker (1995) argues that alcohol-induced disinhibition causes individuals to be less prone to the social controls of normative behavioral expectations and reduces their ability to impose self-restraint. This relative lack of behavioral control makes intoxicated individuals more likely to be either the victim or the offender of violent assaults. The primary reason for this connection is that potential offenders are less likely to restrain emotional responses. In situations where there is a dispute or grievance, people who are intoxicated are more likely to use violence to resolve it. Recent research confirms this general hypothesis, as alcohol consumption seems to nullify the effect of self-control on reactive aggression (Meldrum et al. 2023). Alcohol consumption also raises the likelihood of dying as a victim of violent death. In situations where multiple parties are intoxicated, acting belligerent and aggressive may cause others to respond in kind. This drunken belligerence can contribute to assault and homicide victimization, similar to the concept of "victim precipitated" homicide (Wolfgang 1957).

The propensity toward violence while intoxicated is borne out in the data. In one of the earliest and most influential studies on homicide offending, Martin Wolfgang (1958) found that 64 percent of homicide offenders in Philadelphia from 1948 to 1952 were under the influence of alcohol at time of the fatal assault. More recent studies continue to document the disproportionally intoxicated nature of murder. A meta-analysis found that 48 percent of offenders had consumed alcohol prior to the offense (Kuhns et al. 2014). Additionally, nearly 40 percent of homicide victims had alcohol in their system at the time of their death (Naimi et al. 2016). In nearly half of US homicides, alcohol is in the system of either the perpetrator or the victim (or both).

During the early twentieth century, the public was keenly aware of the role that alcohol consumption played in contributing to violence. A major motivation of the temperance movement that led to the Eighteenth Amendment, otherwise known as "Prohibition," was inspired by domestic violence perpetrated by men who were under the influence of alcohol. Prior to Prohibition, people drank heavily (Miron and Zwiebel 1991), and alcohol consumption was central to understanding high rates of violence in the late 1800s and early 1900s (Felson and Cundiff 2018). Early women's rights groups organized in an attempt to restrict alcohol sales and consumption in an effort to reduce domestic violence (Dannenbaum 1981). If not for the negative side effects of Prohibition, which empowered organized crime, the resulting reduction in alcohol consumption would have probably spurred a decline in homicide victimization as well (Jensen 2000).

Aggregate and historical research in the United States has consistently documented the association between trends in alcohol consumption and homicide. Parker (1995) finds that alcohol consumption trends are significantly associated with homicide rates in the United States, particularly among younger offenders. Historical analyses of the Prohibition era (Jensen 2000) and well as nineteenth- and twentieth-century homicide trends (Batton and Jensen 2002; Felson and Cundiff 2018) demonstrate that alcohol consumption, often captured with the proxy measure of deaths due to cirrhosis of the liver, is consistently predictive of more homicide deaths. Additionally, cross-national research documents that alcohol consumption is a contributor to international variation in homicide rates (Hockin, Rogers, and Pridemore 2018).

To illustrate the historical association between alcohol consumption and homicide, I depict these respective trends in the United States from 1950 to 2021 in figure 3.1. Alcohol consumption is depicted with the dotted line, and the solid line represents the homicide rate. The alcohol data used to construct this figure are drawn from the National Institute on Alcohol Abuse and Alcoholism (NIAAA) (Slater and Alpert 2023). The NIAAA compiles this data through numerous sources but primarily uses state-level alcohol sales data when available. For states and regions where this data are unreported or unreliable, data on alcohol shipments also serve as a source. The NIAAA then uses this sales and shipping data to estimate how much alcohol (in gallons) is being consumed per capita. The homicide data are derived from the FBI's (2022) Crime Data Explorer and historical reports on homicide statistics (Fox and Zawitz 2007).

Figure 3.1 implies that alcohol consumption played a role in the previous increase in homicide during the 1960s and 1970s and may be playing some role in the current one. During the 1960s and 1970s, alcohol consumption and homicide rate trends were increasing at the exact same time. In fact, there is a nearly perfect correlation between the annual rate of gallons of alcohol consumed per capita and the homicide rate between 1950 and 1980 ($r = .97$). The correlation since 1980 has been more modest ($r = .45$), as there is some lag between the decline in alcohol consumption that began in the 1980s and the decline in homicide that occurred in the 1990s. There was also an apparent lag between the

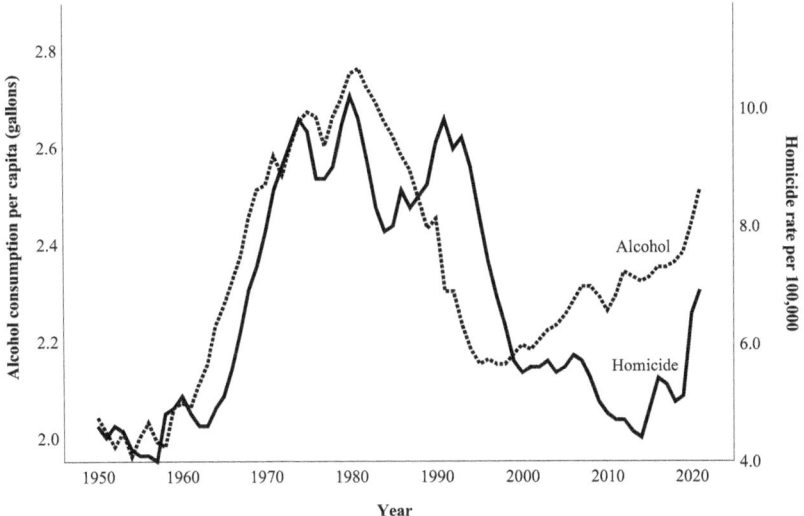

FIGURE 3.1. Alcohol consumption and the homicide rate, 1950–2021

increase in alcohol consumption in the first decade of the twenty-first century and the upward homicide trend in the 2010s. Overall, there is a moderately strong annual association between alcohol consumption and homicide rates from 1950 to 2021 ($r = .76$), suggesting that alcohol consumption is likely to be a factor shaping homicide victimization trends.

How can we account for the weaker association between alcohol consumption and homicide since 1980? Some of the decoupling of these trends during the 1990s may be attributed to the increase in youth violence associated with the crack cocaine epidemic (Baumer et al. 1998). Because the homicide rate trend was seemingly being driven more by an increase in youthful involvement in drug distribution (Cork 1999) rather than alcohol consumption during this era, the impact of declining alcohol consumption was not apparent until the mid-1990s, rather than in the mid-1980s.

The lagged association between alcohol and homicide in the first two decades of the twenty-first century may be due to the decline in other criminal offenses, such as burglary and robbery. As I alluded to in chapter 1, the homicide rate is defying "criminological gravity" by trending in the opposite direction of acquisitive offense patterns. Because the countervailing factor of fewer property-based offenses appears to be contributing to a lower rate of homicide in the early twenty-first century, the impact of the increasing rate of alcohol consumption is not apparent until after 2014.

Additionally, alcohol consumption per capita may not be as deadly as in generations past due to who is but, more importantly, *who is not* consuming it. The NIAAA (2023) estimates that there has been a 58.3 percent reduction in alcohol consumption for youth aged sixteen to seventeen from 2002 to 2021. This decline in youthful intoxication makes the current alcohol binge less deadly than it may have been otherwise. In previous research, Parker (1995) highlights the role of age restrictions on alcohol consumption, which contributed to a reduction in homicide among adolescents and young adults. With fewer youthful drinkers today, the rate of homicides per gallon of alcohol consumed is probably reduced from its peak during the 1980s.

Alcohol Consumption and the 2015–2021 Homicide Epidemic

While US alcohol consumption and homicide trends are not as closely associated as they once were, there are a few pieces of evidence to suggest that alcohol has played a role in the recent homicide epidemic. The first is the timing of the acceleration in alcohol-related deaths, which occurred at the same time as the acceleration of the homicide trend. From 1999 to 2014, the alcohol-related death rate increased by 2.6 deaths per 100,000 population. Then, from 2014 to 2021, the rate of alcohol-related death grew by 6.7 deaths per 100,000. This acceleration after 2014 resulted in an increase of two and a half times more deaths per capita in fewer than half as many years (CDC Wonder 2023). The acceleration of alcohol consumption patterns is also evident in the NIAAA alcohol consumption data. From 1999 to 2014, the number of gallons of alcohol consumed per capita increased by 0.15 (from 2.17 in 1999 to 2.32 in 2014). Then, from 2014 to 2021, there was an increase of 0.19 gallons consumed per capita (2.51 in 2021), which is a larger increase in fewer than half as many years. In both proxy measures of alcohol consumption, we see a similar accelerating pattern at precisely the time that homicide rates began to increase.

There are additional clues in regional patterns in deaths of despair that alcohol consumption is related to the homicide epidemic. As you may recall from chapter 1, homicide mortality in the United States has shifted toward the Midwest, as this region experienced the largest proportional increase in homicide rates of any region since 2014. This pattern of rapidly increasing homicide mortality aligns with a greater proportional increase in deaths of despair in the Midwest during the past few decades. In 1999, the Midwest was tied with the Northeast for the lowest rate of deaths of despair, including deaths from suicide, drug overdose, and alcohol-related causes (20 per 100,000). By 2021, the Midwest had moved into second place, with 63.5 deaths of despair per 100,000, trailing only the Western region (67.4) and experiencing the largest proportional increase of any region in the country.

Table 3.1 depicts the regional change in the rate of deaths of despair and homicide from 1999 to 2021. The numbers depicted in the table represent the percentage change in the rate of death in each region during this period using cause-of-mortality data from CDC Wonder (2023). No region has experienced a greater proportional shift in deaths of despair than the Midwest during the twenty-first century. From 1999 to 2021, the drug overdose death rate has increased by 650 percent, corresponding with the largest increase in suicide (52 percent) and alcohol-related deaths (190 percent) as well. The Midwest has also experienced the largest increase in homicide rate of any region during this time period (46 percent), which suggests that deaths of despair and the current homicide epidemic are related, at least regionally.

Disaggregated homicide victimization trends by age are also suggestive of alcohol's role. Given the decline of youth and young-adult alcohol consumption (NIAAA 2023), the association between alcohol and homicide victimization is more likely to be present among older age groups.

TABLE 3.1. Proportional Change in Deaths of Despair and Homicide by Region, 1999–2021

Region	Suicide (%)	Drug overdose (%)	Alcohol related (%)	Homicide (%)
Midwest	+52	+650	+190	+46
South	+35	+588	+113	+34
Northeast	+33	+438	+109	+17
West	+33	+265	+130	+5

And, in particular, the alcohol-related death patterns among thirty-to forty-nine-year-olds seem to align with their patterns in homicide victimization. To make this comparison, I use CDC Wonder (2023) data on mortality for deaths in the United States from 1999 to 2021. Figure 3.2 depicts trends in alcohol-related deaths (represented by the dotted line) and the homicide victimization rate (represented by the solid line). In the context of this comparison, alcohol-related deaths are used as a proxy measure of heavy alcohol consumption. As you can see in this figure, there is an abrupt increase in alcohol-related deaths in 2015, a year that seemed to mark a turning point for homicide victimization as well. Although the sharp decline in homicide victimization prior to 2010 is not well explained by trends in alcohol-related deaths, there is a close correspondence between these two trends overall ($r = .95$), especially from 2014 onward.[2]

The connection between alcohol consumption and homicide victimization within the same age group is consistent with known homicide offender and victimization patterns. Homicide offenders and victims often overlap in their social and demographic characteristics. While homicide offenders tend to be a little younger than their victims (Broidy et al. 2006), it is often people in a similar age range who are involved in both roles of a violent assault. As excessive alcohol consumption contributed to more middle-aged deaths, it also corresponded with more fatal assaults of people in this group as well.

However, even within this age range, there were some differences across demographic groups. For non-Hispanic White men aged thirty to forty-nine, the relationship was relatively strong (*r* = .89), mirroring the overall association for this age group. However, there is no apparent correlation between the annual rate of alcohol-related deaths and the homicide victimization rate for women (*r* = −.01) during this period. Although there was a modest increase in the female homicide victimization rate between 2014 (2.0 per 100,000) and 2021 (2.9 per 100,000), it was not associated with women's alcohol consumption patterns. This lack of an association is not particularly surprising given gendered homicide offending and victimization patterns. Excessive alcohol consumption among women would not put other women at a significantly greater risk of assault. When women commit homicide, they tend to kill children and their romantic partners (Kellermann and Mercy 1992) and especially their male partners after being threatened with violence or experiencing previous abuse (Jurik and Winn 1990). Accordingly, women's alcohol consumption is not as likely to be predictive of homicide trends in general.

Conversely, male alcohol consumption appears to put women at an increased risk of homicide victimization. The alcohol-related death rate

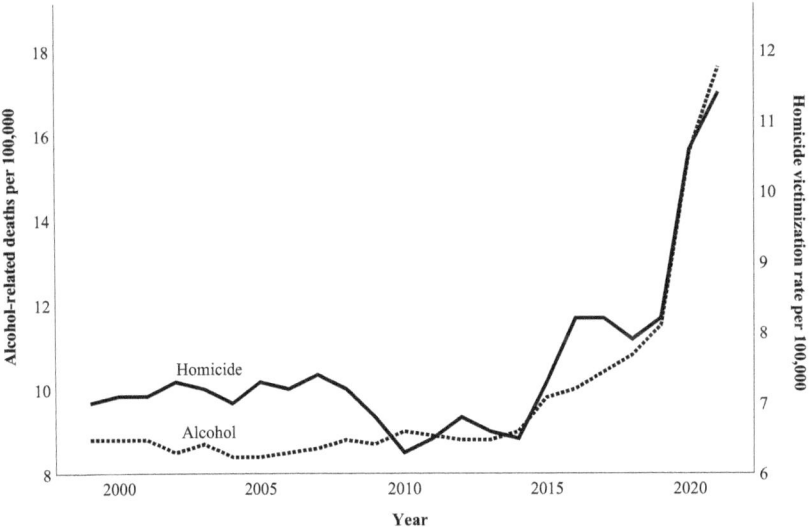

FIGURE 3.2. Alcohol-related death and homicide victimization among people aged thirty to forty-nine

for thirty- to forty-nine-year-old non-Hispanic White males not only is correlated with White male homicide victimization but also shares a moderate association with White female homicide victimization of the same age range ($r = .64$).

The association between alcohol-related deaths and homicide for males aged thirty to forty-nine was not universal across racial and ethnic groups either. For Hispanic men of this age group, the annual correlation between alcohol-related deaths and homicide victimization was only moderately strong ($r = .45$). For non-Hispanic Black men, there was no apparent association between alcohol-related deaths and homicide victimization ($r = -.05$). Overall, the trend in alcohol-related deaths appears to be associated with homicide victimization, but the impact is not universal. The alcohol consumption of men, and particularly non-Hispanic White men between the ages of thirty and forty-nine, seems to be more closely associated with changes in the homicide victimization trend than among other demographic groups.

Without accounting for other factors, these associations are merely suggestive of an association. The same is also true of the *lack* of association between alcohol-related death rates and homicide victimization. Overall, the trends depicted in this chapter are suggestive, supporting the idea that an increase in alcohol consumption has been associated with homicide victimization trends. In chapter 7, I account for additional factors to confirm the arguments made in this chapter that America's drinking problem has contributed to the patterns observed in aggravated assault and homicide.

Conclusion

The evidence presented in this chapter suggests that American malaise is a major component of the recent increase in homicide. The negative emotions that have accompanied American decline have caused a significant number of Americans to cope in self-destructive ways. Depression, stress, and hopelessness have increased in tandem with suicide, drug overdose, and alcohol-related deaths, known as "deaths of despair." Until recently, these self-destructive coping patterns had been largely ignored in relation to patterns in violent crime. This has particularly been the case for alcohol, with almost no media or academic discussion of how patterns in alcohol consumption have contributed to the homicide epidemic. This has been an oversight, as a considerable proportion of both offenders and victims of homicide are intoxicated at the time of the assault. Additionally, there is a historical association between alcohol consumption trends and homicide, including in disaggregated trends of the twenty-first century. These pieces of evidence, coupled with a recent acceleration in alcohol consumption trends, suggest that alcohol has contributed to the homicide epidemic.

In chapter 4, I delve into the other major contributor of American malaise to the increase in homicide: drug abuse. Even more troubling than the increase in alcohol-related deaths is the rapidly increasing rate of drug overdose deaths in the United States. Unlike alcohol-related deaths, the opioid crisis has not avoided public scrutiny and debate. However, there has been a general neglect in the discussion of the impact of drug abuse on recent homicide trends, especially those of 2020 and 2021. In chapter 4, I examine drug abuse as a manifestation of American malaise and its impact on recent homicide trends.

4

Using Drugs

American Malaise, Part II

On the streets, you had to operate with integrity. If you broke your word to someone, he wasn't going to take you to court—he was going to deal with you himself.
—Jay-Z, discussing his experiences as a drug dealer

Attributed to economic decline and physical pain, the opioid epidemic was initially portrayed as a problem disproportionately impacting working-class White Americans. The narrative surrounding the opioid epidemic was set in place by Anne Case and Angus Deaton's (2015) discovery that working-class, middle-aged, (non-Hispanic) White men, disproportionately living in rural and suburban communities, were becoming addicted to prescription pain killers and dying due to overdoses at an alarming rate.

Unlike drug epidemics associated with urban Black users, this drug epidemic garnered sympathy rather than increased severity of criminal penalties (Equal Justice Initiative 2019). Additionally, with an apparent corporate villain (Purdue Pharma) to blame for pushing the highly addictive OxyContin on an unwitting public (US Department of Justice 2020), the opioid epidemic seemed to be more of a story of the greed of pharmaceutical companies rather than user criminality. Even when a subset of politicians and commentators have attempted to tie the opioid epidemic to criminality through a (false) connection to illegal immigration (Bier 2022), their narrative is often one that partially exonerates the drug user as a victim of "open border" immigration policies.

Because the dominant narrative about the opioid epidemic has more often cast drug users as victims of a disease, the connection between drug abuse and crime trends has been partially obscured. On the one hand, this portrayal is a positive step away from the failed "get tough" and "just say no" approach of the 1980s toward a more treatment-based strategy. On the other hand, the softening of public sentiment and the attempt to pursue "harm reduction" strategies obscure its place as a half measure in eliminating the collateral consequences of drug abuse. That is, we are still fighting the "war on drugs" but with somewhat less focus on prosecuting drug users.

The possession, manufacturing, and sale of drugs remain illegal, creating an underground drug market that operates outside government control and regulation. Within this shadow economy, there are no regulations that can be imposed to ensure the quality of drugs, no police intervention in cases of theft or counterfeit goods, no lawsuits that can be brought against those who engage in unfair "business" practices, and no hearings in small-claims court concerning those who fail to pay what each party has agreed on. Regardless of how we decide to treat substance abuse disorders, the underground drug economy continues to exist as a virtual "stateless location" in which government intervention is limited and dispute resolution is enacted through unilateral retribution by the aggrieved party (Black 1983).

The timeline of the opioid epidemic illustrates why America's drug abuse problem has only recently corresponded with an increase in violence. In particular, the drug addiction crisis shifted circa 2012 from legal/quasi-legal prescription drug use to illicit drug abuse facilitated by underground drug markets. In 1996, OxyContin was introduced with an aggressive promotion campaign to doctors that downplayed potential risks of addiction and dependency. The promotional campaign "worked"; by 2004, OxyContin was the most abused prescription opioid (Van Zee 2009). During this early period of the opioid epidemic, there was no clear connection between drug abuse and violent crime trends. Because these drugs were being prescribed legally, violence associated with illicit markets was not as apparent. While there was undoubtedly some illicit secondary market of prescription pills in this era, it did not seem to impact the overall direction of the homicide trend. In fact, there was an overall decline in the homicide rate throughout the early era of the prescription drug epidemic (circa 2000 to 2011).

However, as prescription overdose deaths began to increase, there was growing concern about a big-pharma-manufactured public health crisis. In 2011, the CDC and state officials began to monitor overprescription and cracked down on "doctor shopping" and "pill mills" (Centers for Disease Control 2011). As the supply of legal opioids was curtailed, there was a near-simultaneous expansion of illicit drug markets (McGranahan and Parker 2021). By 2013, the number of heroin overdoses had nearly doubled from the 2011 rate (from 1.4 to 2.7 per 100,000); by 2015, the combined death rate due to heroin and synthetic opioid overdoses had more than tripled (from 2.2 in 2011 to 7.2 in 2015) (Spencer, Miniño, and Warner 2022). During the illicit opioid phase (2012–2021), the homicide rate increased from 4.7 to 6.8 homicides per 100,000 population according to FBI (2022) estimates. Unlike the period in which prescription opioids were the primary driver of drug overdose deaths, the uptick in violence aligns closely with the increase in the abuse of heroin, synthetic opioids, cocaine, and amphetamines, all sold in underground black-market exchanges.

In this chapter, I connect American malaise to the homicide epidemic through a second mechanism: illicit drug abuse and the corresponding expansion of underground drug markets. In chapter 3, I argued that the increase in alcohol consumption was one way in which many Americans have attempted to numb the pain of the decline in their standard of living, economic prospects, and community life. In this chapter, I make a similar argument about the role of cultural malaise in contributing to substance abuse. However, the mechanism connecting drug abuse to violence is slightly different from that of alcohol consumption. While the psychopharmacological effects of drug intoxication may sometimes contribute to violence, the increase in the homicide rate is driven less by the effects of the drugs themselves and more by the expansion of the underground drug market. Before discussing the role that drug abuse and exchange have played in shaping historical and recent homicide trends, I first discuss the causes and evolution of the recent and ongoing drug abuse epidemic.

Pain, Economic Decline, and Drug Abuse

The opioid epidemic began with the increasing experience and treatment of physical pain. The experience of pain is not evenly distributed throughout society, as working-class people are more likely to be employed in occupations that demand physical exertion and have a higher risk of injury. This dynamic was highlighted by Case and Deaton (2020) in their discussion of the association between working-class (non-Hispanic) White pain and deaths of despair. As the rate of reported pain increased, it was heavily concentrated among people without a college degree, which corresponded with a large increase in opioid-addiction-related deaths. This connection between reported pain, opioid addiction, and drug overdose deaths was confirmed by research examining the association between a state's rural physical disability rate and the age-adjusted drug overdose death rate (McGranahan and Parker 2021).

In addition to the experience of pain, there is mounting evidence of the effect of declining economic opportunities on overdose deaths. In an examination of county-level overdose mortality, Atheendar Venkataramani, Elizabeth Bair and Rourke O'Brien (2020) found that the closure of automotive assembly plants was associated with an 85 percent higher rate of county opioid overdose mortality (five years later) than in similar counties where there was no such manufacturing plant loss. This direct impact of the economic decline and despair of the working class is also evident in the lived experiences of those who have survived a drug overdose. The backdrop of community decay and economic decline was present in interviews with people who have overdosed on opioids and survived, as many attributed a portion of their personal struggle with addiction to the hopelessness of the surrounding community's economic prospects (McLean 2016).

When the opioid epidemic shifted from prescriptions to illicit drugs after the CDC crackdown on overprescription (circa 2012), so did the geographical patterns in drug abuse. Initially, the prescription drug epidemic was disproportionately taking place in rural counties that were "left behind." Being "left behind" was indicated by county-level population decline, which was associated with a higher rate of prescription overdose deaths prior to 2012 (Feldmeyer et al. 2022). As the drug abuse epidemic shifted to illicit drugs, it moved to more urban areas, especially those with greater issues associated with "social disorganization," which includes low social capital, vacant homes, and poverty (Peters et al. 2020). It was this shift from legal prescription drugs to illicit drug markets, disproportionately located in distressed urban centers, that turned the drug abuse epidemic into a homicide epidemic.

This shift to impoverished urban locations also included a shift in the demographics of drug abuse deaths. Specifically, a disproportionately White epidemic of prescription opioid abuse turned into a multiracial/multiethnic phenomenon. Prior to this shift in substance abuse patterns, the lower rate of deaths of despair among African Americans was somewhat perplexing, given that one of the primary purported causes of despair was worsening economic prospects for people without a college degree (Case and Deaton 2020). However, as the drug abuse epidemic expanded to illicit drugs, the drug overdose rate for all racial and ethnic groups increased dramatically, with the Black overdose rate exceeding the White rate in recent years.

Figure 4.1 depicts the historical change in the rate of overdose deaths per one hundred thousand population for each of the three largest racial/ethnic groups in the United States (White, Black, and Hispanic).[1] The overdose rate represented in this figure includes all types of drugs, including prescription opioids but also illicit opioids (heroin and fentanyl)

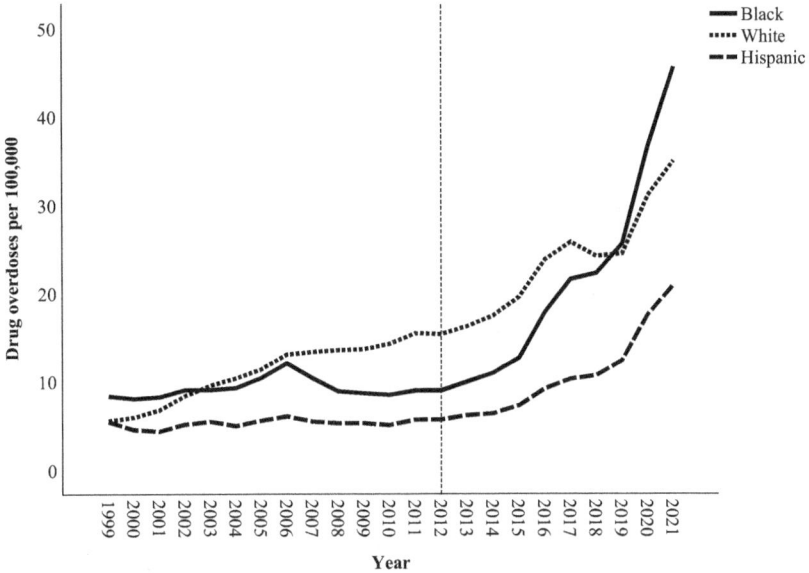

FIGURE 4.1. Racially disaggregated drug overdose death rate, 1999-2021

and non-opioid related drug overdoses as well. A vertical dotted line is placed at 2012, roughly separating the prescription opioid and illicit drug abuse eras. As is apparent in the figure, the White drug overdose death rate had outpaced that of other racial/ethnic groups from 2003 through 2017. In fact, during the prescription drug abuse era prior to 2012, the trend in Black and Hispanic drug overdose rates was relatively flat, indicating that the drug abuse crisis was largely concentrated within White communities.

During the illicit drug era, however, drug abuse became a multiracial and multiethnic disaster. It was only during this era that we see a disproportionate increase in the Black and Hispanic drug overdose death rate. From 2011 to 2021, the Black overdose rate increased by 411 percent. There was also a rapidly accelerating pattern for Hispanics of all races, as drug overdoses increased by 271 percent during this period. Although it is true that there was an increase in the White overdose rate during the same time period, it was not proportionally as large (127 percent).

By 2021, the rapidly accelerating Black overdose rate had surpassed the White rate by more than 30 percent.

The changes in racially disaggregated drug overdose rates both support and contradict Case and Deaton's (2020) arguments about despair and drug abuse. On the one hand, the rapid increase in the rate of Black drug overdose death indirectly supports the idea that economic marginalization and despair are tied to drug abuse. Black workers are in a far worse economic position than their White counterparts (Derenoncourt et al. 2022), which is consistent with their higher rate of drug abuse deaths. On the other hand, it contradicts some of Case and Deaton's specific arguments about the disproportionately White epidemic in deaths of despair. Case and Deaton proposed an ad hoc explanation of why, despite objectively worse economic prospects, Black Americans were seemingly immune from the type of despair that had produced excess deaths in the White community. They argued that Black collective resiliency after generations of maltreatment and struggle created a sort of immunity from deaths of despair. At least in the case of drug overdose deaths, however, this narrative is contradicted by recent trends.

How can we account for this changing racial pattern in drug overdose deaths? It is not entirely clear, but there are a few clues. During the prescription era of the opioid epidemic, the overall non-Hispanic Black drug overdose death rate remained fairly steady, even declining from 2006 to 2010. One likely contributor to this low rate of prescription-opioid-induced death is persistent racial disparities in access to health care. First, Black and Hispanic Americans have a lower rate of health insurance coverage as compared to their (non-Hispanic) White counterparts (Sohn 2017). This makes a doctor visit for pain less likely, which was a major driver of the early phase of the opioid epidemic. Second, physicians are more likely to perceive Black patients as "exaggerating" pain symptoms (Hoffman et al. 2016) and were therefore less likely to prescribe pain medication. In the prescription drug phase of the opioid epidemic, this discriminatory practice may have inadvertently saved Black patients from addiction to highly potent pain killers such as OxyContin.

As the opioid epidemic shifted to illicit drugs, the differential access to health care was no longer a contributing factor in overdose deaths. Whether the rapid increase in Black and Hispanic overdose deaths was due to pent-up demand, such as the feelings of despair and hopelessness noted as part of American malaise, or due to increased access (supply) through illicit markets is unclear. Regardless of the precise reason, the CDC's and state governments' crackdown on the overprescription of opioids in 2011 corresponded with a rapidly increasing illicit drug overdose death rate among minority groups.

By 2021, the opioid epidemic had transformed into a multiracial, polysubstance nightmare. More than one hundred thousand Americans lost their lives to drug overdose in a single year in 2021, which was the deadliest year to date. No longer were these deaths concentrated in one demographic group or geographical enclave. As opioid addiction was driven underground, there was also an increase in both cocaine- and amphetamine (psychostimulants)–related abuse and death (Spencer, Miniño, and Warner 2022). The current drug abuse epidemic is the worst since at least the 1990s and maybe ever. And, like the late 1980s and early 1990s, we should expect the illicit drug trade to contribute to higher rates of homicide. In the next section, I outline the connection between drug abuse and homicide trends.

Background: Drug Abuse and Homicide Trends

Similar to alcohol intoxication, a relatively large proportion of homicides involve either a victim or offender under the influence of drugs. In a study of convicted homicide offenders, more than 46 percent of murderers reported using drugs prior to committing a homicide (Wieczorek, Welte, and Abel 1990). A recent study comparing the characteristics of violent death across homicide and suicide cases found that 41 percent of homicide victims were under the influence of drugs at the time of their untimely deaths; cocaine (16 percent) and heroin (13 percent) were the most common drug intoxicants among homicide victims (Molina and Hargrove 2017). In general, drug abuse appears to put users at an increased risk of being involved in a homicide, as either an offender or victim, as the rate of drug intoxication among people involved in homicides is much higher than for the population at large (Darke 2010).

However, because of the divergent psychopharmacological impacts of specific illicit drugs, a singular explanation cannot be provided for why drug use (in general) puts people at risk of being involved in crime. In fact, opioid intoxication would seemingly reduce the likelihood of committing violent offenses given its sedative effect. It is possible that the intense symptoms of withdrawal or the economic needs produced by the addiction increase involvement in crime (Goldstein 1985). However, the primary violence-inducing effects of drug abuse on crime are believed to be due to an increase in the activity of the illicit drug market.

The connection between drug abuse and violence is largely attributed to the "systemic" issues that surround the underground market for illicit drugs. The illicit drug trade creates social situations and encounters that increase the likelihood of violent and deadly assaults between buyers, sellers, and competitors (Goldstein 1985). In an underground economy in which illegal items are produced and sold, the buyers and sellers are outside typical government protections, including the ability to resolve a dispute by calling on law enforcement or the government. This causes there to be a greater propensity for unilateral dispute resolution in which the aggrieved party uses violence to retrieve disputed property or to enact retribution (Black 1983). Given the illicit drug market's operation outside the law, some drug dealers will take this as an opportunity to "rip off" potential customers, with the knowledge that no one can realistically call on law enforcement (Jacques, Allen, and Wright 2014). Sometimes these attempted thefts contribute to either the dealer or the buyer being shot and killed (Goldstein et al. 1989).

Ironically, the attempts made by law enforcement to suppress illicit drug markets appear to contribute to drug-related homicides. With law enforcement's aggressive pursuit of drug dealers, the specter of potential arrest may cause an escalation of violence between buyers, sellers, and rivals within the drug market in an attempt to avoid apprehension or to eliminate informants (Ousey and Lee 2007). Although separating the amount of drug use and the enforcement of drug laws using arrests as a proxy measure is not always easy, the preponderance of the evidence on drug enforcement suggests that it contributes to more, rather than less, violence associated with illicit drug markets (Werb et al. 2011).

There is a risk of violence not only between buyer and seller but also between members of a gang engaging in drug distribution. As much as gangs pose a threat to the communities they operate in, gang members are also a threat to each other, even within the same group. "Messing up the money" by subordinates—that is, returning less money than the expected yield of drugs sold—could result in low-level street dealers facing violent retribution and even death from their superiors within the gang (Goldstein 1985; Venkatesh 2008).

As the demand for illicit drugs grows, there is a corresponding increase in competition to be the drug supplier. Historically, the best-known example of how the expansion of illicit markets shapes homicidal violence actually involves illegal alcohol sales. Prohibition of alcohol from 1920 through 1933 corresponded with an increase in the homicide rate, despite the fact that alcohol consumption had declined (Jensen 2000). With the prohibition on the manufacture and sale of alcohol, the opportunity for profit for those who were willing to break the law attracted numerous competitors, who used the threat of violence to compete for territory during the "beer wars" (Landesco 1932).

In the contemporary context, gangs fight over the ability to sell drugs or specific "turf" in which only they are allowed to sell. The threat of violence is used both symbolically, to protect the reputation of the gang, and to defend the economic interests of the group. If a rival gang member transgresses the gang's turf for any reason, it is a (potential) provocation for murder to protect the status of the gang (Papachristos 2009). In most cases, gang members see themselves as committing assaults in self-defense, not seeking out violence (Decker 1996). Once an assault is committed, however, retaliatory violence is often soon to follow (Papachristos

2009). This retaliatory violence enables homicide to spread through a process that resembles social contagion. In the city of Chicago from 2006 to 2014, 63.1 percent of the shooting incidents could be attributed to a contagion-like process in which violence spreads like a disease through social networks (Green, Horel, and Papachristos 2017).

Given this competition and spread of defensive violence, illicit drug sales should correspond with an increase in drug-related homicides. During past drug epidemics, the rate of violence increased rapidly. The rise of the crack cocaine market during the late 1980s and early 1990s is often blamed for the spike in homicide that occurred in major US cities (Blumstein, Rivara, and Rosenfeld 2000; Cork 1999). For example, in an analysis of homicides in New York City in 1988, Paul Goldstein and colleagues (1989) found that nearly 53 percent of all homicides were drug related and that 60 percent of these drug-related homicides involved the trafficking of crack cocaine. This period also corresponded with a spike in youth homicides (Fox and Zawitz 2007), as teenagers were recruited by gangs to serve as low-level street dealers (Blumstein 1995; Cork 1999). As the crack cocaine epidemic waned during the 1990s, the homicide rate began to decline in New York City (Chauhan et al. 2011; Messner et al. 2007) as well as in other major cities across the country.

There are some caveats to the straightforward association between the size of the illicit drug market and homicide trends. The crack cocaine markets of the late 1980s and early 1990s were especially deadly, in part because of the youth of the participants. A portion of the 1990s homicide decline can be attributed to the fact that fewer young drug dealers were participating in distribution, which seemed to correspond with a less violent drug market. There is evidence that the association between drug markets and homicide victimization varies, as drug sales are more violent during some periods than others (Ousey and Lee 2007).

The specific dynamics of the current drug market are not the same as during the crack cocaine epidemic. Today, the drug trade is partially facilitated through online transactions (Maras et al. 2023). Additionally, much of the fentanyl production is taking place in China, with the drug then shipped overseas to drug distributors in the US (Gilbert and Dasgupta 2017). More contemporary ethnographic work is needed to determine how the current drug market works to both facilitate and constrain violence associated with distribution. Regardless of the specific divergence from the crack cocaine epidemic, overall trends in drug abuse and drug sales appear to have contributed to the recent increase in homicide victimization.

Drug Abuse and the 2015–2021 Homicide Epidemic

During the opioid epidemic, there has been variability in the apparent impact of drug abuse and sales on violence. Until 2011, the ability to obtain prescription opioids legally (and quasi-legally) limited the impact of drug abuse on crime trends, as those who were abusing opioids often obtained them from pharmacists, not gangs and street dealers. Additionally, as highlighted earlier, drug transactions and abuse were disproportionately taking place in rural and suburban settings, without some of the preexisting issues of poverty and social disorganization apparent in urban areas (Peters et al. 2020). Accordingly, an analysis of counties in the United States from 2006 through 2012 found no impact of the number of prescription opioid pills on homicide arrests (Wentzlof et al. 2021). While there was probably still an underground secondary market of prescription drugs, in which prescription opioids were obtained quasi-legally to then be sold to others illegally, the violence-producing impact of drug sales was not as apparent during the early era of the opioid epidemic.

Conversely, research that either straddles the prescription and illicit drug phases of the opioid epidemic or only examines data after 2012 finds that proxy measures of drug abuse are associated with more shootings and homicides. In an analysis of racially disaggregated county-level data from 1999 to 2015, Richard Rosenfeld, Randolph Roth, and Joel Wallman (2021) found that opioid-related overdose deaths were significantly associated with higher rates of homicide. Additionally, research that examines the increase in homicide in 2015 and 2016 also suggests that there was an impact of increasing opioid abuse. Rosenfeld and colleagues (2017) found that a greater proportion of homicides committed in 2015 and 2016 were "drug related" as compared to the years prior, suggesting that the illicit markets supplying these drugs have contributed to more violent assaults (see also Rosenfeld and Fox 2019). In another county-level study of the change in homicide rates from 2014 to 2016, there was evidence to suggest that the increase in both White and Black homicide victimization rates was associated with variation in fatal drug overdoses (Gaston, Cunningham, and Gillezeau 2019).

There is also indirect evidence linking the drug abuse epidemic to homicide variation at the neighborhood level in 2020. In a study of Philadelphia, Nicole Johnson and Caterina Roman (2022) found that the spike in homicide after the declaration of emergency for the COVID-19 pandemic differed across neighborhoods. Specifically, neighborhoods with higher rates of drug-related arrests experienced a larger increase in homicide in 2020. Overall, research examining proxies for drug abuse during the illicit drug era (beginning circa 2012) has consistently documented an association between drug abuse and homicide.

In addition to the limited research on the topic, there is some supporting circumstantial evidence. Table 3.1 depicts the regional data in deaths of despair from 1999 to 2021. As is apparent in that table, the Midwest experienced the largest proportional change in both drug overdose deaths and homicide deaths. The areas of the country where there has been an emerging drug overdose crisis appear to be the same areas where homicide rates are increasing most rapidly (see also Feldmeyer et al. 2022).

Disaggregated demographic trends by race/ethnicity also provide some suggestive evidence of a drug-induced homicide epidemic. From 2014 to 2021, Whites experienced a 101 percent increase in drug overdose deaths, Hispanics of all races experienced a 230 percent increase, and the non-Hispanic Black overdose death rate increased by 318 percent. A larger proportional increase in drug overdose deaths corresponds with a larger increase in homicide deaths among racial/ethnic groups. For non-Hispanic Whites, there was a 29.2 percent increase, or an additional 0.7 homicides per 100,000 in 2021 compared to 2014. For Hispanics of all races, there was a 52.2 percent increase in homicide victimization, representing 2.4 additional homicides per 100,000 in 2021 as compared to 2014. The non-Hispanic Black homicide victimization rate increased by an astounding 75.9 percent, representing an additional 14 homicides per 100,000 in 2021 as compared to 2014.[2]

There is an especially close association between the trends in Black drug overdose and homicide victimization from 1999 to 2021. The shift in the drug abuse epidemic from prescription to illicit substances was devastating for Black communities across the country, as there have been proportionally more lives lost (per capita) from the twin drug abuse and homicide epidemics than among any other demographic group since 2014. Figure 4.2 visually depicts this association, comparing the rate of Black drug overdose deaths (not involving a homicide or suicide) to the Black rate of homicide victimization from 1999 to 2021 using CDC Wonder (2023) mortality data. The drug overdose death rate is depicted using a dotted line and homicide victimization is depicted with the solid line. It is apparent from the correspondence of these trends that the rapid increase in drug overdose deaths from 2015 onward is closely aligned with the increase in homicide victimization. There is also an apparent deceleration of drug overdose deaths in 2018, which happens to be the year in the midst of the homicide epidemic that the Black homicide victimization rate momentarily declined. The annual overdose death rate and homicide victimization rate are strongly associated within the (non-Hispanic) Black population ($r = .88$).

Overall, the shift in the drug abuse epidemic from rural and suburban communities to distressed urban centers is central to understanding the sudden increase in homicide associated with drug abuse. Neighborhoods with extremely high degrees of poverty concentration and racial segregation are almost exclusively majority Black in the United States. Historically, concentrated poverty and racial segregation are directly

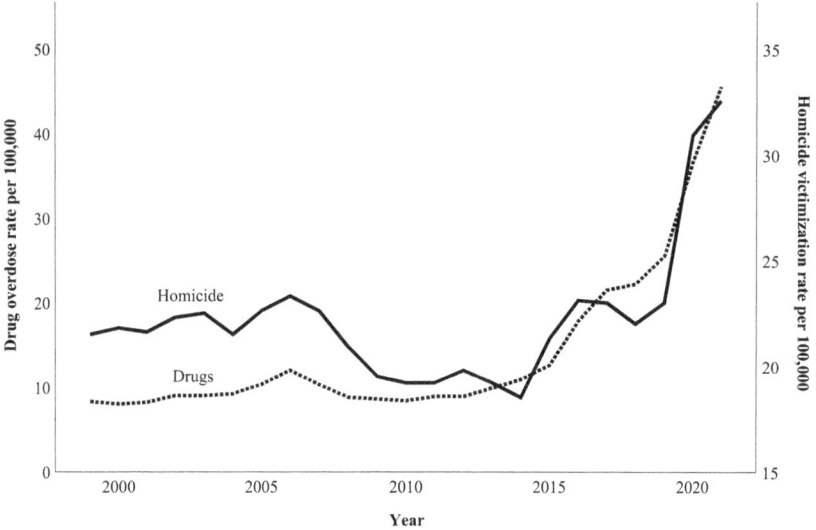

FIGURE 4.2. Non-Hispanic Black drug overdose and homicide death rate, 1999–2021

linked to higher rates of crime and homicide (Massey and Denton 1993; Krivo and Peterson 1996), even prior to the drug abuse epidemic. Given the trends shown in figure 4.2, it seems that as an increase in illicit drug distribution was added to these distressed neighborhoods, it further exacerbated endemic issues with violence.

Another potential reason for this racialized pattern in violence associated with drug abuse patterns is the difference in police response. Despite historically similar levels of drug abuse and addiction between Black and White men, Black men are far more likely to be stopped, arrested, and convicted of drug-related offenses than are their White counterparts. This is partially a function of the different patterns of drug sales, as Black drug dealers are more likely to engage in exchanges in "open-air" settings (Engel, Smith, and Cullen 2012), which are easier for the police to detect. But the disparate rate of arrest also appears to be a function of discriminatory police use of discretion to stop and search Black men under the pretense of "reasonable suspicion" (Gaston 2019). Given that a greater amount of police intervention is associated with higher levels of violence within drug markets (Werb et al. 2011), it is possible that a more aggressive police response has contributed to more violence associated with the illicit drug market involving Black men as buyers and sellers.

Caveats and Remaining Questions

There are still remaining questions about the narrative outlined in this chapter. First, the nature of drug distribution during the current epidemic is not as well-known as during past drug epidemics. In hindsight, the drug distribution in the 1990s proved to be especially violent due to the youthful nature of the boys recruited to sell drugs, many of whom were armed with handguns (Cook 1999). During the current homicide epidemic, the operation of the drug market is still somewhat unclear. It is unlikely to be a perfect carbon copy, as youth criminal involvement and violence today is nowhere near its early-1990s levels. Accordingly, the nature of drug distribution connecting the trends in drug overdose and homicide victimization is probably somewhat distinct from the 1980s–1990s crack cocaine epidemic and warrants further research.

Additionally, following Case and Deaton (2020), I have addressed the increase in drug abuse and overdose using a "demand-side" analysis. That is, I have framed this discussion around the idea that overdose trends are driven by people who feel compelled to buy and use illicit drugs due to the despair caused by American decline. This narrative focuses on declining economic prospects of the users as the underlying cause of an increasing rate of drug abuse and addiction. Conversely, a "supply-side" analysis may emphasize the impact of drug availability and the addictive nature of substance abuse, which may fuel its own demand even without underlying despair. For example, the spike in fentanyl use appears to be partially "supply driven"; users will intend to use other drugs, such as heroin, but end up ingesting fentanyl instead (Duhart Clarke, Kral, and Zibbell 2022). The role of supply-side factors is undoubtedly a portion of the underground markets that needs to be explored further. However, regardless of the precise mechanism explaining the increase in drug abuse, there has been a large and increasing number of Americans who are demanding drugs, and the supply is meeting that demand.

Finally, it should be acknowledged that a portion of the increase in the drug overdose rate is due to increasing toxicity of the substances being abused. Because fentanyl is more deadly per dose that are alternative illicit drugs (Duhart Clarke, Kral, and Zibbell 2022), a portion of the increase in drug overdoses is due to a higher fatality rate rather than more users or an expansion of the drug market. Given the shift in demographics apparent in the drug overdose statistics, as well as the relative stability of the prescription overdose rate during this period (Spencer, Miniño, and Warner 2022), fentanyl overdoses appear to still represent *additional* drug users in more recent years. However, more research is needed to differentiate the increase in the total number of drug users from the increasing toxicity of the drugs being consumed.

Conclusion

The decline in Americans' psychosocial well-being has been dramatic and deadly. As people cope with ongoing societal decline, it has resulted in an epidemic of preventable death. The rising rates of suicide, drug overdose, and alcohol-related deaths have caused a spike in premature mortality, leaving families without loved ones and entire communities devastated by the premature loss of life. As more people coped with their physical and emotional pain through the use of drugs, underground markets expanded. As an unintended consequence of curtailing legal access to prescription opioids, the homicide rate increased rapidly within the burgeoning illicit drug market.

In chapter 5, we will see that the impact of drug abuse has been supercharged by another crisis: the crisis of institutional legitimacy. Political institutions in the United States are perceived as increasingly illegitimate. As a result, Americans have armed themselves in preparation to become their own arbiters of justice. Firearm sales have increased dramatically in recent years, providing more guns to help "resolve" the disputes that arise within underground drug markets. And, similar to previous homicide trends driven by drug sales (Cork 1999), firearms play an outsized role in deaths within the illicit drug market. In chapter 5, I demonstrate that firearms have increasingly become the weapon of choice for deadly assaults during the homicide epidemic.

5

Buying a Gun

The Legitimacy Crisis, Part I

Our founding fathers, they put that Second Amendment in there for a good reason, and that was for the people to protect themselves against a tyrannical government. . . . I hope that's not where we're going, but you know, if this Congress keeps going the way it is, people are really looking toward those Second Amendment remedies.
—Sharron Angle, former member of the Nevada Assembly

Institutional decay and distrust, evident in legitimacy crises suffered by the government and major institutions, have also contributed to the homicide epidemic. When a government is legitimate, it fosters the willing compliance of its citizens. By basing its claim to power on moral rules, adhering to these rules, and resolving disputes between citizens, effective and legitimate governments are able to keep crime rates low (Nivette and Eisner 2013). Accordingly, previous research has often implicated variation in trust in the federal government as central to understanding both increases and decreases in the US homicide rate (LaFree 1998; Roth 2009). Missing from previous research on government legitimacy and crime, however, are the preparations that people make when they begin to distrust their government. In the case of the recent legitimacy crisis, distrust of the government is one of the primary factors motivating Americans to purchase a firearm.

Owning a firearm is a hedge against the monopoly of violence held by the state. Written into the Second Amendment of the United States Constitution is an implicit connection between firearm possession and skepticism about government power. Possession of a firearm is not a guarantee of violent resistance of a tyrannical government but a preparedness for when that time may arise. Of course, people buy and own firearms for reasons other than the eventual overthrow of the government, such as for self-defense against other citizens. However, even in this broader interpretation of gun ownership as enabling self-defense, there is still a skepticism communicated about whether the government can effectively police and protect its citizens.

As political institutions decay and trust in government wanes, there have been a greater number of Americans who have armed themselves with a gun (Carlson 2015, 2023). Over the past fifteen years, firearms sales have increased dramatically. In 2005, around nine million background checks for firearm purchases were conducted and reported to the National Instant Criminal Background Check System (NICS). In 2020, nearly forty million background checks were conducted. And, for the first time in decades, the gun ownership rate has increased (from 2014 to 2021), according General Social Survey (2022) data. An unintended consequence of this gun-buying spree is that the homicide rate, particularly involving deadly assaults committed using a firearm, has increased dramatically during the past decade. According to CDC Wonder (2023) mortality data, 81 percent of homicides in 2021 were committed using a firearm, up from 65 percent in 1999.

To be clear, the argument advanced in this chapter is not that "guns kill people" or that inanimate objects are responsible for homicides independent of human action. This characterization of the association between firearm availability and homicide is probably an intentional strawman intended to deflect any serious discussion of firearm safety policy. It is not that guns kill people, but use of a firearm makes it easier for people to kill people. Gun ownership does not make its possessor inherently more prone to violence, but it makes the violence that they may commit (with that firearm) more likely to have life-threatening consequences.

Accordingly, the best measure for assessing the impact of firearm access on homicide trends is the rate of gun ownership. This statistic is often not available, as there is no national registry for firearms and firearm-related research has often been hampered by government policy, such as the "Dickey Amendment," which constrained federal funds from being devoted to research on gun violence (Rostron 2018). Because of data limitations, proxy measures for firearm ownership are often used to assess the impact of availability. Recent research suggests that proxy measures of firearm possession that use purchase data perform better than conventional measures, such as the firearm-to-nonfirearm suicide ratio, at capturing trends in gun access (Kim and Wilbur 2022). At the national level, the closest approximation of firearm purchase data are background checks for legal gun purchases that are reported to the federal government by licensed dealers.

To assess the availability of firearms, I use a proxy measure of the number of background checks conducted for firearm purchases each year, standardized by population size (per one thousand population). These data are compiled as a count of the number of forms submitted to the National Instant Criminal Background Check System (NICS) to make a legal purchase of a firearm from a registered firearms dealer. Not all background checks will lead to the purchase of a firearm (as some applicants are rejected). Additionally, those who are denied a sale by a registered firearms dealer may turn to nonregistered sources, such as private individuals who are willing to sell firearms to people who would otherwise be barred from owning them, such as convicted felons. This measure will not necessarily capture the number of new firearm owners or changes in the overall firearm ownership rate, as many gun owners have multiple weapons in their arsenal. But this measure provides an (indirect) indication of the degree to which firearms are possessed and are being sold across the country. I supplement this measure with national polling on firearm possession, when available. Before outlining the argument concerning the interconnection between declining government legitimacy, firearm possession, and homicides involving a firearm, I must first contextualize this connection within the broader discussion of legitimacy and governance.

Legitimacy and Governance

There is a long theoretical tradition that links the control of crime with the establishment of a centralized government that holds a monopoly on the capacity for violence. Thomas Hobbes ([1651] 1999) famously argued that the war of "all versus all" in the "state of nature" necessitated a strong central government (a "leviathan") that all citizens feared in order to quell constant interpersonal conflict and criminal predation. The argument that stems from this perspective is that the government serves as a deterrent force that prevents crime through the fear of punishment. To bolster the monopoly of violence necessary to evoke fear, the government must possess deadly weapons that citizens do not have access to, such as firearms. In the case of the United States, this monopoly on violence is somewhat tenuous given the privately held arsenal of its citizens.

Holding a monopoly on violence is also enabled by the consent of the governed. To draw on Max Weber's (1968) definition of the state, the government must possess a monopoly on the *legitimate* use of violence. This definition of the state both contains the ability to inflict overwhelming violence and also emphasizes that the violence used by the government must possess a certain level of legitimacy to foster compliance. Crucially, people must believe that the government is justified in its monopoly of violence. When a truly legitimate government uses physical coercion, this use of force is perceived to be acceptable in the eyes of the public. And, when a government is truly legitimate, it will rarely need to use force or coercion, if at all, to gain citizens' compliance.

By definition, the amount of criminal behavior should vary inversely with the degree of the government's legitimacy. Because the legitimacy of the political order is partially defined as the degree of the public's expression of consent to its authority (see Beetham 2013), crime rates in themselves could be used as an indicator of the government's (lack of) legitimacy. This conceptualization of the legitimacy and crime relationship, however, is tautological, as high crime rates are hypothesized as both the outcome of a lack of government legitimacy and evidence of an illegitimate government.

To avoid this tautology, researchers have examined independent indicators of political or government legitimacy to gauge its impact on compliance with the law. For example, Gary LaFree (1998) and Randolph Roth (2009) have both used public opinion polls concerning trust in government as an indicator of the government's legitimacy, finding that the homicide rate tends to vary inversely with the degree of trust in governmental authority. Using these polls to assess public support of institutions, it would be safe to say that the government and political institutions in the United States are perceived (by many people) to be illegitimate.

The Legitimacy Crisis

If there is one thing that Americans can broadly agree about, it is that our political institutions are poorly run. In January 2022, 72 percent of Americans believed that the country was headed in the wrong direction; fully 76 percent believed that democracy itself was under threat (Murray 2022). These bleak poll results arrive on the heels of one of the worst decades in polling history for the approval of the federal government. Only 39 percent of Americans reported in 2021 that they trust the federal government to handle domestic problems (Brenan 2021). And, although trust in Congress has improved from its all-time low circa 2013 (9 percent), only 18 percent of Americans approved of Congress in 2022 (Brenan 2022a). President Joe Biden's approval rating in many polls has dipped below 40 percent, and his predecessor's approval rating never broke 50 percent (FiveThirtyEight 2022). It is clear that Americans are dissatisfied with the state of their political institutions and the people occupying positions of power within the federal government.

In addition to the general dissatisfaction with the government and its officials, political polarization and, more specifically, negative partisanship have weakened the performance of once-robust democratic institutions. Partisans on both sides no longer see their political opposition as working in good faith to achieve (largely) shared goals through alternative strategies but see the opposition as enemies who seek to destroy the country itself. In this hyperpartisan era, there can be no compromise, as the other side is not only misguided but actively evil. Accordingly, agreeing to basic ground rules to run "free and fair" elections is no longer seemingly possible. Gerrymandering has become more common, especially after the 2010 election, making it difficult for the party out of power to retake a state legislature even if it happens to win a majority of the votes. Additionally, voter-suppression efforts, such as limiting early voting, ending same-day registration, reducing polling hours, removing polling locations, and creating stricter rules surrounding "voter ID," have made it more difficult for citizens to cast a ballot (Brennan Center for Justice 2022).

In 2021, the faith in and respect for elections sunk to their lowest point in modern US history as some members of the losing political party attempted to carry out a coup d'état to maintain power after the Trump administration failed in the courts to overturn the presidential election. A poll conducted during the same year estimated that 34 percent of Americans supported using violence against the government, up from 16 percent in 2010 (Kornfield and Alfaro 2022). Elections in the United States no longer guarantee a peaceful transition of power.

The attempt to disenfranchise and discourage voters, as well as the lack of trust in the fairness and accuracy of elections, has contributed to a democratic system that is more institutionally flawed. International observers have now labeled the United States as a "backsliding" democracy, which attempts to suppress the voting rights of racial/ethnic minorities (International IDEA 2021). And, as the 2021 Capitol riot and coup d'état attempt suggests, Americans have little faith in the results of their own elections. The sudden decline of the United States from being a "defender of democracy" on the global stage to no longer trusting the results of its own elections is a shocking development.

The United States' legitimacy crisis extends beyond just the federal government. There has been a long-term decline in Americans' confidence in institutions in general. Americans still report that they broadly trust a few institutions, such as science and the military, but have become less supportive of both government and nongovernment entities. In addition to the federal government, institutions that have experienced a decline in support during recent years include the media, public schools, the police, the criminal justice system, and religion (Brady and Kent 2022; Gallup 2022). As Americans have become more cynical about and less supportive of institutions designed to adjudicate disputes, they may prepare to take matters into their own hands to resolve grievances as they see fit. One such preparation to hedge on their consent to the state's monopoly of legitimate violence is to buy a gun.

The Legitimacy Crisis and Firearm Purchases

At the same time that trust of the government has declined, firearm purchases have increased. This is unlikely to be a coincidence. Survey results confirm that people who own firearms are more likely to report that they distrust the federal government (Jiobu and Curry 2001). Previous research also suggests that people are more likely to purchase firearms when their confidence in the criminal justice system declines (Young, McDowall, and Loftin 1987). Accordingly, during the gun-buying spree of 2020, it should not be a surprise that people who believed in various antigovernment conspiracies were some of the most likely to purchase a firearm (Lacombe et al. 2022).

Initially, the increase in firearm purchases (beginning circa 2006) was largely driven by Republican partisans adding additional firearms to their preexisting arsenals when Democrats won presidential elections. For example, during the months surrounding the elections of Barack Obama as president in 2008 and 2012, NICS-reported background checks indicated an increase in firearm purchases (LaPlant, Lee, and LaPlant 2021). While the overall proportion of the population that owned a gun actually declined between 2000 and 2014 (Rand 2021), the absolute number of privately owned firearms skyrocketed. Republicans, many of whom already owned firearms, stockpiled additional guns and ammunition in preparation for anticipated firearm restrictions and other forms of perceived government overreach.

Recent research highlights this partisan firearm-purchasing dynamic. Kristina LaPlant and colleagues (2021) found that having a Democratic president in office is associated with a higher rate of firearm sales, particularly in southern states. Additionally, they found that there is a higher rate of firearm purchases after mass shootings and media coverage of mass shootings. The purchase of firearms after a mass shooting is partially due to the fear that the government will unduly restrict access or even confiscate firearms from lawful gun owners.

Similarly, Shawn Ratcliff (2022) found that during Republican presidential administrations, Democrats and independents are more likely to purchase firearms as well. Partisans on both sides of the political aisle seem to be more likely to purchase firearms when their preferred political party is out of power, indicating that firearm purchases are partially driven by a partisan distrust of the government. As historical Pew Research polls indicate, reported trust in government declines dramatically among the partisans of the party out of power. That is, when Republicans gain control of the White House, Democrats report less trust in the government (and vice versa). This distrust translates to a greater likelihood of purchasing a gun (LaPlant, Lee, and LaPlant 2021; Ratcliff 2022).

Over the past two decades, there is an apparent correlation between distrust of the government and the rate of firearm purchases. The Pew Research Center has tracked opinion on the federal government since 1958. "Trust" in the government is measured in this survey as whether people report that they can "trust Washington to do what is right" all of the time or most of the time. In 2021, only about 21 percent reported that they could trust the government most or all of the time, less than half of the twenty-first-century high of 54 percent recorded in 2001 (Pew Research Center 2023). During this general period, firearm purchases (reported to the NICS) per 1,000 population increased from 30.28 in 2000 to 120.28 in 2020, or an astounding 297 percent increase in just two

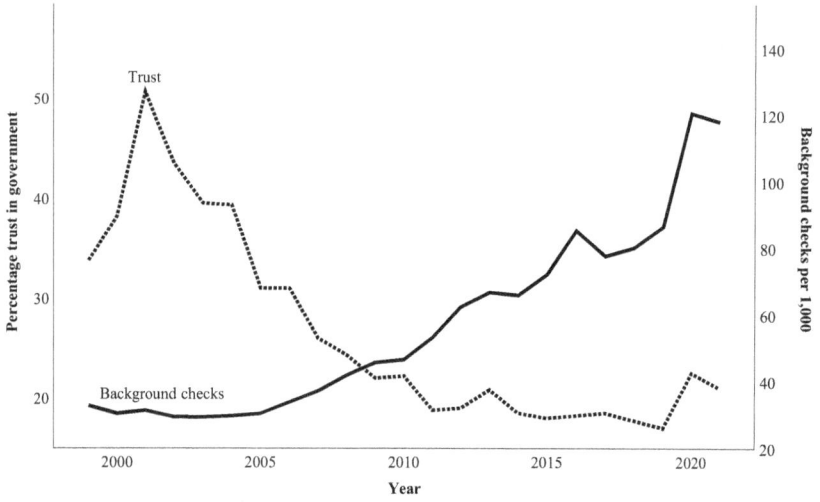

FIGURE 5.1. Percentage who trust government and firearm purchases per capita, 1999–2021

decades. Most of this increase occurred during the 2010s, as the trend in firearm purchases remained relatively flat until 2006 or 2007.

Figure 5.1 traces the trends in trust in the federal government and firearm purchases per capita from 1999 to 2021. The first year in this time series represents the first full year of data collected by the NICS. As is apparent in figure 5.1, as trust in the federal government declined (indicated with the dotted line), there was a sharp increase in the number of background checks for firearm purchases (indicated with the solid line). There is a moderately strong inverse annual correlation between trust in the government and firearm purchases ($r = -.68$), suggesting that as trust in the federal government has declined, people have been more likely to buy a gun as a result.

Similarly, there is also an apparent association between firearm purchases and distrust of the criminal justice system and the police. Figure 5.2 depicts the trend lines in firearm purchases per capita, distrust of the criminal justice system, and distrust of the police from 1999 to 2021. The annual survey data used to depict distrust of institutions were collected by Gallup (2022), which asked respondents to report their degree of confidence in specific institutions or entities. The responses are ranked on a five-point Likert scale from a "great deal" of confidence in the institution to "none." In figure 5.2, I measure "distrust" of the police and criminal justice system by combining the percentage of respondents who answered that they had either "very little" or no ("none") confidence in these institutions. Distrust in the police grew from 10 percent in 1999 to a peak of 19 percent in 2020. Distrust in the criminal justice system has also exhibited a generally upward trend, with the lowest rate reported in 2004 (23 percent) and highest recorded in 2021 (42 percent). Each of these variables (firearm purchases, distrust in the criminal justice system, and distrust in the police) was standardized to a common metric (a Z-score) for the sake of visual inspection of trends. As is apparent in figure 5.2, distrust of the police and criminal justice system increased during the same time as firearm purchases.

The annual bivariate correlations between the distrust reported in these institutions and firearm purchases per capita are relatively strong.

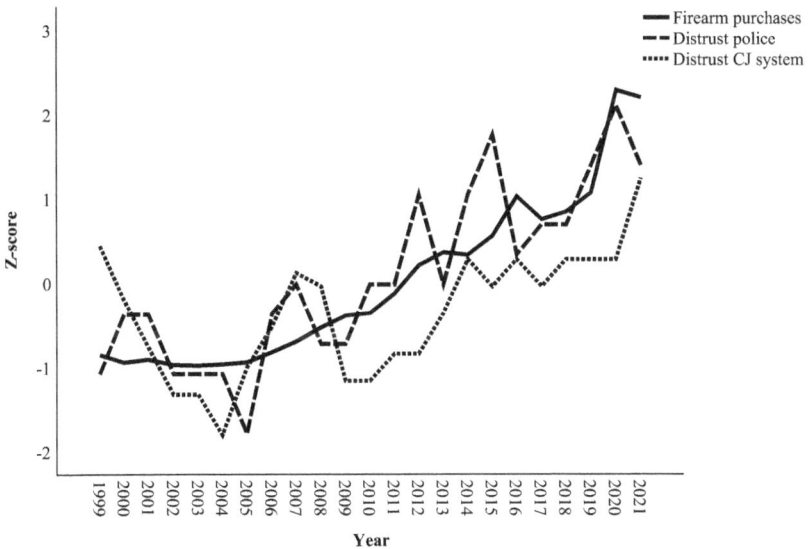

FIGURE 5.2. Standardized trends in distrust and firearm purchases, 1999–2021

There is a moderate positive association between firearm purchases and distrust in the criminal justice system ($r = .68$) and a strong correlation between firearm purchases and distrust in the police ($r = .86$). These associations suggest that as people reported more distrust in the institutions responsible for adjudicating disputes and protecting citizens from crime, they increasingly armed themselves as a result.

Interestingly, the same period in which firearm purchases increased roughly aligns with a shift in gun culture. A recent study by Claire Boine and colleagues (2020) found a sharp increase of firearm ownership culture specifically for the purpose of self-defense after 2004. This fits the general timeline that distrust of the police and criminal justice system began to increase (2004–2005) and was shortly before the increase in firearm purchases began (2006). Additionally, Boine and colleagues document a larger proportion of gun owners motivated by "Second Amendment" concerns in their ownership of firearms around the same time. Both types of gun culture point to a general distrust of the federal government (Second Amendment) or the inability of the government to keep citizens safe (self-defense).

The interrelated dynamics of the loss of trust in government, unpredictable crises, and firearm purchases came into sharp contrast in 2020 and 2021. In March 2020, the announcement that the COVID-19 pandemic had spread to the United States and the subsequent declaration of a national emergency corresponded with over 3.7 million background checks for firearm purchases. To that point, this set a new monthly record in NICS-reported background checks.

Then, in late May 2020, George Floyd's murder by a Minneapolis police officer galvanized Black Lives Matter protests throughout the country. By June, however, some of these peaceful protests had given way to vandalism, looting, and violence. The protests gained more scrutiny as 2020 wore on, with protestors calling for "defunding" or even abolishing the police. Many of those who were aligned against the goals of the protests desired some form of martial law to quell the unrest, including the deployment of the National Guard to Washington, DC (Udall and McGovern 2020), indicative of a belief that the government was either unwilling or unable to restore order. The lack of trust in the police by those who were aligned with Black Lives Matter protestors, coupled with the perceived inaction by the government to quell the protests by those who desired "law and order," corresponded with a spike in firearm purchases. More than 3.9 million background checks for firearms were completed in June 2020, again setting a new monthly record at the time.

Throughout 2020, government responses to the pandemic and protests were perceived to be insufficient by some people and authoritarian by others. Many US states were placed under "lockdown" orders at some point during the pandemic, requiring citizens to stay at home unless they were operating an essential business or retrieving necessary items such as food, gasoline, or medical care. Many Democrats perceived the Trump administration's response to the pandemic to be inept, while Republicans staged protests against state stay-at-home orders and mask mandates, perceived to be government overreach (Zanona 2020). Then, the roles were effectively reversed during the summer protests, as Republicans were demanding the imposition of martial law in major cities, while Democrats perceived the police response to the protests to be heavy-handed and a violation of First Amendment protections of the Constitution (Jalonick, Balsamo, and Tucker 2020). No one seemingly came out of 2020 believing that their government did well at protecting the rights of its citizens, whether that right was to protest, not wear a mask indoors, or operate a "nonessential" business. Unsurprisingly, the total number of background checks for firearm purchases completed in 2020 still holds the annual record.

Firearm purchases continued to accelerate into late 2020 and early 2021, as the aftermath of a highly contested election contributed to an attempted coup d'état. After waiting a week for mail-in ballots to be counted, Joe Biden eventually prevailed in the 2020 presidential election over Donald Trump by a narrow margin in several states. Before any votes were even cast, President Trump had sown doubt about the integrity of the election, claiming that mail-in ballots would be prone to fraud (Seligman 2020). After the election, Trump refused to concede and pressed state election officials to change vote tallies (Amy 2021). After dozens of failed court challenges and little traction in convincing the broader public of widespread voter fraud, supporters of the Trump campaign stormed the Capitol building in an attempt to stop the counting of the electoral votes on January 6, 2021. This act, classified as an "attempted dissident coup" by the Cline Center for Advanced Social Research (2022), is the quintessential event for governments facing a legitimacy crisis. Accordingly, background checks for firearm purchases set monthly records again in the lead-up to (December 2020) and month of (January 2021) the attempted coup, surpassing four million background checks in January 2021.

By tracing these trends in distrust, crises faced by the federal government, and firearm purchases, I do not mean to imply that there is a simple one-to-one relationship. The rate of firearm ownership is impacted by several factors, only one of which is the relative (dis)trust in the government. For example, the rate of firearm ownership used to be much higher than it is today. This was due to many factors, such as a higher percentage of people living in rural areas and recreational practices that are less culturally relevant in recent decades, such as hunting for food or sport. Additionally, the recent gun-buying frenzy has been partially driven by media coverage of mass shootings and political fearmongering about firearm restrictions. However, the combination of relatively low trust in government, social unrest, and sudden destabilizing and unpredictable events during 2020 and 2021 provided the perfect storm for an increase in firearm purchases and higher rates of gun ownership.[1]

Firearms and Homicide

The trend in firearm purchases plausibly explains a portion of the recent increase in the homicide rate. When people purchase a firearm, it is (usually) not their immediate intention to use the recently acquired weapon in a violent crime. In fact, the vast majority of the firearms purchased will never be used in any crime whatsoever. For a small subset of a growing number of gun owners, however, their newly acquired firearm has been used as a murder weapon. By introducing a firearm into a dispute, it increases the likelihood of death for one or more of the combatants. This dispute may have never been anticipated by the purchaser during the sale of the firearm and may have occurred regardless of whether the gun was purchased, but the presence of a weapon can turn a simple assault into a life-threatening situation for all involved. Widespread firearm possession can motivate people to be more polite and less prone to unarmed assaults, but it also can escalate a fistfight into a shootout and, sometimes, a homicide (see Felson, Berg, and Rogers 2014).

The main argument connecting firearm availability to the homicide rate is the "instrumentality" hypothesis. This hypothesis argues that we can assume that the intent to commit homicide is unaffected by the possession of a firearm. However, because firearms are much more efficient killing tools than alternative weapons, it is more likely that the victim of an assault will die. That is, if someone is stabbed during an attempted murder, they are more likely to make it to the hospital alive than if they had been shot (Cook 2018). Even the caliber of the firearm is related to the likelihood of an aggravated assault (shooting) becoming a homicide, as injuries from larger-caliber guns are more likely to contribute to a victim's death than are the wounds inflicted with smaller weapons (Braga et al. 2021).

The instrumentality of firearms also enables more varied types of deadly assaults than alternative weapons do. In assaults without the use of a weapon, people who are physically larger are more likely to carry out an assault and injure their victim (Felson 1996). Firearms nullify this size advantage and allow for violence to be perpetrated by people who would otherwise be overwhelmed by the size and strength of their victim. Additionally, there are some types of offenses, such as drive-by shootings or mass shootings, for which an equivalent offense ranges from difficult to impossible without access to a firearm.

Some researchers have examined whether firearm possession changes social situations in a manner that modifies the propensity toward violence, but the results of this research are less clear. Although it is plausible that the knowledge that the population is heavily armed may serve as a deterrent for some crimes (Lott 2010), the evidence for this hypothesis is relatively scant and in fact mostly contradictory to this claim (Ayres and Donohue 2003; Cheng and Hoekstra 2012; Duggan 2001). Conversely, the psychology literature suggests that the possession of weapons can increase aggressive thoughts and the belief that other people will respond aggressively in ambiguous situations (Benjamin, Kepes, and Bushman 2018). Overall, it is a contested idea that firearms change the propensity of people to commit (or not commit) assaults.

Regardless of the precise mechanism, most research on the topic suggests that greater access to firearms contributes to a higher risk of homicide. A review of the research literature by Lisa Hepburn and David Hemenway (2004) indicates that at every level of analysis, there is a consistent finding that firearm availability increases the probability of homicide. At the individual level, a firearm located in the home is associated with a greater likelihood of homicide death (Wiebe 2003). Examinations of changes in firearm access at the state level also show a correlation between greater firearm access and homicide rates (Siegel, Ross, and King 2013). Finally, in cross-national comparisons of wealthy nations, firearm access is associated with higher rates of homicide (Grinshteyn and Hemenway 2016).

There is some suggestive historical evidence that a decline in access to firearms during the 1990s contributed to the homicide decline. For example, there was a proportionally larger decrease in the rate of homicides perpetrated with a firearm (41 percent between 1993 and 2000) than in homicides committed using another weapon (19 percent) (Rosenfeld 2005). As depicted in figure 5.3, the homicide rate declined (depicted as a solid line) during roughly the same period as the decline in the estimated percentage of households in which a firearm was present (depicted as a dotted line). This figure uses data compiled by the Rand Corporation, available from 1980 to 2016, to estimate the national level of firearm availability in US homes (Rand 2021). In the 1990s, Rand

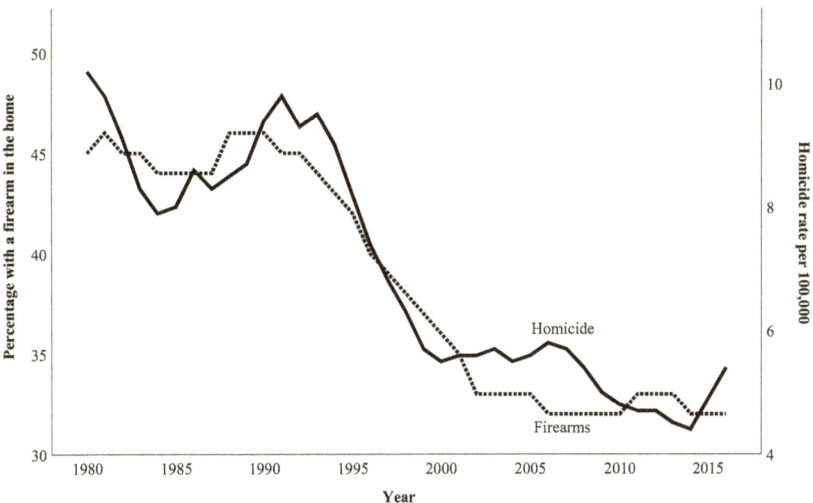

FIGURE 5.3. Firearm availability and the homicide rate, 1980–2016

(2021) estimates that there was a large decline in firearms possession; in 1990, 46 percent of households contained at least one firearm; by 2002, this number was only 33 percent. During the years depicted in the figure, there is a strong bivariate correlation between annual household firearm access and the homicide rate ($r = .95$).

It should be noted, however, that while the majority of research findings document an association between firearm access and homicide victimization, data and methods limitations have prevented strong claims of causality (Kleck 2015). It should also be noted that firearm access does not universally increase the incidence of homicide. Some nations with high degrees of firearm availability have relatively low homicide rates. This indirectly supports the instrumentality hypothesis that firearm availability does not produce violence itself but causes the violent assaults that occur to be more deadly.

Not all guns or gun sales are equally likely to contribute to a homicide. The most concerning element of increasing firearm availability is guns that end up in the possession of felons and other people who are legally restricted from gun possession. Firearms purchased by people convicted of felonies through private sellers account for an outsized proportion of firearm violence (Cook 2018). Additionally, recent research suggests that firearm-related violence needs to be coupled with other predictors of criminal offending to account for homicide patterns. For example, the rate of legal firearms dealers has no overall impact on city-level homicide rates, but cities with a greater degree of social and economic disadvantage have a higher rate of firearm-related homicides (Stansfield et al. 2023). Also, the presence of firearms dealers is more likely to contribute to higher rates of homicide in urban areas but may actually contribute to fewer homicides in suburban settings (Wiebe et al. 2009). Taken together, these findings suggest that, under certain conditions, more access to firearms will lead to a higher rate of homicide; but, under other conditions, the impact of firearm availability will be relatively modest or null. As I show in the next section, the recent increase in firearm access has corresponded with more homicides in which a gun was the weapon of choice.

Firearms and the Homicide Epidemic

During the recent homicide epidemic, firearms have played a central role. From 2014 to 2021, the "excess" homicides have been almost exclusively perpetrated using firearms. Figure 5.4 depicts CDC Wonder (2023) cause-of-death data, splitting the homicide victimization rate by the weapon used in the deadly assault; that is, the homicide victimization rate is depicted according to whether the victim was killed using a firearm or another weapon or method. As indicated with the solid line, the firearm-enabled homicide rate has risen by nearly 62 percent from 1999 to 2021, compared to only 30 percent for the overall homicide rate. Conversely, as indicated with the dotted line, the rate of homicides perpetrated with another weapon/method has declined by 33 percent during this period. Focusing more narrowly on the years of the homicide epidemic, the CDC recorded 10,136 more (excess) homicides in 2021 than in 2014. Of these 10,136 additional homicides, 9,950 were committed using a firearm, implying that 98 percent of the excess homicides were perpetrated using a firearm.

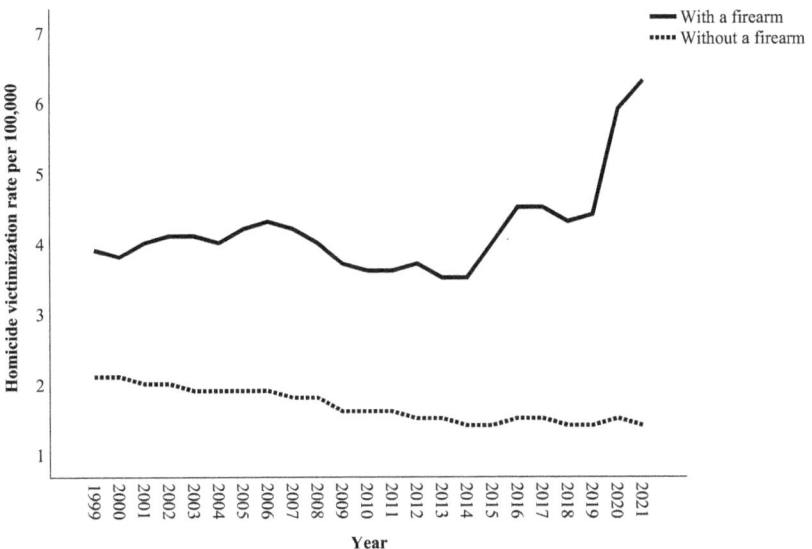

FIGURE 5.4. Homicide victimization rate by weapon, 1999–2021

Some research, but not all (e.g., Schleimer et al. 2021), has implicated firearm access as one of the drivers of recent homicide trends. There is some evidence that the increase in the homicide rate in 2015 was due to an increase in firearm possession in some US cities (Towers and White 2017). Additionally, the increase in the lethality of shootings may have been partially responsible for the increase in deaths, as nonlethal gun violence did not increase at the same rate (Berg 2019; Lauritsen and Lentz 2019). This increased lethality may be due to the increasing caliber size of firearms possessed by Americans (Braga et al. 2021).

Another indication that firearms have played a role in the homicide rate increase is derived from Bureau of Alcohol, Tobacco, Firearms, and Explosives (ATF) data. The ATF collected data on the "time to crime" in 2020, or time from when a firearm is sold to the time that it is confiscated by the police. In 2020, there was a higher percentage of guns purchased during the past six months that were recovered by police in the commission of a crime than during the previous year (Asher and Arthur 2022). This corresponds with research suggesting that not only did

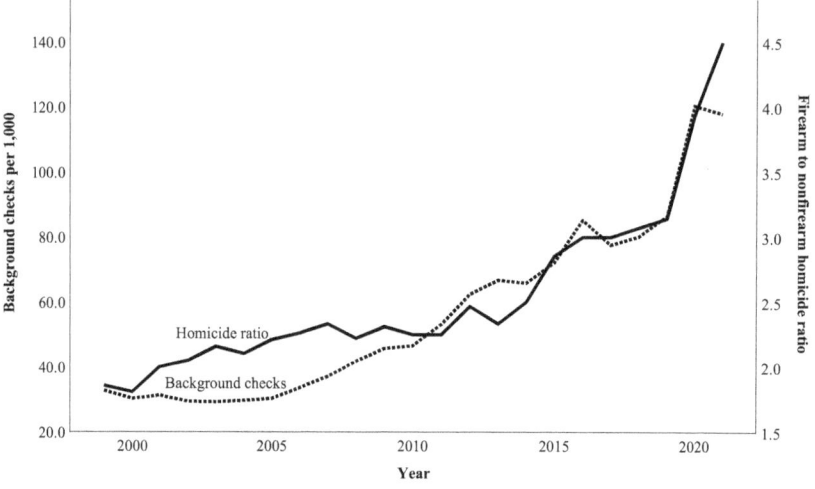

FIGURE 5.5. Firearm background checks and the ratio of firearm to nonfirearm homicides, 1999–2021

police seize more legally purchased firearms but there is an increasing number of privately manufactured firearms as well (Braga et al. 2022).

As firearm availability has increased, guns have become the murder weapon of choice. Figure 5.5 depicts the association between NICS background checks for firearm purchases (per capita) and the ratio of homicides committed using a firearm versus homicides committed using other means. Firearm purchases (background checks) are depicted with a dotted line, while the ratio of firearm to nonfirearm homicides is depicted with the solid line. From 1999 to 2009, the trends in firearm sales and the proportion of homicides committed using a firearm were not closely aligned, although both were generally increasing. However, from 2010 through 2021, the trend lines in firearm availability and the ratio of firearm to nonfirearm homicides are nearly identical. Unsurprisingly, there was a strong ($r = .95$) correlation between the annual rate of firearm sales and the proportion of homicides in which a firearm was used as the murder weapon.

This close association between firearm availability and the homicides in which a firearm was used suggests that the recent gun-buying spree contributed to the homicide epidemic. It is possible that some homicides that would have been committed with other weapons were committed with a firearm given increasing availability. However, because the rate of homicides perpetrated with a firearm has increased faster than the rate of homicides committed with other weapons has declined (see figure 5.4), it appears that firearm access has played a central role in causing gun violence to spike.

Some scholars have suggested that the causality is reversed, as people may buy firearms to protect themselves from a perceived increase in crime (Hauser and Kleck 2013). Yet the public is not very accurate in its perception of crime trends. A majority of Americans believed that the there was an increase in crime during every single year of the 1990s (Brenan 2022b), despite an overall crime *decline* from 1991 to 1999. Accordingly, we would have not expected to have experienced a decline in firearm ownership during the 1990s (see figure 5.3). Additionally, the perception that crime has increased in survey respondents' local community is not strongly associated to the rate of firearm purchases from 1999 to 2021 ($r = .20$).[2] It is certainly possible that fear of crime accounts for a portion of the firearm purchase–homicide association, but public perception of crime trends is often faulty and seemingly less likely to connect the sale and possession of firearms to homicide trends than is the instrumentality of those weapons.

Conclusion

Overall, this chapter addresses the role that the current legitimacy crisis has played in causing more people to purchase firearms. As distrust of the government, criminal justice system, and the police increased, the number of firearms purchased increased as well. This increase in firearm purchases is correlated with an increase in the proportion of homicides committed using a gun; nearly the entirety (98 percent) of the increase from 2014 through 2021 has been due to firearm-facilitated homicides. This higher ratio of firearm to nonfirearm homicides almost perfectly aligns with the increase in background checks, especially after 2010.

However, this association may suggest a type of displacement, in which homicides that would have been committed otherwise were committed using a newly available firearm. It is also possible that there has been a shift in the preference to commit assaults with a firearm that is not strictly due to firearm availability. While it is clear in the preceding figures that homicides in the United States are increasingly perpetrated with a gun, some of this trend may not be due simply to changes in access.

To more definitively assess the impact of firearm purchases on the homicide epidemic, I use multivariate regression analysis in chapter 7 to account for multiple factors influencing crime rates within US states. As is apparent in that chapter, there is evidence that the recent gun-buying spree is associated with an increase in the homicide rate. However, before examining those findings, we must first address the police legitimacy crisis evident in the anti-police-brutality protest movement.

6

Protesting the Police

The Legitimacy Crisis, Part II

> Yesterday, I turned on the TV
> I saw another man down
> He was screaming
> He can't breathe no more
> He held his hands high
> But then he got struck down
> Oh, he got struck down
> I saw the body drop
> On the six o'clock
> —excerpt from the song "6:00" by grandson

Throughout the homicide epidemic, there has been an intense focus on protests and policing. For those who emphasized the impact of de-policing, the protests prevented proactive patrols, thereby reducing deterrence and increasing lawlessness. For those who examined the role of police legitimacy, the impact was attributed to a lack of trust in the police to intervene in community conflicts and crime. As we addressed in chapter 2, de-policing is a poor explanation of the ultimate origin of the homicide epidemic, although de-policing may have exacerbated the increase in homicide rates (see chapter 8). The other side of the de-policing coin is the police legitimacy crisis that was engendered by high-profile incidents of alleged police brutality.

Both the de-policing and legitimacy crisis arguments are aimed at explaining a similar homicide pattern observed in both 2015 and 2020. While the overarching increase in homicide is due to the dynamics described in previous chapters (alcohol consumption, expanding drug markets, and firearm proliferation), there was an apparent "exogenous shock" in homicide trends immediately after protests began. As Richard Rosenfeld (2018) describes, an exogenous shock brings about an abrupt change to the crime trends, due to a sudden shift in social dynamics. In 2015 and 2020, apparent exogenous shocks corresponded with a widespread protest movement against police brutality. In both periods, the homicide rate spiked by historical margins. The sudden increase in violence, beyond what could be predicted within the "normal science" paradigm, warrants further examination.

In this chapter, I address the impact of the police legitimacy crisis. There is some suggestive evidence that during the recent police legitimacy crisis, people were less likely to call on the police to resolve issues within their community (Rosenfeld et al. 2017), potentially fostering unilateral (criminal) resolutions to conflict. Additionally, counties and cities in which the police killed unarmed Black residents had higher rates of homicide in the subsequent years, suggesting that residents were more likely to bypass the police and use unilateral violence to resolve disputes (Gaston, Cunningham, and Gillezeau 2019; Lane 2022). Finally, cities with more Google searches expressing concern about police brutality had higher rates of violent crime (Gross and Mann 2017), suggesting that cynicism about the police was directly connected to more criminal offending. From these pieces of evidence, it would appear that when people distrust the police to intervene in their affairs, there is a higher rate of violent crime.

Following this evidence, I begin the chapter by addressing the conventional argument linking protests to homicide trends through the mechanism of police legitimacy. This perspective suggests that people were less likely to comply with the police or to call on the police to resolve disputes due to the distrust engendered by police brutality. While there is some evidence for this proposition, I argue that the distrust in the police predates the protest movement, making protests less predictive of sudden shifts in the rate of violent crime than we might expect. That is, protest rates may capture a type of police illegitimacy that accounts for stable differences in crime rates across neighborhoods and cities but are less predictive of an abrupt increase in violent crime.

This tentative argument leads to the second major portion of this chapter, linking police brutality to a spontaneous increase in the use of violence due to a "brutalization"-type effect. The protests against police brutality may have *indirectly* impacted the homicide trend by exposing the public to *brutalization*. Instead of a rational weighing of the costs and benefits of committing a murder, as implied by the deterrence perspective (de-policing), or consciously deciding that the police could no longer be trusted to resolve community disputes (legitimacy crisis), the brutalization perspective suggests that the unspoken norms surrounding the use of violence and the sanctity of human life are impacted by witnessing state-sanctioned murder.

The brutalization hypothesis originates from the research literature documenting the disparate impact of the death penalty on homicide rates. Death penalty research is decidedly mixed, as there is no clear conclusion that the imposition of capital punishment impacts the homicide rate (Donohue and Wolfers 2006). In fact, some studies even find that the imposition of the death penalty contributed to more, rather than fewer, homicides (Bailey 1998). The association between executions and homicides is explained as the result of "brutalization." The brutalization effect is hypothesized to "demonstrate that it is correct and appropriate to kill those who have gravely offended us" (Bowers and Pierce 1980, 456). I apply this argument to fit recent incidents of alleged police brutality and the spontaneous increase in homicide offending. Before applying the brutalization effect to sudden spikes in violent offending, however, I summarize the conventional interpretation of the police illegitimacy argument, which directly connects the police legitimacy crisis to the variation in crime.

The Legitimacy Crisis and Crime

Often, periods of social upheaval occur during the same era in which crime rates increase. In Randolph Roth's (2009) historical analysis of the United States, he notes that movements for social justice are a consistent feature of periods in which violence increases. Roth (2009, 469) argues that "nothing increases homicide rates more surely, at least in the short term, than an effort by a dedicated minority to create a more just society." Similarly, Gary LaFree and Kriss Drass (1997) demonstrate that the increase in collective action (usually protests) by African Americans during the 1960s and 1970s corresponded with the largest sustained increase in crime during the twentieth century. Distrust of the government to actually deliver on demands for political empowerment and equality contributes to antisystemic movements, which have consistently occurred during eras of increasing homicide rates (see also LaFree 1998).

There are a few reasons to believe that compromised police legitimacy will contribute to a higher rate of crime. First, if people believe that the law is moral and that the system is "just," they feel compelled to follow the law (Tyler 1990). Conversely, if the police or criminal justice system shows apparent bias, it reduces the perceived morality of the rules, failing to foster willing compliance. Therefore, if the government (or police) lose legitimacy, it causes people to be more likely to commit crime, as the "moral" power of the law erodes (LaFree 1998).

Second, distrust of the police contributes to less effective law enforcement. In particular, people who distrust the police may not report offenses or cooperate with criminal investigations (Sampson and Bartusch 1998), thereby allowing offenders to avoid police custody. In neighborhoods where there is deep distrust of the police, some residents who have information about a crime may be reticent to call the police or even cooperate when questioned (Brunson and Wade 2019; Carr, Napolitano, and Keating 2007). This "no snitching" code is not simply a cultural custom but part of an expression of distrust of a criminal justice system that is perceived to cause as many problems as it resolves (Anderson 1999). As a result, serious and chronic offenders walk free, continuing to victimize people within their community.

A third crime-reducing element of legitimacy is hypothesized to be the public's trust of the state to resolve disputes between parties (Nivette 2014). If an individual is involved in a dispute about a business transaction with another party, the trust that both parties have invested in the government allows them to seek a resolution to this conflict. While the handling of this dispute may be contentious, sometimes leading to civil or even criminal hearings, if both parties accept the outcome of the proceedings as legitimate, the conflict should be resolved without resorting to violence. However, if neither party trusts the government as a legitimate arbiter of justice, they may use "self-help," or unilateral violence, to resolve their dispute (Black 1983).

During the past decade, the years in which there have been widespread protests against police brutality have corresponded with an increase in the homicide rate. As an alternative to the de-policing narrative, the legitimacy crisis perspective suggests that a lack legitimacy in itself could cause the homicide rate to increase. Distrust of the police, including a lack of belief in their practice of procedural justice (Tyler 1990, 2003), a lack of cooperation with police investigations (Sampson and Bartusch 1998), and unilateral resolutions of disputes (Black 1983; Nivette 2014), could cause the homicide rate to increase regardless of a lack of police proactivity. Overall, although not definitive, there is a small body of research that links the police legitimacy crisis to the recent increase in violent crime (Cross et al. 2023; Gaston, Cunningham, and Gillezeau 2019; Gross and Mann 2017; Lane 2022; Rosenfeld et al. 2017).

The Origin of Protest

While it is certainly possible that the police legitimacy crisis has been partially responsible for the spike in homicide, the protests are more of a manifestation of underlying distrust of the police, not the cause of greater distrust. If the police are largely trusted and perceived to be legitimate, even a "police-involved shooting" in which the officer's life was not in apparent danger will be interpreted as an isolated incident—simply the action of a rogue cop. Conversely, people who are already distrustful of the police interpret police-involved shootings through a lens shaded by previous interactions and experiences (Tyler and Wakslak 2004). When the police are perceived to be biased and the criminal justice system is not trusted to offer "justice" to the victims of brutality, people will interpret all citizen and police interactions through this lens. And, as a result, protests will periodically erupt after publicized police shootings due to the preexisting perception that the police (and the criminal justice system) are racially biased.

The incident that most clearly illustrates this dynamic is the 2014 killing of Michael Brown in Ferguson, Missouri. The officer in the case, Darren Wilson, avoided criminal sanctions for shooting and killing Brown. During the trial, the narrative concerning the specific claims made by protestors in the aftermath of Brown's death—namely, that he had his hands up begging the officer not to shoot him at the time that he was killed—were contradicted by the facts of the case (Gass 2015); the protest chant of "hands up, don't shoot," purportedly what Brown begged Officer Wilson before being shot, was inconsistent with the evidence presented in the trial. Because media and public attention almost always focuses on the particular facts of the case, the contradiction of this key claim was perceived to be a repudiation of the Black Lives Matter movement by its detractors.

Essential to understanding the cause of the protests but less sensational, however, was the finding by the US Department of Justice that the Ferguson Police Department had routinely violated the civil rights of its citizens prior to Brown's shooting death. These violations included officers failing to uphold both the Fourth Amendment right against unreasonable search and seizure as well as the Fourteenth Amendment right guaranteeing equal protection of the law to all citizens, regardless of race (US Department of Justice 2015). Therefore, the particular incident in which Brown was killed may not have involved racial bias or even excessive use of force by the officer, but the police officers of Ferguson routinely engaged in racially biased stops and searches and used excessive force. This everyday experience of racial bias provided the lens to interpret Brown's shooting not as an isolated incident but as part of a broader pattern of discriminatory abuse by the police.

The police in Ferguson are not alone in perpetrating discrimination; police departments across the country struggle with racial bias. A recent analysis of more than one million police stops indicates that race still continues to be a factor in the decision to stop and search motorists (Pierson et al. 2020). Additionally, a meta-analysis of the decision to make an arrest also found that police are more likely to arrest minority suspects, even after accounting for relevant factors (Kochel, Wilson, and Mastrofski 2011). Then, once arrested, racial and ethnic minorities are more likely to be detained, convicted, and given longer sentences, even after accounting for legal factors such as prior offending (Franklin and Henry 2020). The majority of the evidence on racial disparities in the criminal justice system suggests that racial bias is still a consistent feature of every step of the adjudication process. Within this context, a police-involved shooting is simply the catalyst that focuses attention and animates anger at the police and the criminal justice system, *but it is not the ultimate cause of distrust in the police.*

A case that illustrates the counterfactual is the shooting death of Gilbert Collar. Collar, an eighteen-year-old college student attending the University of South Alabama, began banging on the window of the campus police station in the early-morning hours of October 6, 2012. Apparently under the influence of drugs, Collar confronted Trevis Austin, one of the campus police officers, in an attempt to fight or attack Austin. Austin shot Collar, who was both naked and unarmed, and Collar later died of his injuries. This case had many of the hallmarks of recent police shootings in which the officer used force that seemingly exceeded what was necessary for self-defense against an unarmed teenager. The apparent lack of an imminent threat to the life of the officer did not lead to a criminal conviction, as Austin was cleared of both criminal charges and civil liability (McKay 2015). Despite the lack of accountability, this case did not spur a protest movement.

Why was the reaction to Collar's death different from that of Brown's? The most likely answer is that Collar was a White student and White people in the United States, in general, have faith in the (local) police and the criminal justice system. Additionally, despite the possibility that this incident could have been interpreted through a racialized lens, as the officer was Black and the victim was White, few people saw this as indicative of racial injustice, as there was no preexisting context of racial discrimination against White people by the police. Accordingly, this incident was metabolized by the public as an isolated tragedy. Many people were critical of the actions of Officer Austin, but this critique did not contribute to a condemnation of policing, let alone a nationwide protest movement.

The respective reactions to the tragic deaths of Brown and Collar illustrate that it is the underlying distrust of the criminal justice system that causes the protest movement, not the other way around. This may be a fairly obvious point, but it is sometimes overlooked in the discussion of the particular "facts" of any case of alleged police brutality. The preexisting experiences and narratives surrounding the relationship between the police and the community determine the reaction to the incident more than the particular facts of the case do. African Americans are less likely to trust the police, which has been true for decades (Jones 2021). This distrust contributes to intermittent protests against police brutality. Protests do not necessarily indicate a new or growing distrust of the police but represent a preexisting deficit of police legitimacy.

Evaluating the Conventional "Legitimacy Crisis" Argument

It is possible that witnessing violence committed by the police serves to further delegitimize them in the eyes of the public. There has been an increasing distrust of the criminal justice system and the police, as documented in chapter 5. Recent research on the aftermath of George Floyd's death suggests that a perceived normative obligation to obey the police declined (Cross et al. 2023). This research, coupled with some suggestive pieces of evidence concerning a decline in calls for assistance (Rosenfeld et al. 2017), would suggest that the historical association noted between protest movements and crime (LaFree 1998; LaFree and Drass 1997; Roth 2009) is due to a straightforward legitimacy crisis.

Yet there are a few potential issues with the conventional legitimacy crisis argument. First, as implied in the preceding discussion of the origin of protests, we should expect there to be more stability than change in perceptions of legitimacy. This is not to deny that the legitimacy crisis has caused some people no longer to involve the police in community affairs and resort to "self-help" or at the very least to prepare to use unilateral violence to resolve disputes by purchasing a firearm (see chapter 5). The majority of the crime-inducing effect of the legitimacy crisis, however, is expected to be time stable, most readily observable between neighborhoods and cities with varying levels of trust in the police. Given the previous evidence on homicide trends (LaFree 1998; Roth 2009), we cannot reject a time-varying effect of legitimacy, but it may be better suited to explain time-stable differences in crime across neighborhoods and cities rather than time-variant crime trends.

A second issue is related to the divergent nature of recent crime trends. Similar to the problem of the de-policing argument presented in chapter 2, the divergence of property-based offenses and the homicide trend presents a problem for perspectives aimed at predicting general trends in criminal offending. Why would a legitimacy crisis contribute to more homicides but not more robberies and burglaries? During previous legitimacy crises, crime rates increased in general (LaFree 1998). If a legitimacy crisis was responsible for the recent increase in the homicide rate, we would also expect there to be an increase in other offenses as well.

Finally, the prevailing policing-based explanations of the protest-homicide association are limited due to their dependence on an intellectualized or overtly conscious response to police brutality. From the de-policing perspective, we are to believe that there is a large number of people who are constantly waiting for an opportunity to murder their neighbors, family members, and/or acquaintances but are otherwise thwarted by (perceived) constant police presence. The de-policing argument does not explain *why* people would be increasingly prone to commit violent assaults but assumes that the desire to murder is more or less constant. Then, perceiving less police proactivity, individuals with this pent-up demand for murder rationally decided that it would be the optimal time to kill their rivals to avoid detection and a potential prison sentence.

The police legitimacy crisis perspective is limited in a similar fashion. This perspective focuses on the trust in the police after acts of alleged brutality, hypothesizing that there are people who willingly complied with the police before witnessing an incident of brutality but then subsequently rejected the legitimacy of the police. Some of these people, no longer trusting the police to intervene in their affairs, took it upon themselves to murder a rival in a situation in which they would have previously called the police to intervene. This, again, presumes that the underlying motivation to kill existed prior to, or is independent of, the police legitimacy crisis and that individuals made a more or less rational decision to murder their rivals rather than call the police.

While some version of these kinds of homicides may have occurred during the homicide epidemic, both perspectives attempt to intellectualize an emotionally charged reaction to police brutality. Whether it is the anger at the unwarranted murder, the sadness created by the loss of young life, or the fear of further police violence, the current discussion about protests, policing, and homicide decouples the traumatic experience of racialized police violence from its emotional core. It also suggests that those who committed acts of violence in the aftermath of the protest movement did so due to some overt calculation, not due to a shift in norms surrounding the use of violence.

In the next section, I suggest that a portion of the homicide spike in the immediate aftermath of highly publicized incidents of alleged police brutality is driven by emotional responses (primarily, anger and fear) and a shift in norms surrounding the use of violence (brutalization). As we began to witness (via recorded video) police officers beat, shoot, and kill on a regular basis, it had a violence-inducing impact on its audience. Instead of affecting the rational decision-making processes by which people make calculations concerning the costs and benefits of committing a murder, it may have shifted subconscious beliefs about the appropriate use of violence. As police brutality filled our television, phone, and computer screens, it may have induced some people who were already predisposed to antisocial behavior, such as those with a prior criminal record, to assault, maim, and kill.

Police Brutality and Brutalization

Despite the shared root word, few people have made the connection between police brutality and the "brutalization" effect. The brutalization effect has primarily been applied to the study of the death penalty in an attempt to explain why, under certain circumstances, there is a higher rate of homicide after the imposition of capital punishment (Shepherd 2005). The brutalization argument hypothesizes that the imposition of the death penalty serves to devalue the importance (sanctity) of human life and allows people to rationalize the killing of people who have aggrieved and offended them (Bowers and Pierce 1980). In the case of police brutality caught on camera, there is not only a devaluation of human life and justification of violence but also a visceral anger and palpable fear. The perception that someone could be shot by a police officer for little to no apparent reason makes the world seem like a violent place in which anyone could be a victim.

The brutalization effect, when applied to instances of alleged police brutality, is hypothesized to operate in a similar, but distinct, manner to an execution. Witnessing police brutality may consciously or unconsciously justify the use of violence (Bowers and Pierce 1980); but, unlike an execution, when a police officer shoots an unarmed man, it also evokes greater fear and anger, as the victim was not condemned to die through the due process of law but by the subjective perception that they were a threat to the officer. Accordingly, we would expect that witnessing police brutality should not only shift the unconscious norms surrounding the use of violence and the sanctity of human life but also create a greater sense of anger, due to the injustice of the violence, and fear that you could be the next victim. It is within this context that people's use of violence is expected to become more prevalent, as the norms against violent assault have been eroded and the public is angry and fearful about becoming victims of violence themselves.

Public brutalization is hypothesized to be an *indirect* outgrowth of the protest movement. The protest movement directs public attention toward instances of brutality or a lack of racial justice within the criminal justice system. When protestors draw attention to a particularly egregious act of alleged brutality, they may inadvertently influence others to imitate the officer's violence. When the police shoot an unarmed man in the back, kill a lawful gun owner during a routine traffic stop, or kneel on a man who begs for his life until he can no longer breathe, it may appear to some people, particularly Black men, that violence is simply part of life in America. The fear evoked by the idea that the police, or anyone, could kill you for any reason at any moment provides a fertile ground for defensive violence. And, as we have seen from the defenses of police officers accused of lethal brutality, it requires little provocation to make someone fear that their life is in danger, justifying a lethal response to any perceived threat, whether real or imagined.

The incident of alleged brutality often comes with a video recording that will be shared, on the news or social media. Many of us witnessed the video of Walter Scott being shot in the back by a police officer after a traffic stop. There is a widely shared video showing the aftermath of an incident in which Philando Castile informed an officer of his legal firearm, only to be shot dead in front of his girlfriend and child. We all witnessed, in excruciating detail, George Floyd beg for his life while a Minneapolis police officer kneeled on his neck until he was no longer conscious. Unlike alleged incidents of police brutality of the past and government executions of the present, we all witness state-sanctioned violence in the smartphone and social media era.

The damaging psychological impact of publicized incidents of police brutality has already been documented in recent research. African Americans are five times more likely to worry about police use of excessive and lethal force than are their White counterparts (Graham et al. 2020). The distress and trauma of witnessing violence has caused hyperalertness, fear of death, and a lack of effective coping with the constant stream of police-brutality incidents. These incidents seem to evoke a response resembling posttraumatic stress disorder (PTSD) (Hawkins 2022). Black youth who are exposed to videos of police violence have greater odds of sleep disturbance, attributable to increased emotional distress (Jackson, Fix and Testa 2024). The racialized trauma of witnessing videos of police brutality impacts Black people at a young age who are growing up in an era when videos of the violence can be easily witnessed on social media (Williams 2021).

For young people and people who are already predisposed to violence (such as those with previous criminal records), the witnessing of police brutality may influence the decision to react violently to a perceived threat. Similarly, in the literature on patterns of self-harm, media depictions of suicide seem to induce young people who are already predisposed to suicidal ideation to be more likely to kill themselves in the proceeding days and months (Romer, Jamieson, and Jamieson 2006). In the case of "suicide contagion," it is not necessarily a conscious calculation that influences young people to imitate depictions of self-harm. Instead, it is a subtle influence that may escape conscious awareness. Those who were influenced to commit suicide may not even have acknowledged that they were impacted, but the high-profile depiction of suicide may have provided implicit "permission" to take their own life.

Additionally, in areas with high rates of crime, there may be a general fear of violence, facilitating the rapid spread of homicide after an incident of police brutality. Jeffrey Fagan, Deanna Wilkinson, and Garth

Davies (2007, 692) refer to an "ecology of danger" in which violence spreads due to perceived threats to safety. For many people living in economically disadvantaged neighborhoods across this country, there is a thin line between demonstrating credible deterrence against violence and becoming the perpetrator of violence (Anderson 1999). After a publicized act of police brutality, the fear of violence may be palpable, causing an increase in the use of defensive violence as a result. In the following pages, I more closely examine a couple of incidents that illustrate the potential impact of brutalization on recent homicide trends.

Baltimore, 2015

On April 12, 2015, Freddie Gray made eye contact with a Baltimore police officer and subsequently fled on foot. The officers perceived this as reason to pursue Gray as a suspect, search him, and arrest him for (allegedly) carrying a "switch blade," which has been subsequently disputed. The aftermath of this confrontation was caught on video and widely circulated. Gray, apparently injured and under duress, was forcibly placed in the back of a police van. The "rough ride" to the police station resulted in a neck injury that severed his spine. Gray died of these injuries on April 19, 2015 (Peralta 2015).

By the time that Gray had died, there was already a preexisting protest movement against police brutality that had highlighted similar incidents. Not only had Michael Brown been shot and killed during the previous year, but there were several other incidents of alleged police brutality that had been caught on camera. Laquan McDonald was shot and killed in Chicago despite walking away from officers in October 2014 (Alm 2019). Twelve-year-old Tamir Rice had been shot and killed in a Cleveland park by a police officer who apparently mistook a toy gun for a real firearm in November 2014 (Ali 2017). Then, the murder of Walter Scott was caught on camera as a North Charleston (South Carolina) police officer shot Scott in the back several times as he was fleeing from a routine traffic stop in April 2015 (Vann and Ortiz 2017).

In this context of growing anger about Black youth and men killed by the police, the death of Freddie Gray corresponded with an immediate spike in the Baltimore homicide rate. Prior to the incident, there was an average of 18.1 homicides per month in the city (May 2013 to March 2015). After Gray was killed in April 2015, the number of homicide deaths jumped to a new average threshold of 28.8 by the next month. The homicide rate remained elevated in Baltimore for years after this incident (Sweet, Alexander, and Alexander 2020).

While it is certainly true that arrests declined in Baltimore at the onset of protests and riots after Gray's death, signaling a police pullback, the increase in shootings (140 percent) and homicides (92 percent) (from April 20 to July 12, 2015) exceeded the increase in other offenses that would indicate the effect of a lack of police proactivity, such as robbery (31 percent) and automobile theft (52 percent) (Morgan and Pally 2016). The immediate and disproportionately violent response to Gray's death suggests a brutalization effect of witnessing police violence. While it is difficult to measure whether police violence directly caused the residents of Baltimore to devalue the sanctity of life and respond to perceived threats with violence, the sudden increase in shootings and homicides is broadly consistent with this hypothesis.

Minneapolis, 2020

Another incident that fits a brutalization-effect-like pattern occurred in Minneapolis in 2020. An unintended consequence of the pandemic-related restrictions in 2020 was the amount of time people spent at home watching videos and sharing news stories online. This attention amplified stories that may have otherwise been missed and provided further context to see the murder of George Floyd not as an isolated incident but as part of a broader pattern of racialized violence in the United States. In particular, the shooting of Ahmaud Arbery, an unarmed Black jogger who was pursued and shot by White men in an unprovoked attack, increased public scrutiny on racial injustice within the criminal justice system.

The murder of Arbery occurred in February 2020, with no immediate national attention. Initially, the men who killed Arbery were not charged with his murder. However, a leaked video in May contradicted their claims of self-defense (Andone 2021). The ensuing public outcry resulted in (eventual) murder and hate crime convictions for the men involved (US Department of Justice 2022). The obvious implication of the lack of an initial prosecution for Arbery's murder is that if the public had not witnessed the video and demanded justice, Black men could be murdered by White men with impunity.

The attention to Arbery's death provided the context for immediate outrage when the video of George Floyd's murder was shared on social media later that month. The media report of Floyd's death also initially downplayed the actions of the man who killed him, reporting that Floyd had an unspecified "medical incident" (Levenson 2021). When the video of the incident was circulated the next day, protests erupted immediately. It appeared that, for the second time in a month, Black men could be murdered with impunity without the public exerting pressure on the criminal justice system. The protests of the incident and lack of prosecution of the officer escalated to riots. On May 28, rioters burned the Minneapolis Third Precinct police station to the ground. The public was so incensed by the murder of Floyd and attempts to cover it up that a majority of Americans reported that they supported the burning of the police station (Impelli 2020). It was not until the next day that former police officer Derek Chauvin, who was eventually convicted of Floyd's murder, was arrested (Levenson 2021).

A recent study of violence in Minneapolis in the wake of Floyd's death provides suggestive evidence of a brutalization effect within the city. Ryan Larson, N. Jeanie Santaularia, and Christopher Uggen (2023) found that there was a sevenfold increase in firearm assaults in the period immediately after Floyd's murder, disproportionately concentrated in neighborhoods with social (racial) disadvantage. They found that this sudden spike in violence is not explained by changes associated with the pandemic or policing (de-policing). The publicized murder of Floyd by itself seemed to spark anger, fear, and, accordingly, violence in its wake. Although the authors do not specifically attribute this spike in shootings to the brutalization effect, they argue that the correspondence of neighborhoods in which there was violence in the aftermath of the Floyd protests with the sites of uprisings against police brutality in the 1960s "speak[s] to the traumatizing effects of police violence in the short- and long-term" (Larson, Santaularia, and Uggen 2023, 12).

In both Baltimore in 2015 and Minneapolis in 2020, there was an immediate spike in violence in the aftermath of highly publicized incidents of alleged brutality caught on camera. The spike in offending was disproportionately violent. The immediate increase in shootings and homicides suggests that brutalization had served to devalue the lives of others, which was coupled with anger and fear. This effect was concentrated among people who were already more prone to violence—especially those living in economically and socially disadvantaged neighborhoods. While it is not definitive, the effect of publicized brutality appears to be the culprit.

Directions for Future Research

The impact of police brutalization on recent homicide trends is still speculative at this point. There are additional elements missing in determining when police brutality will independently contribute to an increase in violent assaults and homicides. There are also counterexamples in which there was no spike in homicide after a highly publicized "police-involved shooting." For example, after the 2016 killing of Philando Castile in Minneapolis, there was no apparent increase in criminal offending. It is not entirely clear why some police shootings would inspire a sudden burst of violence while others do not.

An underappreciated, but certainly relevant, portion of a hypothesized brutalization effect is a measure of community and individual predisposition. For most people witnessing police violence, there is little impact on their likelihood of committing a murder. However, neighborhoods with high degrees of economic and social disadvantage, as well as people already more prone to violence, are more likely to be influenced by the brutalization effect. It was almost exclusively in the most disadvantaged neighborhoods where a sudden spike in violence occurred in Minneapolis (Larson, Santaularia, and Uggen 2023), implying that most communities are effectively "immune" from the brutalization effect.

For additional guidance on incidents that are most likely to spark an increase in violence, we can also draw on the brutalization literature concerning the death penalty. This literature suggests that in places where the death penalty is regularly used, there is no apparent brutalization effect. It is only where capital punishment is an infrequent occurrence where a spike in homicide occurs as a result of an execution (Shepherd 2005). This pattern suggests that at the beginning of a protest movement, videos of police brutality will have an outsized impact on the murder rate. As publicized incidents of brutality become more frequent, the public may become desensitized, and no further violence can be attributed to witnessing police violence.

Future research on the impact of police brutality on violent crime should delve into three relevant elements of the brutalization effect. The first element is a preexisting narrative. In both 2015 and 2020, the incidents of alleged police brutality highlighted in the preceding section fit into a larger narrative about the devaluation of Black life and the impunity of a White killer. Without this preexisting context, the incident of alleged police brutality could be interpreted as an individual tragedy committed by a rogue officer, not a collective affront to racial justice.

The second element involves the publicity of the incident. If there is video of the incident that is shared with the public, we would expect a larger impact than if it were not publicized or recorded. This is essential for establishing both the impact of the police legitimacy crisis on crime and the brutalization effect. While previous research suggests that cities and counties where residents were killed by the police had higher homicide rates (Gaston, Cunningham, and Gillezeau 2019; Lane 2022), the potential missing element is the level of public awareness of these killings.

Finally, there needs to be some consideration of exhaustion. After a long period of protest and several highly publicized incidents, there will probably be a diminution of the brutalization effect or even no effect whatsoever. This may explain the lack of an apparent impact of police brutality as the protest movement progresses. Ultimately, more research is needed to definitively conclude that the brutalization effect caused sudden spikes in homicide in 2015 and 2020 as well as to establish this pattern beyond fitting the general facts of a few incidents.

Conclusion

In this chapter, I have advanced the argument that the police legitimacy crisis contributed to the homicide epidemic. This contribution, however, is not as straightforward as often depicted in the previous research literature. Distrust of the police is endemic within some communities around the country, meaning that the protest movement probably has little influence on the opinions of those who are most cynical of the police. Therefore, distrust of the police is more likely to have a time-stable impact on variation in homicide rather than predict a sudden spike in shootings. In chapter 8, I return to this argument.

Given that a stable level of distrust may not explain the sudden rise in violence, I argue that the protest movement may have had an indirect impact through the brutalization effect. By drawing attention to incidents of police brutality, the protest movement exposes the public to state-sanctioned violence. In addition to providing a devaluation of human life, witnessing police brutality evokes the emotions of anger and fear, which lend themselves to the use of violence. For this reason, we should expect the immediate aftermath of high-profile incidents of police brutality to evoke a disproportionately violent response. However, as I outlined earlier, further evidence is needed to definitively conclude that brutalization was one of the primary causes of the sudden spikes in violent crime.

Now that I have laid out the argument as to how the decline in Americans' well-being and institutions has contributed to the homicide epidemic, I test (some of) the contentions I have made throughout the book. In chapter 7, I assess the impact of drug overdose deaths, alcohol consumption, and firearm purchases on trends in homicide and other criminal offenses, testing the assertions that I made in chapters 3 through 5. In doing so, I demonstrate that these factors can explain why homicide (and, to a lesser extent, aggravated assault) have increased at the same time that robbery and burglary rates have declined.

7

Alcohol, Drugs, and Guns

An Analysis of State-Level Crime Trends, 2010–2021

The homicide drop was great while it lasted.
—Richard Rosenfeld and James Alan Fox, discussing the 2015–2016 homicide rate increase in "Anatomy of the Homicide Rise"

After generally declining for more than two decades, the homicide rate suddenly spiked in 2015 and increased intermittently, peaking in 2021. In previous chapters, I have argued that the historical reversal in the alcohol consumption trend, the deadliest drug addiction epidemic in US history, and an increase in firearm purchases have contributed to the homicide epidemic. With more people drunk, buying drugs from street dealers, and having access to deadly weapons, the expectation is that there will be a greater number of violent altercations, resulting in more deaths due to assault. This chapter more systematically assesses the impact of alcohol consumption, drug abuse, and firearm accessibility on recent crime trends.

To test the impact of guns, drugs, and alcohol on crime, I use multivariate fixed-effects regression analysis on data representing US states from 2010 to 2020. These years represent the period immediately before (2010–2014) and during (2015–2020) the homicide epidemic, mirroring the timeline and trends depicted in figure 1.1. Unfortunately, due to data limitations in the FBI crime statistics for 2021, I am unable to include this year in the analyses. Notably, some states still feature incomplete crime data for 2021 at the time of writing. To supplement these data, I perform an additional analysis spanning from 2010 to 2021 on homicide rates using CDC Wonder (2023) mortality data on deaths caused by assaults.

The analysis presented in this chapter comports with the "normal science" study of crime trends (Rosenfeld 2018). Each of the factors just listed has previously been identified as having an impact on historical homicide trends (see chapters 3 through 5) and is expected to exert a fairly consistent impact on crime over time. Unlike the exogenous shock(s) of 2020, the results are expected to be reproduced during different time periods and are not dependent on a sudden or unexpected change in social dynamics.

As is apparent from the tables presented in this chapter, the impact of drugs, alcohol, and guns differed across criminal offenses. The differential impact of these factors on specific criminal offense trends helps to resolve one of the unique characteristics of the homicide epidemic, which is that the increase in aggravated assault and homicide occurred at the same time as a decline in property crime and property-motivated offenses. As highlighted in chapter 1, the rate of homicide and aggravated assault has increased since 2014, but the rates of both burglary and robbery have declined during this same period. Because firearm purchases, drug abuse and sales, and alcohol consumption are more closely associated with the homicide rate than with robbery and burglary, the results suggest that these factors are central to understanding divergent crime trends during the homicide epidemic.

The sample for this analysis includes all US states. States were selected as the unit of analysis because there were complete data for each of the three primary factors examined (alcohol, drugs, and guns). There are analyses at a lower level of aggregation on some of these specific factors, such as a recent analysis on county-level drug overdose and homicide trends (Rosenfeld, Roth, and Wallman 2021), but the data on firearm purchases and alcohol consumption are not available with this level of geographical detail. Additionally, some of the sources I draw on do not include data for Washington, DC, and it is therefore not included in the final sample.

Variables and Data Sources

I examine four types of criminal offenses: each state's annual rate of *homicide, aggravated assault, robbery,* and *burglary*. These data are derived from the publicly available FBI (2022) Crime Data Explorer. I have selected these crimes as they are among the most consistently and accurately reported to the police (Rosenfeld 2009) and represent distinctive types of criminal offenses. Some previous analyses have examined the total violent crime rate (or property crime rate) as an outcome, but as is apparent in the results shown in this chapter, trends in each offense had slightly different sets of predictors. Examining the overall violent crime trend would obscure the specific factors influencing recent homicide trends.

Homicides included in the FBI (2022) data are all reported incidents of murder and nonnegligent manslaughter. These data represent criminal homicides, excluding noncriminal assaults such as those carried out in legally permissible self-defense. In supplemental analyses, I also examine CDC homicide data, derived from the publicly accessible CDC Wonder (2023) database. The state-level data for the CDC extend to 2021. CDC data include all deaths by assault, regardless of legal determination of criminality.[1]

In addition to homicide, I also examine trends in three other offenses. "Aggravated assault" is defined as an unlawful attack that results in "severe or aggravated" bodily injury. "Robbery" is defined as the attempt to take an item of value from someone through the use or threat of force. "Burglary" is defined as the unlawful entry with the intent to commit a felony or theft (FBI 2022). All crimes are converted to a rate by dividing the number of reported offenses by each state's population size and then multiplying this number by one hundred thousand.

Table 7.1 presents the change in these crimes from 2010 to 2020. Note that the statistics presented in this table are a mean across the fifty states and are not weighted for population size; these are not the national crime rates but an average across the states in the sample. Also, the CDC

TABLE 7.1. State Mean and Percentage Change of Outcome Variables, 2010–2020

Variable	2010	2020	% change from 2010 to 2020
Homicide rate (FBI)	4.12	6.03	+46.4
Aggravated assault rate	240.61	277.08	+15.2
Robbery rate	90.43	57.20	−36.7
Burglary rate	666.26	316.06	−52.6
Homicide rate (CDC)*	4.61	7.27	+57.7

* For the CDC data, the final year of homicide data is 2021, not 2020. The other crime measures end in 2020. The percentage change is calculated from 2010 to 2021.

homicide data extend to 2021, not 2020 as the other crime rates. Similar to figure 1.1, it is apparent that state mean homicide and aggravated assault rates increased during the previous decade, while the mean rates of robbery and burglary across US states declined.

I use proxy measures to capture the increase in illicit drug sales, alcohol consumption, and firearm availability. My proxy for the increase in illicit drug sales is the annual *drug overdose* death rate for each state. While previous research has specifically analyzed one type of drug, such as opioid overdoses (e.g., Rosenfeld, Roth, and Wallman 2021), I make no distinction in the type of drug overdose in these statistics. This allows me to account for the sale and abuse of any type of drug. This proxy measure for drug sales and abuse is utilized under the assumption that the increase in deaths rates is *primarily* a function of an increase in illicit drug abuse and users. In this measure, I include only drug overdoses that were unintentional, undetermined, or attributed to other causes, such as a substance abuse disorder. I exclude drug overdoses recorded as homicides and suicides in these data. The data for the state drug overdose death rate are derived from the CDC Wonder (2023) database.

Alcohol consumption data are derived from the National Institute on Alcohol Abuse and Alcoholism (NIAAA) (Slater and Alpert 2023). NIAAA data provide a yearly measure of alcohol sales, supplemented by shipping data, to estimate the amount of alcohol consumed per capita in a given year and are therefore used in the final analysis.[2]

Firearm purchases data capture the number of background checks for legal firearm sales, standardized by one hundred thousand population, made by registered firearms dealers and reported to the NICS (FBI 2023). This proxy measure is an attempt to capture the relative change in firearm access over time. However, this measure is not a perfect representation of firearm access, as it captures purchases made by people who already own firearms, which would not meaningfully increase their access to a firearm. This measure also fails to capture firearm purchases that are made illegally and by nonregistered dealers. The ideal measure would be the total proportion of the population owning or having access to a firearm or, potentially, a measure of new firearm purchases by first-time buyers including both legal and illegal sales. However, given the data limitations and a dearth of alternative sources, this measure is the best available proxy to capture annual variation in the demand for firearms, providing an indirect indication of the rate of firearm possession.

Additional variables are included in the regression models presented in this chapter to serve as controls for relevant factors. Demographic control variables include *percentage age fifteen to twenty-nine, percentage Black, percentage Hispanic*, and *population size*, all derived from the CDC Wonder (2023) database, which uses US Census Bureau state population estimates. These measures are employed to assess the degree to which population characteristics of each state impact the crime rate, which is common in this type of research.

To capture economic deprivation, the crude *infant mortality rate* is also derived from the CDC Wonder (2023) database. Infant mortality has been used as a proxy measure of poverty in cross-national analyses of homicide (Pridemore 2008) and is also highly correlated with income inequality (Olson et al. 2010). This makes infant mortality a good proxy measure of social exclusion and economic deprivation, which are often hypothesized to contribute to crime. Notably, it was a more consistent predictor of crime trends than was the poverty rate as estimated by the US Census Bureau in my preliminary analyses (not shown). The other economic variables that are included in these models are *Gross*

Domestic Product (GDP) per capita and the *unemployment rate*. These data are derived from the Bureau of Economic Analysis (2022b) of the US Department of Commerce and the Federal Reserve Bank of St. Louis (2022b), respectively.

To account for changes in "routine activities" (e.g., Cohen and Felson 1979), I also include variables representing the *labor-force participation* rate, derived from the Federal Reserve Bank of St. Louis (2022a), and the *percentage retail workers* as a proportion of the entire labor force, derived from the Bureau of Economic Analysis (2022a). These measures are included as proxies of two potential contributors to the decline of burglary and robbery rates. For the proposed impact of labor-force participation on burglary trends, the underlying idea is that a decline in labor-force participation contributes to fewer opportunities for burglary, as more people at home during the middle of the day should increase guardianship against burglary (Cantor and Land 1985). In relation to the hypothesized retail employment and robbery association, the expectation is that if there are fewer in-person financial transactions, there should be fewer opportunities to locate attractive targets for robbery.

Finally, to account for changes in the incapacitation of offenders, I include the *incarceration rate* in each state. Incarceration rate data are derived from various annual reports released by the Bureau of Justice Statistics of the US Department of Justice (e.g., Carson 2022). The effect of the incarceration rate is included in both the contemporaneous year and lagged by one year. The lag captures change in the incarceration rate in the year prior, such as in 2009 in relationship to the state crime rate in 2010. The lagged measure is typical of research on the impact of incarceration to account for simultaneity bias, or the idea that increases in crime could contribute to a higher incarceration rate in the same year, thereby contributing to a positive rather than negative association of incarceration with crime (Spelman 2000). I include both measures of incarceration (contemporaneous and lag) in the following models.

TABLE 7.2. State Mean and Percentage Change of Independent Variables, 2010–2020

Variable	2010	2020	% change from 2010 to 2020
Drug overdose rate	11.64	27.95	+140.1
Alcohol consumption	2.39	2.53	+5.9
Firearm purchases (per capita)	6,000.44	13,137.56	+118.9
Percentage age 15 to 29	22.01	21.05	−4.4
Percentage Black	10.62	11.25	+5.9
Percentage Hispanic	10.65	12.44	+16.8
Population size (in thousands)	6174.90	6615.20	+7.1
Infant mortality rate	626.41	543.17	−13.3
GDP per capita (in thousands)	47.20	59.84	+26.8
Unemployment rate	8.75	7.40	−15.4
Labor-force participation rate	65.23	62.13	−4.8
Percentage retail workers	10.50	9.86	−6.1
Incarceration rate	435.39	331.72	−23.8
Incarceration rate (lagged)	438.30	387.82	−11.5

Table 7.2 provides the mean of each of the variables included in the model at the beginning (2010) and end (2020) of the period of analysis. I also provide an indication of the overall trend in each of these variables during this period by including the percentage change. While the difference between 2010 and 2020 represents the overall trend, there are some trends that have featured notable reversals during this period that are not captured within the table. As noted previously, the homicide and assault rates declined from 2010 to 2014 but then increased from 2014 to 2020. Another notable trend reversal is noted in the unemployment rate. While the unemployment rate has declined (overall) from its peak in 2010, the unemployment rate increased dramatically in 2020 due to COVID-19-related restrictions. The percentage change provides the overall indication of the direction of these trends during the period under study, which is an important consideration when examining the direction of their impact (coefficient) on crime trends in the following regression models.

Analysis Method

To analyze the data, I use multivariate fixed-effects panel regression analysis. This procedure estimates the impact of change over time on the outcome variable (crime rate), while simultaneously accounting for other relevant factors. This approach more closely assesses causality than tracing national trend lines and examining bivariate correlations. By examining change within each individual state, the association between the variables of interest (drug overdose, alcohol consumption, and firearm purchases) and the crime rate approximates a quasi-experimental design by comparing the same state with *itself* at a different point in time. Fixed-effects regression models also account for time-stable differences between states.

Additional controls were included when estimating the final models. First, I account for the linear impact of time, which assesses the impact of annual change from 2010 to 2020 on the crime rate.[3] This is an attempt to account for factors that vary systematically with time that could influence the crime rate but are not available to include in the analysis. Additionally, I first-difference the panel data in an attempt to achieve stationarity.[4] This means that I subtract the current year's data from the previous year's data; each data point represents annual change from the previous year. Each of the regression models estimated in tables 7.3 and 7.4 employ robust standard errors to help account for heteroskedasticity bias. Finally, I include a "period effect" for 2020 to account for the exogenous shocks of the pandemic and protests during that year.

Results

The results of these models are presented in table 7.3. This table presents the unstandardized coefficient as well as the standard error in parentheses. All coefficients that exceed the conventional cutoff point for statistical significance are marked using either one ($p < .05$) or two ($p < .01$) asterisks within the table. As is apparent in table 7.3, there is a

TABLE 7.3. Predictors of Crime Trends, 2010–2020

Variable	Model 1: Homicide	Model 2: Aggravated assault	Model 3: Robbery	Model 4: Burglary
Drug overdose rate	.04** (.02)	.18 (.37)	.15 (.16)	−.28 (.55)
Alcohol consumption	1.43* (.64)	40.84* (13.71)	.33 (8.53)	31.03 (28.83)
Firearm purchases (per capita)	.001* (.0004)	.01 (.01)	.003 (.005)	.04 (.03)
Percentage age 15 to 29	.16 (.34)	1.30 (12.93)	4.63 (3.91)	−15.44 (29.03)
Percentage Black	−.99 (.99)	−30.03 (25.03)	−2.62 (8.74)	−3.10 (37.60)
Percentage Hispanic	.16 (.80)	28.22 (31.11)	−15.40 (7.64)	99.81* (30.20)
Population size (in thousands)	−.001 (.001)	−.01 (.02)	−.002 (.01)	−.15* (.06)
Infant mortality rate	.001* (.001)	.01 (.02)	.01 (.005)	.05** (.02)
GDP per capita	.01 (.02)	−1.19 (.63)	−.35 (.31)	−5.24** (.92)
Unemployment rate	.02 (.06)	−2.91 (1.69)	−.85 (.85)	−2.35 (4.08)
Labor-force participation	.10 (.06)	2.16 (1.51)	.83 (1.08)	6.11 (3.68)
Percentage retail workers	.78 (.40)	21.27* (9.07)	10.35** (3.32)	−25.60 (14.90)
Incarceration rate	−.01** (.002)	−.12** (.05)	−.03 (.03)	−.29** (.08)
Incarceration rate (lagged)	.0002 (.001)	−.08 (.05)	−.05* (.02)	−.55** (.09)
R-squared	.24	.25	.09	.17

$N = 500$; * = $p < .05$; ** = $p < .01$

statistically significant impact of the drug overdose death rate, alcohol consumption, and firearm purchases on annual change in the homicide rate. These significant effects persist even after accounting for the other variables included in the model, the linear impact of time, and the 2020 period effect. This finding allows us to have more confidence that the homicide epidemic was partially the result of increases in drug abuse, alcohol consumption, and firearm availability.

To interpret the results in tables 7.3 and 7.4, it is important to keep in mind the direction of the regression coefficient as well as the overall trend in the crime rate (presented in table 7.1) and trend in the variable (presented in table 7.2). When the coefficient, crime trend, and variable trend are all positive (or all negative), this eases interpretation, as the overall impact of the variable on the crime trend can be surmised from the direction of the coefficient. As is the case for the effects outlined in the previous paragraph, all (drugs, alcohol, and guns) were increasing, and each variable had a positive effect on the homicide rate. This lends to a relatively straightforward interpretation, as these factors have contributed to the increase in homicide.

If one of the three (direction of coefficient, crime trend, or variable trend) is in the opposite direction of the other two, however, it complicates the interpretation of the substantive effect on the crime trend. For example, if the coefficient of a variable is positive (table 7.3) but the trend declines from 2010 to 2020 (table 7.2), it would suggest that this variable is partially responsible for the crime rate falling. This is the case for the effect of infant mortality on the homicide rate. Given the declining trend in infant mortality during this period (13.3 percent decline), the positive coefficient of infant mortality on the homicide rate in Model 1 of table 7.3 suggests that the homicide trend would have increased even more if it were not for a decline in infant mortality (poverty) during the era. This finding implies that the homicide epidemic would have been even more deadly if it had occurred during an era in which poverty rates were either stable or increasing.

The other statistically significant predictor of annual variation in the homicide rate (Model 1) was change in the contemporaneous incarceration rate. The negative coefficient, coupled with a decline in the prison population (23.8 percent decline) during this period, implies that the decline in incarceration has contributed to more homicides. While the falling incarceration rate cannot explain the timing of the homicide epidemic, as it has been declining nationally since 2009, it does appear that it has impacted the homicide trend. Overall, the results presented in

Model 1 of table 7.3 confirm the impact of drugs, alcohol, and guns on homicide trends within US states and also suggest that a decline in incarceration played some role as well.

The results for annual variation in aggravated assault are located in Model 2 of table 7.3. Similar to the homicide model, alcohol consumption is a significant predictor of aggravated assault, and the decline in the incarceration rate is associated with the increase in aggravated assault. However, the other findings in this model differed somewhat from the homicide model. The percentage of the labor force composed of retail workers was significantly and positively associated with aggravated assault. Because retail workers as a percentage of the labor force declined during this period (6.1 percent decline), this finding implies that a decline in in-person financial transactions served as a countervailing force against the increase in assault rates. That is, the aggravated assault rate is predicted to have increased even more if the rate of in-person financial transactions had remained at 2010 levels throughout this period.

In Model 3 of table 7.3, we find that few variables predict annual variation in the rate of robbery. As expected in accordance with the routine activities perspective, the percentage of the labor force working in retail was positively associated with robbery. Given the decline in the percentage of retail workers during this period, this finding is consistent with the idea that there were fewer opportunities ("attractive targets") for profitable robberies due to the decline of in-person transactions. Additionally, the lagged impact on incarceration was significantly and negatively associated with robbery. Because the (lagged) mean incarceration rate declined during this era (9.5 percent decline), this implies that robbery rates would have declined *even more* if incarceration rates had remained stable (or increased) from 2010 onward.

Finally, the results for annual change in the burglary rate are located in Model 4 of table 7.3. Two factors are acting as countervailing forces to the decline in burglary: the increase in the Hispanic population and declining incarceration rates. The interpretation for the effect of the percentage Hispanic on the burglary rate is unclear, as city-level findings imply that a larger Hispanic population is often associated with less crime (see chapter 8), the opposite of what is found here. The negative and significant impact of incarceration rates (and the one-year-lagged effect of incarceration rates) suggests that burglary rates would be even lower if incarceration rates had remained at 2010 levels. The factors that contributed to the decline in the burglary rate are a decline in infant mortality (poverty), an increase in population size, and an increase in GDP per capita.

CDC Homicide Data Analysis, 2010–2021

Because (reliable) FBI data do not extend to 2021 at the state level at the time of writing, I conducted a supplemental analysis of homicide deaths using CDC Wonder (2023) mortality data. Unfortunately, I can only examine homicide rates, as the CDC provides only cause-of-death data, not general crime data. Model 5 in table 7.4 uses the same model specifications as Model 1 of table 7.3 in examining annual change in homicide rates but extends the time series by an additional year for each variable.

The results between the models using FBI and CDC homicide data are similar, with a few notable exceptions. Beginning with the similarities, the impacts of alcohol consumption, drug overdose deaths, and firearm purchases are all significantly associated with the homicide rate. Additionally, the contemporaneous negative association between the incarceration rate and homicide is also significant in Model 5 of table 7.4, which was also the case in Model 1 of table 7.3. The consistency of these effects using a different measure of homicide victimization and across a slightly different time period suggests that these findings are robust.

Key differences from the FBI model (Model 1 versus Model 5) include the impact of infant mortality, which only nears statistical significance ($p = .11$) in the model predicting CDC homicide trends but was a significant predictor of homicide using FBI data. Percentage Hispanic and labor-force participation are significant in the CDC model (table 7.4) but not the FBI model (table 7.3). Labor-force participation's decline and

TABLE 7.4. Predictors of the CDC Homicide Rate, 2010–2021

Variable	Model 5: CDC homicide
Drug overdose rate	.04**
	(.01)
Alcohol consumption	1.58**
	(.52)
Firearm purchases (per capita)	.001*
	(.0004)
Percentage age 15 to 29	−.54
	(.40)
Percentage Black	−.07
	(.62)
Percentage Hispanic	1.41*
	(.56)
Population size (in thousands)	−.0001
	(.0005)
Infant mortality rate	.001
	(.001)
GDP per capita	−.03
	(.03)
Unemployment rate	.03
	(.05)
Labor-force participation	.14*
	(.06)
Percentage retail workers	.54
	(.32)
Incarceration rate	−.01**
	(.002)
Incarceration rate (lagged)	.002
	(.002)
R-squared	.27

$N = 550$; * = $p < .05$; ** = $p < .01$

positive association with homicide suggests that it is acting as a countervailing force against the homicide rate increase, although the precise explanation of this effect is unclear.

As we will see in chapter 8, the effect of percentage Hispanic on crime rates at the state level is contradicted by city-level analyses suggesting a *lower* rate of crime predicted by larger Hispanic populations. It is possible that at the state level, changes in the Hispanic population are capturing a latent poverty measure or social disorganization effect that is not well accounted for within these models. Because the rate of Hispanic infant mortality tends to be lower than would be expected given the relatively high level of poverty among Hispanics (Hummer et al. 2007), it is possible that using infant mortality as the proxy measure of poverty does not adequately capture a greater degree of economic disadvantage within this group. It is also possible that in states in which Hispanic population growth is greatest, there is greater change/disorganization in community dynamics, resulting in a decline of collective efficacy (e.g., Sampson, Raudenbush, and Earls 1997). Further research is needed to clarify the differences in these findings across the state (chapter 7) and city (chapter 8) levels of analysis.[5]

Explaining Divergent Crime Trends

Overall, these results provide insight into a neglected area of the homicide epidemic: the divergence in crime trends. The results presented in this chapter show a significant impact of drug overdose rates, alcohol consumption, and firearm purchases on homicide but not on robbery and burglary. Unlike deterrence or economic deprivation, which should have a nearly universal impact on the direction of crime trends, the offense-specific impact of these variables on violent assaults provides an explanation as to why there has been an increase in aggravated assault and homicide but not in property-based offenses.

The only other consistent contributor of the increase in homicide rates from these models is declining incarceration rates. The negative and significant association, coupled with the declining trend (table 7.2), provides evidence that fewer people in state prisons contributed to the homicide increase. However, depending on the lag (contemporaneous or one-year lag), the incarceration rate was also significantly and negatively associated with robbery and burglary rates, both of which declined during this period. A decline in the incarceration rate has apparently exacerbated the homicide epidemic but cannot explain the divergent crime patterns or seemingly the direction of crime trends in general.

The results presented in this chapter also help to explain the continued decline in robbery and burglary. Given the decline of retail workers, there appear to have been fewer opportunities to commit robberies. Following the logic of the routine activities perspective, the decline in this proxy for in-person transactions suggests that there are fewer "attractive targets" for robbery, as an increasing number of economic transactions take place online. Finally, Model 4 of table 7.3 shows that improving economic conditions, captured by increases in GDP per capita and declines in infant mortality (poverty), appear to have contributed to a decline in the burglary rate during this period.

Conclusion

In this chapter, I have provided further evidence that the manifestations of American decline, including drug abuse, alcohol consumption, and firearm purchases, have contributed to the recent homicide epidemic. I have also partially explained the contradictory trends in criminal offending. Homicide trends were predicted by a different set of factors than were robbery and burglary trends. Additionally, the increase in alcohol consumption partially explains the increase in the aggravated assault rate as well. There were other contributors to the homicide epidemic, such as the decline in the incarceration rate, but the lack of incapacitation could not explain the divergence in crime trends, as it exerted a fairly uniform impact across different types of offenses. For example, the effect of the incarceration rate was similar for both homicide and burglary, yet the mean state homicide rate increased by 46.4 percent during this period while the mean burglary rate declined by 52.6 percent. The results of these models suggest that incarceration can prevent crime but is not terribly predictive of the overall direction of crime trends.

In chapter 8, I revisit the most notable year of the homicide epidemic: 2020. In particular, I revisit two themes that could not be included in this analysis of state-level trends: the impact of protests and de-policing on crime rates. As I discussed in chapter 2, protest-related de-policing in 2020 did not begin until after the national homicide rate began to increase. However, as I show in chapter 8, a lack of police proactivity in making weapons-related arrests predicts larger increases in homicide across US cities. Additionally, cities with a higher rate of protest had a higher overall rate of homicide in 2020.

8

Protests, Policing, and Crime

A City-Level Examination of 2020

For too many American communities, it's not as bad as the 1990s, it's worse.
—Magic M. Wade, referring to firearm-related violence in "Not as Bad as the '90s?"

In 2020, the homicide rate increased by the largest annual margin in recorded US history. The homicide rate increased from 5.1 homicides per 100,000 population in 2019 to 6.5 in 2020, a total increase of 1.4 homicides per 100,000. Since 1950, the largest recorded annual increase in the homicide rate was only half as large (0.7 homicides per 100,000), which last occurred from 1989 to 1990 (Fox and Zawitz 2007). The 2020 homicide rate increase was also proportionally the largest in recorded history, as the national homicide rate leaped by more than 27 percent in a single year. The previous record was the 11 percent increase from 1967 to 1968 (Fox and Zawitz 2007), which occurred in the wake of the assassination of Martin Luther King Jr. and subsequent urban uprisings and rebellions.

In chapter 7, I confirmed the impact of alcohol, drugs, and guns on the homicide epidemic, all of which played an apparent role in 2020. Each of these three American vices increased more rapidly in 2020 than in any other year in recent history, which can partially explain the spike in homicide. However, the state-level data analyzed do not capture one of the most discussed concepts in both the academic literature and popular media. Specifically, what was the effect of de-policing and the police legitimacy crisis?

This chapter provides a city-level assessment of these competing perspectives in relation to the homicide rate increase in 2020. Previous research has rarely attempted to simultaneously examine these two concepts in competition with each other. There is partial support for both perspectives, although the most consistent predictor of a larger homicide rate increase is the degree of city-level economic and social disadvantage. Before presenting these analyses, I first contextualize the homicide rate increase in 2020, including a comparison with the 1990s for cities experiencing the highest rates of homicide.

City-Level Homicide Rates, 2020

The crime narrative in the United States has long been stuck in the 1990s. For some people, New York City is perpetually an example of a city with "out-of-control" crime rates. In 2023, the US House Judiciary Committee held a hearing in Manhattan, ostensibly to call attention to the crime-victimization problem specific to New York City. In this hearing, Republican members of Congress accused their political opponents of having "pro-crime, anti-victim" policies (Sisak 2023).

While this was a farcical political stunt, it serves to demonstrate how much the prevailing narrative about crime is still stuck in the 1990s. The homicide rate in New York City was approximately 18 percent lower than the national average in 2020 (author's calculation), and at the time of this congressional hearing, New York City had a lower homicide rate than most large cities across the country. In fact, New York City had a lower homicide rate than entire states across the South and Midwest. If the House Judiciary Committee was actually interested in investigating policies that had contributed to high rates of homicide instead of making a political stunt, they would have visited Louisiana, Mississippi, or Missouri and their emerging centers of violent crime victimization that had recently set new records for homicide, including Baton Rouge, Jackson, and St. Louis.

Because of the decade's outsized place in the public imagination, the 1990s serve as a good point of comparison for recent homicide patterns.

For some cities, the homicide rate in 2020 broke all previous records, including those set during the crime-plagued early 1990s. Table 8.1 presents the twenty cities with the highest 2020 homicide rates. The homicide data are derived from the FBI's (2022) Crime Data Explorer and only include cities that (a) initially reported homicide data to the FBI for 2020 and (b) had a population of at least one hundred thousand residents. In total, this produced data for 299 cities. Notable cities that are not included in this list are Atlanta and Philadelphia, both of which have faced significant issues with violent crime in recent years but did not initially report reliable data to the FBI. The relative change in the homicide rate per one hundred thousand from 2019 to 2020 is located in the middle column of table 8.1. Presented in the left column is an indication of whether the homicide rate in 2020 exceeded all annual rates recorded in the city in the 1990s. For many cities on this list, homicide victimization in 2020 not only was as bad as it was during the 1990s but was worse. Of these top twenty cities, eleven exceeded all annual homicide rates recorded in the 1990s.

Even though some cities on the East Coast still face significant issues with crime, their respective homicide rates were well below historical highs in 2020. Washington, DC, went from often being the "murder capital" of the United States in the 1980s and 1990s to falling out of the top ten in homicide victimization (now eighteenth). The cities of New York (ranked 157 of 299) and Newark (ranked thirty-second), which were once near the top of the list, have completely fallen out of the top twenty.

In the Midwest and South, the shift in homicide has been in the opposite direction. Cities located in Missouri, Ohio, and Louisiana have emerged to take top spots on this list. In 2020, Louisiana had three cities claim a top-ten spot (New Orleans, Baton Rouge, and Shreveport), while Missouri boasted two cities in the top ten (St. Louis and Kansas City). Ohio had three cities reach the top twenty, two of which recorded fewer homicides in 2020 than in some of the worst years during the 1990s (Cleveland and Dayton) but had a higher homicide rate due to population decline during the intervening decades. Some cities in the eastern part of the US still remain on this list (Baltimore, Richmond,

TABLE 8.1. Highest City-Level Homicide Rates per One Hundred Thousand Population in 2020, Compared to the 1990s

City	Homicide rate 2020	Change in homicide rate 2019 to 2020	Higher than 1990s?
1. St. Louis, MO	88.36	+23.88	Yes
2. Jackson, MS	69.70	+22.39	Yes
3. New Orleans, LA	51.61	+20.68	
4. Baltimore, MD	51.01	−7.51	
5. Detroit, MI	49.30	+7.53	
6. Baton Rouge, LA	46.56	+14.86	Yes
7. Memphis, TN	44.48	+14.68	Yes
8. Cleveland, OH	42.26	+16.04	Yes*
9. Shreveport, LA	37.34	+18.65	
10. Kansas City, MO	35.40	+4.77	Yes
11. Dayton, OH	32.88	−4.14	Yes*
12. Milwaukee, WI	32.42	+16.01	Yes
13. North Charleston, SC	32.00	+9.57	Yes
14. San Bernardino, CA	31.27	+10.04	
15. Cincinnati, OH	30.21	+8.20	Yes
16. Chicago, IL	28.79	+10.40	
17. Richmond, VA	28.42	+4.18	
18. Washington, DC	27.78	+4.32	
19. South Bend, IN	27.49	+13.76	Yes
20. Little Rock, AR	24.76	+6.54	

* Fewer total homicides than a year during the 1990s but higher homicide rate in 2020 due to population decline.

and Washington, DC), but even these cities are technically located in the "South," according to CDC classification, leaving zero cities in the East region and only one (San Bernardino) from the West in the top twenty. Nine of the cities in the top twenty were located in the Midwest, and ten were located in the South.

Research on the 2020 Homicide Spike

The order of the list of the most homicidal cities in the United States in 2020 is indicative of both stability and change. Even on this list of the most homicide-plagued cities, there are two (Baltimore and Dayton) that experienced a homicide *decline* in 2020. Of the 299 cities with over one hundred thousand residents and sufficient/complete data, 208 experienced an increase in homicide, 10 experienced no change, and 81 experienced a decline. Overall, approximately 70 percent of the cities in the sample experienced an increase, but there is a remarkable amount of variation in both the overall homicide rate and change in the homicide rate across these cities.[1] Despite all cities experiencing the same national events that wreaked havoc in 2020, the effects on homicide were not universal. Before assessing the impact of city characteristics on crime, I address the nationwide events of 2020 and how they may have influenced overall crime trends.

Stay-at-Home Orders and COVID-Related Restrictions

Ben Stickle and Marcus Felson (2020) called the COVID-19 restrictions the "largest criminological experiment in history." As a result of this experiment, Stickle and Felson believed that the rapid change in "routine activities" due to the pandemic-related restrictions would contribute to a drop in crime. It initially seemed like this criminological experiment had reduced crime victimization. Because there were fewer people in public spaces and away from their homes, which are key components in understanding the opportunity to commit crime, fewer offenses were reported at the beginning of the pandemic (Stickle and Felson 2020).

Additionally, in many countries around the world, pandemic-related stay-at-home orders corresponded with a decline in crime. Analyses of data from twenty-seven cities across twenty-three countries demonstrated clear reductions in assault, burglary, robbery, and theft in the immediate days and months after COVID-related restrictions on movement had been put into effect. The overall homicide trend line was relatively flat within this sample, with some cities experiencing an increase but most experiencing either no change or a decline. Assessed as a whole, there was a significant homicide-reducing effect of social distancing orders within this international sample (Nivette et al. 2021).

In the United States, however, this was the deadliest "criminological experiment" in history. While not all of the increase could be attributed to the stay-at-home orders and other restrictions associated with the pandemic, there were 5,434 excess deaths due to assault in 2020 as compared to 2019, according to CDC Wonder (2023) mortality data. The increase in homicide would not have been anticipated from this experiment, as the lack of ability to travel freely should have restricted the opportunity to commit violent assaults, particularly those that take place between acquaintances and strangers.

Americans, however, were often noncompliant with stay-at-home orders in 2020 and, increasingly, with laws against murder. Although the findings have not been universal, depending on the city observed, the implementation of stay-at-home orders corresponded with more, rather than fewer, shootings, assaults, and homicides. Research in some cities, such as Los Angeles, did not document any impact of stay-at-home orders on gun violence (Campedelli Aziani, and Favarin 2021). However, in other cities, such as Buffalo (Kim and Phillips 2021) and New York City (Kim 2022), the timing of the pandemic-related restrictions corresponded with more shootings. With varying degrees of certainty, Bridgeport, Cincinnati, Grand Rapids, Indianapolis, Milwaukee, Portland (OR), Seattle, and Albuquerque all experienced an increase in their respective homicide rate with the implementation of stay-at-home orders (Murray and Davies 2022). Ironically, but not entirely unexpectedly, the relaxation of stay-at-home orders also corresponded with an increase in shootings and homicides across several US cities (Murray and Davies 2022; Kim 2024).

There are several potential reasons why COVID-19 restrictions were associated with a spike in violent assaults. As I have suggested or implied in previous chapters, the anxiety and despair of the early pandemic corresponded with a sudden increase in firearm sales, drug overdoses, and alcohol-related deaths, each of which corresponded with the timing of the increase in homicide (see also figure 2.2).

It appears that stay-at-home orders increased domestic violence, but their role in the homicide increase is debatable. Evidence from several cities indicates that being kept inside during the pandemic caused tension and seemed to contribute to more domestic abuse (Piquero et al. 2021). Yet, evidence is scant that there was an increase in domestic-violence-induced homicides (Miller, Segal, and Spencer 2022). Although women were at a somewhat greater risk of victimization in 2020 than in 2019, the majority of the increase in homicide victimization occurred among men (CDC Wonder 2023), who are proportionally less likely to be the victims of domestic-violence-related murders.

There were other changes during the initial phase of the pandemic as well. In many jurisdictions, "nonessential" businesses were ordered to be closed, putting millions of Americans out of work. The sudden spike in unemployment was temporally associated with an increase in violent crime (Schleimer et al. 2022). However, because the increase in the unemployment rate occurred almost simultaneously with the implementation of stay-at-home orders (Kim 2024), it is difficult to assess whether it was unemployment, the stay-at-home orders, the disruption to daily life, or a combination of all three that caused homicide rates to increase.

It should be noted that while the beginning of the pandemic was associated with an increase in violent crime, particularly aggravated assault and homicide, there was a simultaneous decline in property-based offenses. In particular, with more people staying home during the day, there were fewer opportunities to commit thefts and other property crimes. Accordingly, the beginning of the pandemic corresponded with a decline in residential burglary and robbery (Ashby 2020; Rosenfeld and Lopez 2021).

Conversely, the specific pressures of the pandemic exerted the opposite effect on motor-vehicle theft. As fewer people were using their cars to commute to work and prices of used cars skyrocketed due to the COVID-19-related slowdown in manufacturing in the United States, automobiles became an increasingly valuable item to steal, often left unattended for days on end as people worked from home. Accordingly, motor-vehicle theft was the one type of property crime that exhibited a sharp increase during the pandemic in some cities (Mohler et al. 2020; Rosenfeld, Abt, and Lopez 2021).

Protests and Policing

The other notable exogenous shock of 2020 was the nationwide anti-police-brutality protests. At the same time that protests had erupted across the country in response to the murder of George Floyd, there was also an increase in violent assaults (Rosenfeld and Lopez 2021). This apparent association set the stage for many people to blame the protestors for the sudden surge in homicide. However, as I outlined in chapter 2, the homicide rate in 2020 was already elevated prior to the George Floyd protests. The timeline linking protests and increases in crime remained compelling nonetheless (Cassell 2020; Lopez and Rosenfeld 2021).

As summarized previously, there is mixed evidence on the role of de-policing on crime in 2020. There have been at least two studies that found evidence supporting the de-policing hypothesis (Kim 2024; Nix et al. 2024) and two studies that suggest that the police pullback had little to no effect on crime rates (Larson, Santaularia, and Uggen 2023; Roman et al. 2023). It is certainly plausible that a lack of police proactivity contributed to higher rates of crime, but it is far from definitive.

An alternative policing-based explanation for the timing of the homicide increase is that there was a legitimacy crisis. I previously discussed this perspective in chapter 6. The general argument is that as people withdrew their trust from the police, they were less likely to involve the police in disputes and cooperate with authorities to solve crimes in their neighborhood. During the 2015–2016 increase in homicide, there was some indirect support for this proposition (Gaston, Cunningham, and Gillezeau 2019; Gross and Mann 2017; Rosenfeld et al. 2017), and the protests in 2020 appear to be associated with increases in homicide offending (Kim 2024). While this association has more consistent support in the academic literature than the de-policing argument does, the evidence is still limited, and the precise mechanisms remain unclear.

Overall, the existing research literature has largely focused on the disruptions to daily life in 2020 caused by the pandemic and protests. Research has largely examined the timing of either the pandemic-related restrictions or the protests and the spike in the homicide rate. The analysis presented in this chapter *does not* address the timing of these events but instead examines the characteristics of cities that experienced a greater increase or higher rate of crime in 2020.

Methods and Analyses

In the rest of this chapter, I compare the effects of the police legitimacy crisis and de-policing within the same analysis. In the results presented here, I use the proxy measures of the police legitimacy crisis (protests) and de-policing (fewer arrests and fewer police) to measure their effects on the change in crime rates from 2019 to 2020.

The sample for this analysis is 299 US cities (population of at least one hundred thousand) with complete crime data for both 2019 and 2020. The crime data include *homicide, aggravated assault, robbery*, and *burglary*, all derived from the FBI's (2022) Crime Data Explorer. The outcomes analyzed here are the change in crime rate from 2019 to 2020. This sample comprises all regions of the country, although not all states are represented, as some states do not have a single city with at least one hundred residents. Due to missing data, the overall multivariate regression analyses do not always include the full sample of all 299 cities.

Table 8.2 includes the 2020 city-level mean and change in crime rates from 2019 to 2020 for this sample. Crime rates are all measured as offenses per one hundred thousand population. Similar to the overall crime trends in 2020, the homicide and assault rates increased while the mean burglary and robbery rates declined within this sample. It should be noted that these rates are not weighted by population size, meaning that this does

TABLE 8.2. Crime Rates (per One Hundred Thousand) in 299 American Cities, 2019–2020

Crime	2020 rate / standard deviation	Change in rate 2019 to 2020
Homicide	9.52 (10.91)	+2.35
Aggravated assault	376.94 (300.69)	+46.19
Robbery	117.89 (89.73)	−14.35
Burglary	412.41 (242.96)	−28.89

not represent the true rate of crime but the mean of all city crime rates combined. The standard deviations are included in parentheses.

The primary factors of interest are the police legitimacy crisis and de-policing. I measure the police legitimacy crisis as the *protest rate* per one hundred thousand population in each city in 2020. Protest data are derived from the Armed Conflict Location & Event Data Project (ACLED 2022). These data are collected by aggregating news reports about protests, riots, violence, and military actions. The data set includes dates, classifications of event types, and location of protests, which allows researchers to assess when and where events took place across the country. From these data, I calculated an overall protest rate for each city in 2020, which includes all events classified as protests or riots.

I also separately examined the protest rate from May 25, 2020, onward, eliminating all protests that were specifically for other purposes, such as protests for teachers and students, anti-lockdown protests, and Antifa and Proud Boy demonstrations, among others. I included protests that were pro-policing, as it is sometimes unclear whether these are counterprotests against Black Lives Matter and other anti-police-brutality protests. Substantively, both protest measures (overall versus May 25 and after) had a similar association with de-policing (table 8.3) and city-level crime rates (table 8.4), so I used the overall protest rate in the final analyses.

There were several ways in which I captured de-policing. First, I included the *change in police per capita*, which captures whether the city had more, the same, or fewer police officers per capita in 2020 than in 2019; a higher number on this metric implies more police per capita in 2020. According to the de-policing argument, an increase in police per capita is expected to have a *negative* association with the crime rate.

I also examined the change in arrest rates for different offenses from 2019 to 2020 to capture de-policing. Specifically, I aimed to assess a decline in arrests that are indicative of a lack of proactive policing. In the case of most violent offenses, the police investigate a crime after it is reported, causing there to be little impact of proactivity on overall felony arrest rates. As an alternative, I examined offenses for which relatively few arrests would be made without proactive policing: drug arrests and weapons arrests. For *de-policing weapons*, I subtracted the number of weapons arrests made in 2020 from the number made in 2019, standardized by one hundred thousand population. For *de-policing drugs*, I subtracted the number of drug arrests conducted in 2020 from the number in 2019, standardized by one hundred thousand population. These de-policing (weapons and drugs) variables are expected to have a *positive* association with crime rates.

Before describing the control variables included in the final analyses, I present bivariate correlations assessing whether protest activity in each city was associated with de-policing. Overall, the impact of the city-level protest rate on de-policing measures is rather modest, as is apparent in table 8.3. This lack of a strong city-level impact of protests is unexpected, as it was purportedly the protests that caused police to be less proactive. However, because there was a nationwide protest movement in 2020, there could have been a general impact on de-policing that was not apparent in variation of protests across individual cities. The only statistically significant correlation between the protest rate and de-policing was apparent for drug arrests. The other associations with city-level protest rates were not statistically significant. Therefore, the police legitimacy crisis and de-policing may be operating somewhat independently within these cities, as protests were only associated with a decline in drug arrests. There is a statistically significant association

TABLE 8.3. Bivariate City-Level Correlations between Protests and De-policing, 2019–2020

Variable	Protest rate	De-policing weapons	De-policing drugs	Change in police per capita
Protest rate	1			
De-policing weapons	.02	1		
De-policing drugs	.16*	.27*	1	
Change in police per capita	.01	–.03	–.05	1

N = 272; 253 for correlations with "change in police per capita"; * statistically significant at the .05 level

between de-policing weapons and de-policing drugs in table 8.3, but similar to the association between protests and de-policing drugs, the strength of this correlation was relatively weak.

I included control variables in the final analysis to account for other differences across cities. These data are primarily derived from the US Census Bureau's (2022) American Community Survey. The data for these variables represent the single-year estimate of 2019. These variables include *population size* (transformed by the natural logarithm), *percentage aged fifteen to twenty-four, percentage Hispanic, percentage of males divorced, percentage with a college degree* (over twenty-five), and *percentage houses occupied*.

I also constructed a *disadvantage index* of correlated variables broadly measuring economic and social disadvantage. In part, this index was constructed to reduce issues associated with collinearity bias (see Land, McCall, and Cohen 1990) but also to capture the general effect of cities experiencing economic and social disadvantage. These variables include the percentage of people living below the poverty line, the percentage of children living below the poverty threshold, the percentage of the population that is Black, and the percentage of households headed by a single mother. To construct this variable, I use a confirmatory principal components analysis to determine the degree to which each variable of the common factor of "disadvantage" was indicative of this concept. Each of these factors was indicative of the same component, which I labeled as the "disadvantage index."[2]

Additionally, I included two dichotomous variables to account for the specific state or regional characteristics of each city. There is longstanding precedent to examine regional impacts on homicide variation within the United States. Traditionally, researchers have noted a higher rate of homicide in the South (Hackney 1969). However, I account for whether the city is located in the geographical *Midwest*, indicated with a 1 for a midwestern location and 0 for a non-midwestern location. Primarily, I do this to capture some of the variation in homicide from factors that are not included in the model (increasing issues with drugs and alcohol) but that are partially responsible for the increase in homicide.

Additionally, to account for the degree to which COVID-19 restrictions were more disruptive in some states than others, I included a variable indicating the stringency of state restrictions. *Stringent COVID restrictions* in 2020 are indicated with a 1 to indicate that the state averaged above a 45 on James Doti's (2021) index. Cities within states with less than a 45 were coded a 0. Ideally, I would also account for unemployment, but city-level data were not available for each city. In preliminary analyses, it appeared that homicide rates were actually inversely associated with the available city unemployment rate data. Table 8.4 includes the descriptive statistics for each of the variables just discussed.[3]

There are a couple of things to note in the descriptive statistics. First, the negative mean of de-policing weapons implies that the average city in this sample actually had *more* weapons arrests in 2020 than in 2019. This is probably due to the record number of firearm sales noted in previous chapters, providing more opportunities to commit weapons-related offenses. While the impact of increased firearm availability in 2020 does complicate the interpretation of this variable as representing "de-policing," it is still true that cities with positive numbers on this metric had fewer firearms arrests made in 2020 than in 2019 despite the increased proliferation of firearms, suggesting some degree of de-policing of weapons offenses within a subset of cities.

TABLE 8.4. Descriptive Statistics of Variables

Variable	Mean	Standard deviation	Minimum and maximum
Protest rate	11.58	11.61	0.0, 71.47
De-policing weapons	−4.74	29.98	−373.03, 97.21
De-policing drugs	115.25	152.77	−337.56, 914.37
Change in police per capita	−.01	.12	−.6, 1.0
Disadvantage index	0	1.0	−1.88, 2.96
Population size (in thousands)	308.60	601.95	100.64, 8,253.21
Percentage houses occupied	91.26	4.59	74.3, 99.0
Percentage aged 15 to 24	14.57	4.44	6.9, 41.0
Percentage with college degree	35.26	14.09	11.65, 79.99
Percentage divorced males	9.13	2.58	2.9, 16.8
Percentage Hispanic	27.18	20.90	1.5, 96.0
Midwest	.15	.36	0, 1
Stringent COVID restrictions	.41	.49	0, 1

Results: Change in City-Level Crime Rates, 2019 to 2020

In table 8.5, I present the results of weighted least squares (WLS) regression models on the change in crime rates from 2019 to 2020 across the cities in this sample. WLS regression analysis accounts for systematic differences in data quality. Especially in the case of homicide, the annual change in the crime rate within more populous cities is much less prone to large annual changes than in smaller cities. Therefore, the models assessing change in crime rates from 2019 to 2020 are all weighted by population size. Table 8.5 presents the standardized regression coefficients, with larger coefficients (in absolute terms) representing a larger effect size, allowing readers to make apples-to-apples comparisons. An asterisk accompanies any effect that was statistically significant at the 95 percent confidence level ($p < .05$), and two asterisks represents statistical significance at the 99 percent confidence level ($p < .01$). Note that only 249 cities were included in the final analysis due to missing data.[4]

The models presented in table 8.5 include the standardized WLS regression coefficients examining the change in crime rates from 2019 to

2020. As is apparent in Models 1 through 4 of table 8.5, stable city-level characteristics appeared to shape the change in homicide from 2019 to 2020 more than either the protest rate or de-policing did. In particular, the largest effect on the city-level increase in the homicide and aggravated assault rate was exerted by the disadvantage index. On average, cities with a greater amount of social and economic disadvantage experienced a larger increase in homicide in 2020.

After accounting for relevant controls, the protest rate was not a statistically significant predictor of change in homicide from 2019 to 2020 (Model 1 of table 8.5). Instead, the de-policing of weapons was a significant predictor of a larger city-level increase in the homicide rate. This is consistent with previous research that has linked directed patrols aimed at confiscating illegal weapons to a reduction in the rate of weapons-related crime (Koper and Mayo-Wilson 2006). However, neither the

TABLE 8.5. WLS Standardized Coefficients of Change in City-Level Crime Rates, 2019 to 2020

Variable	Model 1: Homicide	Model 2: Aggravated assault	Model 3: Robbery	Model 4: Burglary
Protest rate	.01	.001	−.05	.02
De-policing weapons	.22**	−.15*	.16*	.22**
De-policing drugs	−.05	−.12	.11	.01
Change in police per capita	.07	.07	−.06	−.22**
Disadvantage index	.54**	.50**	−.15	−.16
Percentage houses occupied	−.13	−.08	.21**	.03
Percentage 15 to 24	−.19**	−.12*	.18**	−.03
Percentage with college degree	.03	.08	.18*	.33**
Percentage divorced males	−.02	.03	.21**	−.02
Percentage Hispanic	−.24**	−.22**	.08	.16*
Midwest	.23**	−.03	.07	−.03
Stringent COVID restrictions	.05	−.04	−.18*	.05
R-squared	.40	.34	.25	.38

$N = 249$; * $p < .05$; ** $p < .01$

de-policing of drug offenses nor a smaller police force predicted variation in homicide across cities.

After the disadvantage index, one of the strongest effects in the model was the percentage of the population that is Hispanic in each city, which was *negatively* associated with city-level change in homicide. These results suggest that cities with larger Hispanic populations experienced a smaller increase (or even decline) in homicide in 2020. Additionally, a higher percentage of the population aged fifteen to twenty-four was predictive of a smaller homicide increase. The variable accounting for the regional impact of the Midwest was a significant predictor of a larger increase in the homicide rate.

Similar results were noted for change in aggravated assault (Model 2 of table 8.5), with two notable exceptions. Surprisingly, the de-policing of weapons was *negatively* and significantly associated with annual change in aggravated assault, suggesting that cities experiencing more de-policing of weapons offenses had *fewer* aggravated assaults. While the precise mechanism that explains this association is unclear, it does imply that weapons arrests took guns out of the hands of people desiring to use them in an assault. While this interpretation is speculative, it is consistent with the disparate impact of weapons arrests on these two types of violent offenses. Another change from the homicide model (Model 1) is that a midwestern location had a nonsignificant association with change in aggravated assault. The disadvantage index (positive) and percentage Hispanic (negative) were still the strongest predictors, while percentage of the population aged fifteen to twenty-four was also predictive of fewer assaults.

Model 3 of table 8.5 presents the findings for change in the robbery rate from 2019 to 2020. The results of this model are notably different from the model examining homicide, as annual change in the robbery rate was predicted by almost an entirely different set of predictors. The percentage of homes occupied, percentage with a college degree, percentage divorced males, and population aged fifteen to twenty-four were predictive of a greater city-level increase in the robbery rate. Surprisingly, more COVID-19 related restrictions were associated with fewer robberies in 2020 as compared to 2019. The one similarity to the homicide model is that de-policing of weapons was a statistically significant predictor of change of both robbery rates and homicide rates.

Finally, in the model examining change in the burglary rate (Model 4 of table 8.5), percentage with a college degree, percentage Hispanic, and de-policing of weapons were all positively and significantly associated with the change in the burglary rate, while the change in police per capita was negatively associated with burglary. Given the impact of *both* the de-policing of weapons offenses and change in police per capita, the clearest evidence of the de-policing effect was actually for burglary, a crime that declined in 2020.

Overall, the strongest predictor of the surge in homicide and aggravated assault at the city level appears to be stable levels of economic and social disadvantage. While this is not surprising, it has rarely been discussed in the context of the recent increase in homicide. This result implies that cities that have substantial problems with poverty and racial segregation were the most predisposed to a sudden surge in violence in 2020. These preexisting social conditions allowed the homicide epidemic to spread quickly, as it was far more deadly in cities with a higher concentration of disadvantage than elsewhere. It appears that the United States' long-standing issues of social exclusion and concentrated poverty provided the perfect context for the largest homicide rate increase in its history.

I did find that de-policing played a role in the homicide surge in 2020. The models presented here indicate that proactive policing of weapons offenses may have kept guns off the street that would otherwise have been used in homicides. However, it should be reemphasized that de-policing of weapons offenses was not associated with the protest rate across the cities in this sample, suggesting that annual change in arrest rates may have been either influenced by national coverage of protests or idiosyncratic factors at the city level that are not well understood and unrelated to police scrutiny (protests).

A city's protest rate was not predictive of a larger increase in the homicide rate after accounting for other relevant factors. In a model comparing only protests and de-policing-related variables (not shown), there was some indication that the protest rate contributed to an increase in homicide. However, after accounting for relevant control variables, there was no apparent impact of protests on annual change in any criminal offense. This is contradictory to the conventional explanation that people withdrew support from the police and no longer involved them in resolving disputes (LaFree 1998; Rosenfeld et al. 2017). However, as we will see in the next set of models predicting the overall rate of crime in 2020, there is support for the idea that protest rates represent a time-stable distrust of the police and contribute to higher rates of crime. In the next section, instead of examining city-level change in crime rates from 2019 to 2020 (as presented in table 8.5), I examine the predictors of the overall crime rate in 2020.

Results: Predictors of City-Level Crime Rates in 2020

The results presented in table 8.6 examine variation in overall crime rates in 2020 across US cities. These regression models are estimated using ordinary least squares (OLS) regression techniques, as there should be less extreme variability in the overall crime rate than there is in the change in the crime rate from 2019 to 2020 (i.e., table 8.5). Each of the outcome variables (crime rates) is transformed using the natural logarithm to approximate a normal distribution.[5]

The results in table 8.6 show that the protest rate is significantly predictive of not only the overall homicide rate in 2020 but also aggravated assault, robbery, and burglary rates. This is consistent with the idea that the police legitimacy crisis provides the context for higher rates of crime, as fewer people cooperate with or call on the police to resolve disputes. This finding suggests that the cities experiencing a greater crisis in police legitimacy have had higher rates of crime in general.

Because overall crime rates tend to be correlated, there are few differences across the models for homicide, aggravated assault, robbery, and burglary. As displayed in table 8.6, the factors that were consistently

TABLE 8.6. OLS Standardized Coefficients of City-Level Crime Rates, 2020

Variable	Model 5: Homicide	Model 6: Aggravated assault	Model 7: Robbery	Model 8: Burglary
Protest rate	.15**	.26**	.30**	.26**
De-policing weapons	.05	.02	.03	.05
De-policing drugs	−.06	−.08	.02	.02
Change in police per capita	.02	−.04	−.05	.03
Disadvantage index	.50**	.31**	.33**	.16
Population size (ln)	.25**	.29**	.32**	.25**
Percentage houses occupied	−.03	−.04	−.02	.03
Percentage 15 to 24	−.06	.07	−.09	.05
Percentage with college degree	−.25**	−.35**	−.24**	−.22*
Percentage divorced males	−.03	.13*	−.04	.13
Percentage Hispanic	−.21**	−.19**	−.06	−.24**
Midwest	.01	.06	.02	.03
Stringent COVID restrictions	.01	.05	.23**	.20*
R-squared	.54	.62	.50	.34

$N = 249$; * $p < .05$; ** $p < .01$

associated with crime rates are the protest rate, economic/social disadvantage, population size, people with a college degree (inversely), and a larger Hispanic population (inversely).

There were a few exceptions to this general pattern. The robbery rate was not associated with the size of the Hispanic population, and the burglary rate was not associated with the disadvantage index. Additionally, the percentage of divorced males was significantly predictive of aggravated assault but of no other offense. Finally, stringent COVID-19 restrictions did not seem to impact homicide or aggravated assault but were significantly association with higher rates of robbery and burglary. Interestingly, COVID-19-related restrictions were not predictive of change in crime rates examined in the previous analysis of change from 2019 to 2020 (see table 8.5). In fact, stringent COVID-19 restrictions were associated with a greater *decline* in robbery from 2019 to 2020. The effect noted on the overall 2020 robbery and burglary rate may be due to other similarities between the states that were most likely to place stringent restrictions on their populations in 2020, such as greater population density, although this remains unclear.[6]

Implications of the Findings

The findings presented in this chapter contribute to a few conclusions about the homicide epidemic. First, it is apparent that the increase in the rates of homicide and aggravated assault was larger in cities with higher levels of economic and social disadvantage. This is consistent with research that has implicated disadvantage as a primary cause of crime (e.g., Krivo and Peterson 1996; Sampson, Raudenbush, and Earls 1997). One of the reasons for the spread of violence in the United States in 2020 is the country's preexisting issues with racial and economic inequality. Cities that had the greatest amount disadvantage had the largest increase in violence (homicide and aggravated assault) and also had higher rates of crime in general in 2020 (table 8.6). This was by far the most consistent finding and the strongest effect noted within this chapter.

Second, the protest rate, a proxy for the police legitimacy crisis, was predictive of the 2020 homicide rate across US cities. Despite being associated with higher rates of crime overall (table 8.6), the protest rate was not predictive of a larger increase in homicide from 2019 to 2020 (table 8.5). This finding is consistent with the implications of the discussion in chapter 6. Protests are an indicator of preexisting distrust of the police, which predates the protest movement. The protest rate was not significantly associated with change in crime rates from 2019 to 2020, as discontent with the police was not unique to 2020. This interpretation is also evident in the fact that the protest rate in 2020 had a similar bivariate correlation with the city-level homicide rate in 2019 ($r = .32$), the year prior to the George Floyd protests, as it did in 2020 ($r = .33$).

Finally, I find some support for the de-policing argument. This support is less straightforward than depicted in the research literature and the media. Surprisingly, there were actually *more* arrests for weapons offenses in 2020 than in 2019 among the cities in this sample. Accordingly, there was not clear evidence of de-policing in general. Additionally, de-policing of weapons was not correlated with the protest rate, contrary to the notion that police officers were more reticent to make arrests due to the intensity of scrutiny within their particular city. However, I did find that cities that were less aggressive in policing weapons offenses had a larger increase in their respective homicide rates from 2019 to 2020. While I cannot say that these findings provide unequivocal support for a de-policing argument, given the higher rate of arrests and the lack of a connection to the city-level protest rate, it does appear that changes in policing of weapons were associated the spike in homicide in 2020.

Conclusions

The results of these analyses provide some additional clues about the most notable year of the homicide epidemic. This chapter provides evidence that the spike in homicide in 2020 was facilitated by the United States' preexisting conditions of racial and economic inequality, as captured in the disadvantage index. The police legitimacy crisis and de-policing also played some role, albeit not as straightforward as previously depicted. Both distrust of the police and police reticence to make weapons arrests partially contributed to the record-breaking rates of homicide in 2020.

This chapter adds to the growing literature that distrust of the police has contributed to higher rates of crime during the past decade. This chapter documents the impact of distrust of the police, as measured by the city-level protest rate, on higher rates of crime, consistent with a conventional argument concerning waning legitimacy (e.g., LaFree 1998). However, more fine-tuned analyses concerning the precise timing of the spike in homicide are required to assert more confidently that a portion of this impact is due to the brutalization effect of witnessing state-sanctioned violence. Assessing the brutalization effect that I discussed in chapter 6 was beyond the scope of the data I collected for the city-level analyses I presented in this chapter.

In the conclusion that follows, I summarize the overall findings presented in this book and outline some of its implications. I provide tentative predictions about crime trends in the near future as well as highlight the lessons of the recent homicide epidemic for forecasting crime trends.

Conclusion

Attempting to Predict Future Crime Trends

It is difficult to make predictions, especially about the future.
—attributed to Yogi Berra

The 2015–2021 homicide epidemic is unlike any crime trend in modern US history. The homicide rate has seemingly defied criminological gravity, trending in the opposite direction of property-motivated offenses. Instead of representing an overall increase in crime, the decline in burglary, robbery, and larceny has dramatically diverged from the spike in homicide since 2014. Additionally, despite teenage offending hitting historical lows during the past decade, a surge in violent crime occurred anyway, unlike the youth-driven spike that occurred in the 1990s. Put simply, the homicide trend has defied expectations by suddenly increasing during an era of low and falling overall crime rates.

This unprecedented increase in the homicide rate has been the result of an American decline that many people acknowledge but few have fully examined in relation to crime victimization. As many Americans lost hope for their future, some turned toward drugs and alcohol to numb their literal and figurative pain. In the case of the drug abuse epidemic, underground drug sales supercharged an already burgeoning prescription opioid epidemic and converted a public health crisis into a tsunami of death, from both overdose and violent assault. Additionally, as more middle-aged Americans consumed alcohol, there was a corresponding increase in both aggravated assault and homicide rates.

Distrust of major American institutions also contributed to the homicide epidemic. As people lost trust in the federal government, criminal justice system, and the police, they increasingly purchased firearms. As firearm sales increased, there was a corresponding surge in gun violence. Of the excess homicides in 2021 as compared to the baseline established in 2014, 98 percent were committed using a firearm. The proliferation of firearms accelerated crime problems associated with alcohol consumption and illicit drug sales to cause the highest rate of homicide in more than twenty years or, in the case of the Midwest, the highest rate of homicide in more than forty years.

Additionally, the "exogenous shocks" of anti-police-brutality protests probably explain part of the timing of the upward homicide trend. The spikes in homicide after the death of Freddie Gray in Baltimore in 2015 and George Floyd in Minneapolis in 2020 provide some initial indication of a brutalization effect caused by witnessing state-sponsored violence. This interpretation is not definitive, but the crime patterns in the aftermath of these killings, which cannot be accounted for by changes in policing (Larson, Santaularia, and Uggen 2023), point to a sudden shift in the homicide trend resembling an exogenous shock. Pertinent to 2020's record-breaking homicide increase, I find partial support for the idea that both de-policing and the police legitimacy crisis exacerbated the homicide epidemic.

Overall, the decline in psychosocial well-being evident in increasing alcohol and drug abuse has contributed to more people under the influence of mind-altering substances as well as a growing propensity for the underground exchange of illicit drugs. The decline in American institutions helps to explain the proliferation of firearms. Additionally, the protest movement against police brutality sensitized the public to witnessing violence perpetrated by the police, setting the stage for a brutalization effect. Without this decline in America's hope for the future and its belief in its institutions, the homicide rate in 2021 would have been among the lowest in recorded history. Instead, some cities and states across the country set new homicide records.

The Mosaic Big Picture

The narrative advanced in this book is one that addresses the big picture of overarching US crime trends over the past decade. This narrative attempts to encapsulate the primary social forces responsible for the recent homicide epidemic. There is great value in focusing on the big picture, as it has the potential to inform ongoing debates about crime and policing in recent years. Without examining the big picture in relation to crime in general (Rosenfeld 2018) or crime trends specifically (Baumer, Vélez, and Rosenfeld 2018), criminologists often lack an explanation of the patterns in crime that entice public interest and debate, leaving them on the sidelines when policy decisions are made.

However, this big-picture narrative partially obscures the mosaic it represents. The homicide epidemic has not equally impacted everyone across the country, making the account outlined in this book more relevant for some groups and less so for others. At times, I hint at these differences across demographic groups, such as in the discussion of the disproportionate toll that the drug abuse crisis has wrought on the African American community in relation to both drug overdose deaths and homicide victimization. Yet the overall statistics and findings at national, state, and city levels of analysis presented in this book do not adequately capture the mosaic of experiences that different communities and neighborhoods have had with crime during the past decade.

Some research has already documented the concentration of recent homicide trends within smaller subsets of the country. For example, in an analysis of homicide trends in Philadelphia, New York, and Los Angeles during the COVID-19 pandemic, John MacDonald, George Mohler, and P. Jeffrey Brantingham (2022) found that a vastly disproportionate amount of the increase in shooting victimization occurred within 10 percent of census-block groups. This finding implies that a small subset of neighborhoods experienced a sudden surge of violence during the pandemic, while many neighborhoods were largely immune from an increase. The authors also document the disproportionate increase in shooting victimization among Black and Hispanic residents, suggesting that racially disaggregated trends may diverge somewhat from the overarching trends presented in this book.

For many people across the United States, the crime wave was simply something that they watched on television and scrolled through on social media. There are parts of the country where homicide rates declined during this period and neighborhood residents who were actually safer in 2021 than in 2014. For a large portion of American citizens, there was no noticeable change in their community's level of violent crime. Often, the narrative about crime in "big cities" was used to push a political agenda and was not motivated by a genuine fear of crime victimization in cities where many of the "concerned citizens" did not even reside. Even in cities where the homicide rate hit record levels, many residents were safely nestled in newly gentrified neighborhoods where crime victimization was not a major concern.

Across a nation as large as the United States, a single narrative about crime trends will obscure the differences across communities. Future research should further interrogate the smaller population fragments that make up the national mosaic to refine the claims made in this book and outline precisely *where* the homicide epidemic took place.

Attempting to Predict the Future

While some of the claims made in this book are still tentative, we can place them in the context of past research in order to make predictions about future crime trends. In particular, the findings of this book should be addressed in the context of crime-trend research of the 1990s. The 1990s will always play an outsized role in our understanding, or lack thereof, of crime trends. The success in apparently solving the "crime problem" during this era attracted the attention of both the media and academics alike. Researchers from seemingly every academic discipline and vantage point provided an explanation of the "Great American Crime Decline" (Zimring 2007); there are at least twenty-four distinct explanations of crime trends during the 1990s (Tcherni-Buzzeo 2019), making it difficult to separate the signal from the noise. That is, there is no definitive model to predict future crime trends but simply a series of mildly plausible perspectives on what happened during the 1990s.

The study of crime trends has often been hampered by a lack of a comprehensive framework or theory. In its place, there is a proliferation of novel, single-factor explanations (Baumer, Vélez, and Rosenfeld 2018). After the "discovery" of the 1990s crime decline, a number of such hypotheses hinged on a single historical coincidence that occurred during the same era as a change in the direction of the crime trend. These "magic bullet" hypotheses included a decline in environmental lead (Nevin 2000), the legalization of abortion during the decades prior (Donohue and Levitt 2001), and the relaxation of firearm restrictions (Lott 2010), all of which were widely debated during the era. Yet, as we try to understand the recent homicide epidemic, these factors appear either to be irrelevant or even to have portended a sharp decline in homicide at the exact time in which homicide rates increased. By moving past single-factor explanations, we can create a body of research and (hopefully) a scientific understanding of crime trends rather than compiling a list of unique circumstances that occurred during the 1990s.

Eric Baumer, Maria Velez, and Richard Rosenfeld (2018) suggest that researchers studying future crime trends should examine general factors in an attempt to develop a predictive framework. These factors include changes in social controls, shifts in criminal propensities and motivations, and changes to settings and situations that lend themselves to crime. I believe that this framework is a good place to start but could be informed by some lessons from the recent homicide epidemic. In the following pages, I address each of these in greater detail and then highlight areas for elaboration and expansion.

Changes in Social Controls

The first general factor identified by Baumer and colleagues (2018) is the change in social control. By far, the most popular genre of explanation during the crime wave is that there has been a lack of formal social control. Not only is it a plausible explanation of the increase in crime, but it has the added benefit of enabling us to advocate to "punish more and understand less" (Garland 2001) at a time that we are collectively fearful about crime victimization.

As we have seen with the homicide epidemic, however, weakened social controls are not as helpful in predicting the direction of crime trends as anticipated. In chapter 7, I showed that the decline in incarceration rates since 2010 has contributed to more criminal offending. Yet, for robbery and burglary, the near-continuous decline in the incarceration rate since 2010 has *not* produced an increase in the overall crime trend. In chapter 8, there appeared to be some impact of the de-policing of weapons offenses on the homicide increase, but it was associated with *fewer* aggravated assaults in 2020. Formal control mechanisms have some impact on the crime rate but are less clearly predictive of the overall *direction* in crime trends.

Trends in informal social control are more difficult to assess. Informal social control could include things like supervision of teens, community interventions, or the prosocial pressure of peer groups. There is no indication that these types of controls have been waning during the homicide epidemic, although it is possible that community intervention groups (e.g., Sharkey 2018) could have been thwarted by COVID-19 fears and restrictions in 2020. Given the general lack of teenage involvement in crime and the increase in the supervision of teenagers (Baumer, Cundiff, and Luo 2021), the initial conclusion is that informal social control may impact overall crime trends but is less clearly linked to the recent homicide increase.

Shifts in Criminal Propensities

The second factor identified by Baumer and colleagues (2018) is the change in criminal propensity. Based on prominent theory within criminology (Gottfredson and Hirschi 1990), the authors attempted to reconcile two of the most often discussed 1990s historical circumstances that were examined as the cause of the crime decline: the reduction in childhood exposure to environmental lead (Nevin 2000) and the legalization of abortion (Donohue and Levitt 2001). In both cases, the children of the late 1990s were predicted to be less prone to either brain damage, in the case of environmental lead, or abuse and neglect, in the case of the legalization of abortion, than in the decades prior. In both cases, we would predict that teenagers in the second half of the 1990s and onward would have greater degrees of self-control and, thereby, a lower propensity toward crime. However, we still do not have a definitive measure of trends in self-control at the aggregate level (Baumer, Vélez, and Rosenfeld 2018). We also have no indication that societal levels of self-control suddenly dipped circa 2015.

In the case of violent assaults, an additional factor impacting criminal propensity is the influence of alcohol and drugs. As was evident throughout this book, the increase in substance abuse was tied to a higher rate of homicide. Because of the influence of these mind-altering substances, offenders are less prone to social or self-control. Whether it is aggressive and belligerent behavior sometimes associated with alcohol consumption, a substance-altered state that impacts decision-making, or the felt need to commit a crime to obtain money to feed a drug habit due to the symptoms of withdrawal, substance abuse increases the risk of violent assault. This is consistent with recent research that suggests that self-control is thwarted by intoxication (Meldrum et al. 2023).

Overall, changes in criminal propensities should be a fruitful place to start in examining crime trends. We should not think of it as simply different "types" of people with stable criminal propensities, such as low self-control. Instead, we also need to consider how alcohol consumption and substance abuse can influence the propensity toward offending to assist in the prediction of future trends in crime.

Changes in Settings and Situations

Finally, Baumer and colleagues (2018) identify changes in social settings as potentially predictive of crime trends. Formalized in the classic work of Lawrence Cohen and Marcus Felson (1979), "routine activities theory" highlights the basic elements necessary for a crime to occur: a motivated offender, a suitable or attractive target, and the lack of a capable guardian. This perspective has been highly influential and largely supported by research examining trends in property offenses. In what has become known as the "security hypothesis," the decline in the rate of burglary and automotive theft in the 1990s is associated with increasing security measures (Farrell, Tilley, and Tseloni 2014). As the "capable guardian" was built into more cars, homes, and electronic devices, property crime rates fell precipitously.

The arguments laid out in this book are influenced by the routine activity perspective. Specifically, instead of examining robbery, aggravated assault, and homicide together as a measure of "violent crime," I analyzed each offense separately, as they are each the result of a unique combination of motivated offenders, suitable targets, and capable guardians. One reason that robbery has declined appears to be that there are fewer economic transactions occurring in person, as implied by the findings in chapter 7, which show that the decline in retail employment is significantly associated with state robbery rate trends. Robbery is impacted by fewer people carrying cash (Gandelman, Munyo, and Schertz 2023) as well as increased security measures embedded within phones and other electronic devices. There are simply fewer attractive targets and more capable guardians. But the trends in aggravated assault and homicide are somewhat less affected by these dynamics.

Instead, there are other situations and settings that have made homicides more likely during the recent homicide epidemic. Specifically, there has been an increase in illicit drug transactions, which are sometimes rife with violent retribution (Goldstein et al. 1989). These transactions have the possibility of fostering robberies as well, but, at least in the crimes reported to the police, there was no apparent impact of drug overdose on the robbery rate. The expansion of the drug market is a change in social settings and situations that contributes to an increase in violence, in the form of homicide, as is evident in chapter 7.

Overall, the impact of changes in social controls, criminal propensities, and social situations and context can partially explain recent crime trends. However, this framework could be supplemented with additional relevant factors. As I outline in the following pages, changes in the capability of offenders and stable social conditions that lead to the contagious spread of violence also need to be considered.

Capability of Offenders

One element missing from the framework just outlined (i.e., Baumer, Vélez, and Rosenfeld 2018) involves the capability of the offender. This was especially relevant in the findings pertaining to the impact of firearm sales on homicide. Following the logic of the "instrumentality hypothesis," we would not expect firearms to produce additional assaults (necessarily) but cause the assaults that occur to be more deadly. This implies a continuum of offender *capability*. Offenders who are unarmed are much less capable (on average) of murdering their victim than are offenders who are armed with a gun. The proliferation of high-capacity, large-caliber firearms during the past decade has caused offenders to have a greater degree of capability of murdering their assault victims. Additionally, the capability to produce lethal violence is somewhat independent of offenders' intention or motivation. The death of a combatant is just as related to the capability to inflict harm as it is to the intention of the offender. Offenders' capability may vary with other offenses as well, possibly suggesting an additional factor in predicting crime trends in general.

Stability of Criminogenic Settings and Social Contagion

Additionally, as implied by the findings presented in chapter 8, there are stable social conditions that contribute to crime trends as well. In

Baumer and colleagues' (2018) discussion of crime trends, their primary focus is on factors that change over time. Yet the cities that were most susceptible to an increase in homicide and aggravated assault in 2020 did not experience a significantly greater increase in their degree of social and economic disadvantage. Instead, their stable levels of deprivation corresponded with a larger increase in violent crime. It is not just change but time-stable characteristics of cities, states, and countries that can either constrain or facilitate a crime trend. In fact, a study of the increase in shootings across four cities (Chicago, Los Angeles, New York, and Philadelphia) in 2020 and 2021 suggests that a portion of the increase in shootings resembled the spread of a social contagion (Brantingham et al. 2021).

Accordingly, it could be that some social settings can facilitate a crime wave, while others exert controls that thwart criminal offending. In 2020, some nations experienced an increase in homicide as a result of the pandemic; but the spike in homicide in the United States was much larger, in both absolute and relative terms, than in any other wealthy democracy (see also Rogers 2024). While the factors outlined in chapters 3 through 6 present a plausible explanation, the US spike in homicide was also facilitated by its "underlying conditions," namely, persistent issues with economic inequality and racial segmentation/segregation.

In settings with issues relating to social inequity or other preexisting criminogenic conditions, violence is more likely to spread. Contagious models imply that violence itself contributes to more violence. One version of social contagion is similar to the spread of a literal virus, requiring individuals to be in close proximity for violence to spread. Research examining social networks has documented the contagious impact of a single shooting, setting off a self-propelling cycle of retribution (Papachristos, Wildeman, and Roberto 2015). These models imply that violence within a social network will ricochet throughout the network long after an initial assault or homicide takes place.

Another version of the social contagion of violence was outlined in chapter 6, addressing the "ecology of danger" (Fagan, Wilkinson, and

Davies 2007). In these contexts, the belief that you could be a victim of violence is constant, motivating the use of defensive violence. This facilitates the spread of violence within communities with high levels of economic and social disadvantage.

Implications for Future Crime Trends

The findings presented in this book also provide some insight into the direction of the homicide trend in the near future. Crime trends are notoriously difficult to predict, but we can use recent observations to make tentative predictions about the next few years. Overall, I believe that the homicide rate in 2021 hit its peak (for now) and will decline. There are already some initial data from the FBI (2022) that show that the national homicide rate declined in 2022 from its 2021 peak. In the following pages, I outline a few reasons why I believe this trend will continue.

Alcohol, Drugs, and Guns

By tracing the trends that caused the homicide epidemic, we can find areas for optimism. While it is true that the United States is still (arguably) in the midst of a societal decline, some of the violence-producing trends that accompanied this decline are plateauing or even reversing direction. Most notably, we have seen a decline in firearm purchases every single year since 2020, according to NICS data (FBI 2023). In 2020, 39.7 million background checks were conducted for firearm purchases. In 2021, this number fell by about a million background checks (38.9 million). By 2022, the number of background checks declined again, falling to 31.6 million. The initial numbers for 2023 (29.9 million) suggest a similar level of firearm purchases as 2022. Although there are still more background checks for firearms purchases per capita than prior to the pandemic (28.4 million in 2019), there is clear evidence of decline in firearm purchases.

Additionally, the drug abuse epidemic is (hopefully) starting to stall, resulting in fewer underground drug transactions. There is some evidence of a decelerating drug overdose crisis. It is still too early to say that there has been a decline in drug abuse, but the higher proportion of fentanyl deaths and a slowing increase in the rate of overdose (National Center for Health Statistics 2023) suggest that fewer people are using drugs, thereby reducing the number of illicit drug transactions. The deceleration of drug abuse deaths last occurred in 2018, a year in which the homicide rate declined, albeit slightly. Deaths from drug overdoses are estimated to have declined in 2023 (Centers for Disease Control 2024). It is too early to tell if the drug abuse crisis is about to experience a long-term decline, but there are reasons for optimism concerning the plateau in overdose deaths.

There is also evidence of a decline in alcohol consumption in 2022. Both the number of alcohol-related deaths (CDC Wonder 2023) and the number of gallons of alcohol consumed per capita (Slater and Alpert 2024) declined in 2022. The provisional CDC Wonder (2023) data for 2023 also hint at a further decline in alcohol-related deaths.

Overall, while the evidence is still somewhat unclear, the decline in firearm sales, plateau in drug overdose deaths, and decline in alcohol-related deaths provide reasons for optimism. The homicide rate declined in 2022 and will probably decline in 2023 given these trends. If there is a sustained decline in gun sales, drug abuse, and alcohol consumption, we should expect a sustained decline in homicide in the near future and an end to the homicide epidemic.

Criminological Gravity: The Decline of Acquisitive Crimes

There are other reasons to believe that the homicide rate will decline during the next few years. If alcohol consumption, drug abuse, and firearm access are no longer increasing, the other factors that typically drive homicide trends should exert a greater effect. As I alluded to in chapter 1, homicide trends from 2015 to 2021 were defying criminological gravity. Most notably, a decline of property-based offenses, including burglary, motor-vehicle theft, and robbery normally would correspond with a declining homicide trend (Rosenfeld 2009). During the homicide epidemic, crime trends have defied this pattern; robbery and burglary rates declined by about 40 percent from 2014 to 2021, and yet the homicide rate increased by nearly 55 percent. Unlike the increase in homicide in the 1960s or even in the late 1980s–early 1990s, the current era features homicide trends moving in the opposite direction of acquisitive crimes.

As property-based offenses continue to decline, criminological gravity will eventually pull the homicide trend toward it. There are several reasons to believe that property-based offenses will continue to decline. Beginning with "attractive targets" for theft, there is a decline in the number of people who carry cash and easily fungible items of value (Faverio 2022). Research examining the impact of transferring payments to a card-based system demonstrates that this has contributed to fewer thefts (Wright et al. 2017). Additionally, more transactions have moved online, and more items of value are possessed in virtual accounts or in the cloud. This has not stopped theft but moved where it takes place (Tcherni et al. 2016). Crucially, thefts that take place online do not have the same propensity to contribute to interpersonal violence. Therefore, in consideration of historical precedent and previous research, the homicide rate should eventually more closely align with trends in robberies and burglaries, which still appear to be in the midst of a decades-long decline.

The Decline of Youth and Young-Adult Offending

A final reason why homicide rates will probably decline in the near future is the lower offending propensity of youth and young adults. In the early 1990s, one of the reasons that the homicide rate was so high was youth offending. The homicide offending rate doubled for teenagers (aged fifteen to nineteen) between 1985 and 1990 and increased by nearly 40 percent for young adults (aged twenty to twenty-four) (O'Brien and Stockard 2009). However, since the 1990s, there has been a general decline in youth and young-adult involvement in crime, a decline that has accelerated during the past decade. During the first two decades of the twenty-first century, youth offending of all types declined even further, attributable to a decrease in unstructured time for socialization, less alcohol consumption, and less inclination toward risky activities in general (Baumer, Cundiff, and Luo 2021).

As youth offending continues to decline, it portends a future of lower rates of crime as youth age into adulthood. This is not to imply that youth offending and victimization were not components of the 2015–2021 homicide epidemic; especially for Black male youth and young adults (aged fifteen to twenty-four), the increase in homicide victimization from 2014 to 2021 (nearly 73 percent) outpaced the increase for the population overall (59 percent) (CDC Wonder 2023). It does imply, however, that adolescents and young adults are less involved in violent assaults than they have been in the past, particularly as compared to the early 1990s. Given the lower propensity of offending in the current youth cohort (Neil and Sampson 2021; Tuttle 2024), there may be a rapid decline in overall offending as members of Gen Z age into their thirties and forties. That is, the kids who are growing up and abstaining from criminal offending in their teens are less likely to become serious offenders during adulthood, causing the crime rate among adults to decline due to an age-related desistance.

Caveats and Unanswered Questions

Of course, the account of the homicide epidemic presented in this book is not without its limitations. One question that could be asked concerns the basis for the motivation of recent crime trends. Why has an economically inspired malaise caused an increase in alcohol and drug abuse but not an increase in property-based offenses?

There is not a perfect answer to this question. One potential answer is implied in the changing nature of where valuable items are located, which is increasingly online. Because online thefts are poorly tracked, it is possible that an online crime wave has occurred and there are no data to document it (Tcherni et al. 2016). Additionally, the type of despair and hopelessness of the present is somewhat distinct from in the past. In the early 2020s, the recorded poverty rate has neared historical lows (Shrider and Creamer 2023). The despair of the present appears to be more of an outgrowth of *relative* rather than *absolute* deprivation. Most Americans are not so desperate as to lack the basic necessities for survival, as is the case of absolute deprivation. Instead, they see a future in which home ownership, financial security, and other hallmarks of middle-class life are just out of reach and seemingly getting farther away each year. This relative deprivation may be more impactful on substance abuse patterns, exerting a specific impact on aggravated assault and homicide but not property-based offenses. However, more research is needed to confirm this hypothesis.

Another potential criticism of this book could target my (relative) dismissal of the effect of policing and imprisonment on crime trends. It is true that cities in which there was evidence of de-policing had a larger increase in homicide in 2020 (see chapter 8). However, this instance of de-policing occurred in the midst of an already accelerating rate of homicide (see chapter 2). Additionally, the decline in the incarceration rate also corresponded with a higher rate of homicide from 2010 to 2021 (chapter 7). Yet there was a similar, if not stronger, effect of incarceration rates on both robbery and burglary trends, suggesting that the impact of incarceration does a poor job of explaining the direction of crime trends. Overall, I reconcile these findings by arguing that a "lack" of punishment probably made the homicide epidemic more severe but is not ultimately responsible for the direction of the overall homicide trend. That is, if policing practices and incarceration rates had remained constant from 2010 onward, the homicide epidemic would have still occurred but would have been less severe.

I also think it is not perfectly clear as to why 2015 was the turning point in the homicide epidemic. Although we began to see a divergence between homicide and acquisitive crime trends as early as 2012 (see figure 1.3), it was not until 2015 that the homicide rate spiked. While I have discussed this in the context of the brutalization effect and the spike in

Baltimore's homicide rate during the immediate aftermath of the death of Freddie Gray, this is the most speculative element of my homicide epidemic explanation. It is also possible that the acceleration of firearm purchases, alcohol consumption, and drug overdose deaths could have finally exceeded the countervailing forces of declining property and teenage offending for the first time in 2015. Possibly, it was the brutalization effect coupled with an acceleration of alcohol consumption, drug abuse, and firearm sales. But I cannot be sure.

In general, more research is needed to confirm several of the claims made in this book. I have provided a high-level summary of the trends across the United States over the past decade that contributed to the homicide epidemic. I have used aggregate data to confirm my hypotheses and have largely been vindicated by my findings. However, more detailed analyses of the impact of drug abuse and drug-related homicides, alcohol consumption and homicide offending and victimization, the mechanism(s) by which offenders obtain firearms, and a more systematic analysis of the brutalization effect of publicized police violence could all contribute to a more comprehensive understanding of the causes of the homicide epidemic.

Conclusion

Predicting the future is difficult, but by paying attention to the past, we may be able to develop a more comprehensive model of crime trends. The recent increase in the homicide rate has provided some important lessons for scholars attempting to understand variation in crime. While the task of forecasting crime will always be somewhat difficult given the effect of exogenous shocks, paying careful attention to the past can assist criminologists in being better able to forecast the trends of the future, contributing to the advancement of the normal science of crime trends.

ACKNOWLEDGMENTS

I would like to thank the anonymous reviewers as well as Ilene Kalish and the rest of the New York University Press editorial team for their helpful comments on earlier versions of this book.

NOTES

CHAPTER 2. THE LIMITED IMPACT OF "DE-POLICING"

1   There are 168 cities in this sample. Each of the following cities had sufficient data in the FBI database for at least two of the three years and is included in the final sample. I highlight the cases in which homicide data for the cities were missing or deemed unreliable when compared to alternative sources in the following list. These data were collected from the FBI's (2022) Crime Data Explorer in early 2024. These cities include Abilene (TX), Albuquerque (NM), Alexandria (VA), Amarillo (TX), Anchorage (AK), Ann Arbor (MI), Athens-Clarke County (GA), Aurora (IL; 2021 missing), Austin (TX), Bakersfield (CA; 2021 missing), Baton Rouge (LA), Boise (ID), Boston (MA), Boulder (CO), Bridgeport (CT), Brownsville (TX), Buffalo (NY), Cambridge (MA), Cary (NC), Cedar Rapids (IA), Charleston (SC), Charlotte-Mecklenburg (NC), Chattanooga (TN), Chico (CA; 2021 missing), Cincinnati (OH), Clearwater (FL; 2021 missing), Cleveland (OH), College Station (TX), Colorado Springs (CO), Coral Springs (FL), Corpus Christi (TX), Dallas (TX), Davenport (IA), Dayton (OH), Denver (CO), Des Moines (IA; 2021 unreliable), Detroit (MI), Durham (NC), El Paso (TX), Elizabeth (NJ), Eugene (OR), Fargo (ND), Fayetteville (NC), Fort Collins (CO), Fort Wayne (IN), Fontana (CA; 2021 unreliable), Fort Lauderdale (FL; 2021 missing), Fremont (CA; 2021 missing), Fresno (CA), Gainesville (FL; 2021 missing), Garland (TX), Grand Rapids (MI), Greeley (CO), Green Bay (WI), Greensboro (NC), Hampton (VA), Hartford (CT), Henderson (NV), Hialeah (FL; 2021 missing), High Point (NC), Honolulu (HI), Houston (TX), Huntington Beach (CA; 2021 missing), Independence (MO), Indianapolis (IN), Irving (TX), Jackson (MS, 2021 missing), Joliet (IL, 2021 unreliable), Kansas City (MO), Killeen (TX), Knoxville (TN), Lafayette (LA), Lansing (MI), Laredo (TX), Las Cruces (NM), Las Vegas (NV), Lexington (KY), Lincoln (NE), Little Rock (AR), Los Angeles (CA; 2021 missing), Louisville (KY), Lubbock (TX), Madison (WI), Manchester (NH), McAllen (TX), McKinney (TX), Memphis (TN), Meridian (ID), Mesquite (TX), Miami (FL; 2021 missing), Midland (TX), Milwaukee (WI), Minneapolis (MN), Modesto (CA; 2021 missing), Murfreesboro (TN), Naperville (IL), Nashville (TN), New Haven (CT), New Orleans (LA), Newark (NJ), Norfolk (VA), Norman (OK), Oakland (CA; 2021 missing), Odessa (TX), Oklahoma City (OK), Omaha (NE; 2021 missing), Orange (CA; 2021 unreliable), Orlando (FL; 2021 missing),

Pasadena (CA; 2021 missing), Paterson (NJ), Pembroke Pines (FL; 2021 missing), Philadelphia (PA), Phoenix (AZ; 2021 missing), Pittsburgh (PA; 2021 missing), Plano (TX), Pomona (CA; 2021 missing), Portland (OR), Providence (NH), Raleigh (NC), Reno (NV), Renton (WA), Richmond (VA), Riverside (CA; 2021 missing), Rochester (NY), Rockford (IL), Sacramento (CA; 2021 missing), Salinas (CA; 2021 missing), Salt Lake City (UT), San Antonio (TX), San Diego (CA), San Francisco (CA; 2021 missing), San Jose (CA; 2021 missing), Sandy Springs (GA), Santa Clarita (CA; 2021 missing), Santa Rosa (CA; 2021 missing), Savannah-Chatham (GA; 2020 missing), Scottsdale (AZ), Seattle (WA), Shreveport (LA), Sioux Falls (SD), South Bend (IN; 2021 unreliable), Spokane (WA), Springfield (MA), Springfield (MO), St. Paul (MN), St. Petersburg (FL; 2021 missing), Syracuse (NY; 2021 missing), Tallahassee (FL; 2021 missing), Tampa (FL), Temecula (CA; 2021 missing), Tempe (AZ; 2021 missing), Toledo (OH), Topeka (KS; 2020 unreliable), Tucson (AZ; 2021 missing), Tulsa (OK), Tyler (TX), Vallejo (CA; 2021 missing), Vancouver (WA), Visalia (CA; 2021 missing), Waco (TX), Washington (DC; 2021 unreliable), Waterbury (CT), Wichita (KS), Wichita Falls (TX), Wilmington (NC), Winston-Salem (NC), Worcester (MA), and Yonkers (NY).
2 The results displayed in table 2.1 include unstandardized regression coefficients and standard errors. All models are estimated using robust standard errors. The sample size was 459 observations (city-years) in Models 1 and 2 and 457 observations in Model 3.

CHAPTER 3. GETTING DRUNK

1 These mortality estimates were generated from the publicly available CDC Wonder (2023) mortality database. Suicide deaths include all deaths due to "intentional self-harm" (mortality codes X60–X84). Alcohol-related deaths are derived from the "Drug/Alcohol Induced Causes" menu, including alcohol poisoning (X45, X65, and Y15), but also "all other alcohol-induced causes." Most notably, these causes of death include code K70, which represents diseases of the liver related to alcohol consumption. Drug overdose deaths are also derived from the "Drug/Alcohol Induced Causes" menu. For drug overdose deaths, I only include unintentional drug poisonings (X40–X44), drug poisonings of undetermined causes (Y10–Y14), and "all other drug-induced causes," which in some cases, include addiction-related mental illnesses (F11–F16). I explicitly exclude suicide deaths related to drug overdose, as these deaths are captured elsewhere, and homicide deaths (X85) in which drug poisoning was used to perpetrate a fatal assault.
2 As with figure 3.1, the data for figure 3.2 used to depict alcohol-related deaths are derived from "Drug/Alcohol Induced Causes" menu, including alcohol poisoning (X45, X65, and Y15) but also "all other alcohol-induced causes," including deaths from code K70, which represents diseases of the liver related to alcohol consumption. Homicide victimization rates are also derived from CDC Wonder data

(codes X85–Y09). To make disaggregated racial comparisons, I harmonized the bridged-race (1999–2020) and single-race data (2018–2021). I treated the bridged-race data as the standard and calculated the proportional difference between death estimates during the overlapping years (2018–2020), then used this proportional difference to harmonize the 2021 estimate with a bridged-race standard of the previous years.

CHAPTER 4. USING DRUGS

1 The overdose death rates depicted in figure 4.1 for Hispanics of all races, non-Hispanic Blacks, and non-Hispanic Whites are calculated using CDC Wonder (2023) mortality data. These include all drug poisonings that were unintentional (X40–X44) or undetermined (Y10–Y14) and miscellaneous drug-induced causes that do not include either homicide or suicide. To harmonize the bridged-race data (1999–2020) and single-race data (2021) collection methods by the CDC, I calculated the differences in estimated rates during the years when these two protocols overlap (2018–2020). I calculated the average difference between estimates and used this to harmonize the 2021 estimate to the bridged-race estimates of 1999 to 2020. Note that there is no need to harmonize the data for Hispanics of all races as the bridged-race and single-race estimates organized by ethnicity are identical.

2 Note that the 2021 single-race non-Hispanic Black homicide victimization rate was harmonized with the 1999–2020 bridged-race homicide rate by examining the years of overlap between the two methods of racial classification (2018–2020). If we made the less "apples-to-apples" comparison between the bridged-race non-Hispanic Black homicide victimization rate in 2014 and the single-race classification in 2021, the increase is 83 percent rather than 76 percent. Homicide statistics are derived from mortality due to "assault" using CDC codes X85–Y09.

CHAPTER 5. BUYING A GUN

1 It should be noted that the monthly record for the greatest number of background checks for firearm purchases occurred in March 2021. It is unclear why the number of firearm purchases continued to increase, although it may have been a combination of the $1,400 stimulus checks provided by the Biden administration and renewed media discussions about potential firearm restrictions after a mass shooting (see Alcorn 2021).

2 The data used for this correlation between the firearm purchases and crime perceptions come from historical Gallup polls (Brennan 2022b); specifically, the statistic used here is the response that there was "more" crime in the US or community than there was the year before. The missing years of survey data were imputed using linear interpolation. The correlation between the national perceptions of crime and firearm purchasing trends ($r = .52$) is stronger than that

of community crime perceptions and firearm purchasing ($r = .20$), although it is unclear why national trends would be more likely to motivate firearm purchases than perceptions about crime within one's local community.

CHAPTER 7. ALCOHOL, DRUGS, AND GUNS

1 The CDC homicide data are derived from the CDC Wonder (2023) database. The mortality codes for this data are X85–Y09. From 2010 to 2013, data for Vermont were missing due to fewer than ten homicides committed in the state, as the CDC suppresses small values to protect individual privacy. For these years, I imputed nine homicides for each. I did this to avoid missing data, especially due to the fact that these data would not be missing "at random" but because the homicide rate was lower than the other years in the time series.

2 Initially, I had used data on alcohol-related mortality derived from the CDC Wonder (2023) database, but I opted for NIAAA data because it provides a more contemporaneous proxy measure of alcohol consumption. Many of the people who succumb to alcohol-related deaths die due to the slow progression of cirrhosis of the liver, which may take several years of heavy alcohol consumption to result in a death, thereby producing an unspecified lag between drinking alcohol and the indicator of alcohol consumption (death). In supplemental analyses (not shown), there was no statistically significant impact of annual alcohol-related deaths as recorded in the CDC Wonder (2023) database on state-level homicide trends during this time period. This lack of an association was somewhat surprising, as prior research has used the proxy measure of deaths due to cirrhosis of the liver to predict historical homicide trends (Batton and Jensen 2002; Jensen 2000), which is the primary cause of alcohol-related death in the CDC Wonder (2023) statistics. Additionally, in chapter 2, the national trends in the increase in alcohol-related deaths occurred at the same time as the increase in homicide victimization in 2019 and 2020.

3 Accounting for the linear impact of time on the dependent variable is an attempt to account for omitted variable bias. Omitted variable bias is a pervasive issue in multivariate regression analyses with no perfect solution (Clarke 2005). However, this approach accounts for potential confounding systematic changes in the dependent variable operating in accordance with the passage of time that are not accounted for with other covariates.

4 First-differencing is a common practice in the analysis of panel data to achieve stationarity. "Stationarity" refers to the idea that the components of the data should not vary over time, such as the mean and standard deviation. Typically, each time series would be assessed in relation to its stationarity using a unit root test. However, a small sample size (with regard to panel years) prevents effective assessment of nonstationarity in this sample. Accordingly, first-differencing is used as a precaution to account for nonstationarity bias under these circumstances, following the example of previous research (Messner, Raffalovich, and

Sutton 2010). An added benefit of first-differencing the data is that it reduces potential issues of collinearity bias as well. There was no evidence of collinearity bias within the data after first-differencing each time series.

5 In each of the homicide models displayed, alcohol, drugs, and guns contributed to a significant amount of the explained variation in homicide trends. In Model 1 of table 7.3, the control variables accounted for only 10 percent more variance explained above what was accounted for by trends in alcohol, drugs, and guns alone (14 percent). There is a similar dynamic in Model 5 of table 7.4, as 17 percent of the 27 percent variance explained was explained by alcohol, drugs, and guns. While it is certainly true that changes in the incarceration rate accounted for a significant portion of the variance explained within the homicide models as well, these results provide further confirmation of the arguments advanced in chapters 3 through 5.

CHAPTER 8. PROTESTS, POLICING, AND CRIME

1 The 299 cities included in this sample were selected using the criteria of having at least one hundred thousand residents in 2020 and possessing complete data for crime-related variables. The city-level crime data were derived from the FBI's (2022) Crime Data Explorer in 2021 and early 2022. The list of cities in this samples is included here, with an asterisk indicating that this city was not included in the final analysis, which includes only 249 of these 299 cities. The cities in the sample include Abilene (TX), Akron (OH), Albuquerque (NM)*, Alexandria (VA), Allen (TX), Amarillo (TX), Amherst Town (NY)*, Anaheim (CA), Anchorage (AK), Ann Arbor (MI), Antioch (CA), Arlington (TX), Arvada (CO), Athens-Clarke County (GA), Aurora (CO), Aurora (IL)*, Austin (TX), Bakersfield (CA), Baltimore (MD)*, Baton Rouge (LA), Beaumont (TX), Bellevue (WA), Bend (OR), Berkeley (CA), Billings (MT), Boise (ID), Boston (MA), Boulder (CO), Bridgeport (CT), Broken Arrow (OK), Brownsville (TX), Buffalo (NY), Burbank (CA), Cambridge (MA), Cape Coral (FL), Carlsbad (CA), Carrollton (TX)*, Cary (NC), Cedar Rapids (IA), Centennial (CO), Chandler (AZ), Charleston (SC), Charlotte-Mecklenburg (NC), Chattanooga (TN), Chesapeake (VA), Chicago (IL)*, Chico (CA), Chula Vista (CA), Cincinnati (OH)*, Clarksville (TN), Clearwater (FL), Cleveland (OH), Clovis (CA), College Station (TX), Colorado Springs (CO), Columbia (MO), Columbia (SC), Columbus (OH), Concord (CA), Coral Springs (FL), Corona (CA), Corpus Christi (TX), Costa Mesa (CA), Dallas (TX), Daly City (CA), Davenport (IA), Davie (FL)*, Dayton (OH), Denton (TX), Denver (CO), Des Moines (IA), Detroit (MI), Downey (CA), Durham (NC), Edinburg (TX), El Cajon (CA), El Monte (CA), El Paso (TX), Elgin (IL)*, Elizabeth (NJ), Elk Grove (CA), Escondido (CA), Eugene (OR), Evansville (IN)*, Everett (WA), Fairfield (CA), Fargo (ND), Fayetteville (NC), Fontana (CA), Fort Collins (CO). Fort Lauderdale (FL), Fort Wayne (IN), Fort Worth (TX), Fremont (CA), Fresno

(CA)*, Frisco (TX), Fullerton (CA), Gainesville (FL), Garden Grove (CA), Garland (TX), Gilbert (AZ), Glendale (AZ)*, Glendale (CA), Grand Prairie (TX), Grand Rapids (MI), Greeley (CO), Green Bay (WI), Greensboro (NC), Gresham (OR), Hampton (VA), Hartford (CT), Hayward (CA), Henderson (NV)*, Hialeah (FL), High Point (NC), Hillsboro (OR), Hollywood (FL)*, Honolulu (HI)*, Houston (TX), Huntington Beach (CA), Independence (MO), Indianapolis (IN), Inglewood (CA), Irvine (CA), Irving (TX), Jackson (MS)*, Jacksonville (FL)*, Jersey City (NJ), Joliet (IL)*, Jurupa Valley (CA)*, Kansas City (MO), Kent (WA), Killeen (TX), Knoxville (TN), Lafayette (LA), Lakeland (FL), Lakewood (CO), Lakewood Township (NJ)*, Lancaster (CA)*, Lansing (MI), Laredo (TX), Las Cruces (NM)*, Las Vegas Metro (NV), League City (TX), Lees Summit (MO), Lewisville (TX), Lexington (KY), Lincoln (NE)*, Little Rock (AR), Long Beach (CA), Los Angeles (CA), Louisville Metro (KY)*, Lowell (MA), Lubbock (TX), Madison (WI)*, Manchester (NH), McAllen (TX), McKinney (TX), Memphis (TN), Meridian (ID), Mesa (AZ), Mesquite (TX), Miami (FL), Miami Gardens (FL), Milwaukee (WI)*, Minneapolis (MN), Miramar (FL), Modesto (CA), Moreno Valley (CA)*, Murfreesboro (TN), Murrieta (CA), Nampa (ID), Naperville (IL)*, Nashville (TN), New Haven (CT), New Orleans (LA), New York (NY)*, Newark (NJ), Newport News (VA), Norfolk (VA), Norman (OK), North Charleston (SC), North Las Vegas (NV), Norwalk (CA)*, Oakland (CA), Oceanside (CA), Odessa (TX)*, Oklahoma City (OK), Olathe (KS*), Omaha (NE), Ontario (CA), Orange (CA), Orlando (FL), Overland Park (KS)*, Oxnard (CA), Palm Bay (FL), Palmdale (CA)*, Pasadena (CA), Pasadena (TX), Paterson (NJ), Pearland (TX), Pembroke Pines (FL), Peoria (AZ), Peoria (IL)*, Phoenix (AZ), Plano (TX), Pomona (CA), Pompano Beach (FL)*, Port St. Lucie (FL), Portland (OR), Providence (RI), Pueblo (CO), Raleigh (NC)*, Rancho Cucamonga (CA)*, Reno (NV), Renton (WA), Rialto (CA), Richardson (TX), Richmond (CA), Richmond (TX), Richmond (VA), Riverside (CA), Rochester (MN), Rochester (NY), Rockford (IL), Roseville (CA), Round Rock (TX)*, Sacramento (CA), Salem (OR), Salinas (CA), Salt Lake City (UT), San Angelo (TX)*, San Antonio (TX), San Bernardino (CA), San Diego (CA), San Francisco (CA), San Jose (CA), San Mateo (CA), Sandy Springs (GA), Santa Ana (CA), Santa Clarita (CA)*, Santa Maria (CA)*, Santa Rosa (CA)*, Scottsdale (AZ), Seattle (WA), Shreveport (LA), Simi Valley (CA), Sioux Falls (SD), South Bend (IN), Sparks (NV), Spokane (WA), Spokane Valley (WA), Springfield (IL)*, Springfield (MA), Springfield (MO), St. Louis (MO), St. Paul (MN), St. Petersburg (FL), Stamford (CT), Sterling Heights (MI), Stockton (CA), Sugar Land (TX), Sunnyvale (CA), Surprise (AZ), Syracuse (NY), Tacoma (WA), Tallahassee (FL), Tampa (FL), Temecula (CA)*, Tempe (AZ), Thornton (CA), Thousand Oaks (CA)*, Toledo (OH), Torrance (CA), Tucson (AZ), Tulsa (OK), Tyler (TX), Vacaville (CA), Vallejo (CA), Vancouver (WA), Ventura (CA)*, Victorville (CA)*, Virginia Beach (VA), Visalia (CA), Vista (CA)*, Waco (TX),

Warren (MI), Washington (DC)*, Waterbury (CT), West Covina (CA), West Jordan (UT), West Palm Beach (FL), West Valley (UT), Westminster (CO), Wichita (KS), Wichita Falls (TX), Wilmington (NC), Worcester (MA), and Yonkers (NY).

2 These four variables (poverty, childhood poverty, percentage Black, and single motherhood) all loaded onto a single component with an Eigenvalue of 2.92. Each of the variables loaded on the single component at or above the threshold of 0.7. All other components had an Eigenvalue of less than 1.

3 In preliminary analyses, I examined the bivariate correlations between these variables to examine potential issues with collinearity bias. None of the bivariate associations exceeded the cutoff for concern ($r = .8$). Further checks for collinearity bias were conducted using the Variance Inflation Factor (VIF) in each model. There were no apparent issues with collinearity bias within these models.

4 Additional preliminary analyses included examining whether the dependent variable was normally distributed. The annual change in city crime rates approximated a normal distribution, and there was no noted issue with heteroscedasticity in post hoc analyses.

5 It should be noted that a few cities in the sample had zero reported homicides in 2020. This caused complications, as the dependent variable for table 8.6 was transformed using the natural logarithm, initially causing these cities to be recorded as "missing." In order to retain them within the data, I added 0.1 to the homicide rate of each city in the sample before transforming the data with the natural logarithm.

6 For the models presented in tables 8.5 and 8.6, post hoc analyses were conducted to check for common issues in multivariate analysis. I examined the predicted and residual values to check for heteroscedasticity. One model (Model 5) presented some apparent issues with heteroscedasticity, due to the cases for cities reporting a homicide rate of zero before adding 0.1 and transforming the distribution with the logarithm. After eliminating these cities from the model, the results were substantively the same and no longer presented heteroscedasticity issues. I also examined influential outliers for the models presented in tables 8.5 and 8.6. There were no substantive differences in the homicide model after excluding cases that exceeded the Cook's distance cutoff (4/n) for homicide. However, there were some departures in other models. For example, in the aggravated assault model (Model 6 of table 8.6), there was a significant and inverse association between de-policing of drugs and aggravated assault when outliers were not included. In the robbery model (Model 7), percentage of the population aged fifteen to twenty-four was inversely associated with robbery. There were no substantive differences in the burglary model (Model 8) noted after eliminating outliers. Overall, the main substantive findings were largely robust to changes in sample composition and model specification.

REFERENCES

ACLED (Armed Conflict Location & Event Data Project). 2022. "Data Export Tool." https://acleddata.com.

Agnew, Robert. 1992. "Foundation for a General Strain Theory of Crime and Delinquency." *Criminology* 30 (1): 47–87.

———. 2006. *Pressured into Crime*. Los Angeles: Roxbury.

Alcorn, Chauncey. 2021. "Gun Background Checks Soar to Record in March Following Mass Shootings and Gun-Control Bills." *CNN*, April 1, 2021. www.cnn.com.

Ali, Safia Samee. 2017. "Tamir Rice Shooting: Newly Released Interview Reveals Cop's Shifting Story." *NBC News*, April 26, 2017. www.nbcnews.com.

Alm, David. 2019. "'16 Shots' Revisits the Murder of Laquan McDonald, and Its Aftermath." *Forbes*, June 11, 2019. www.forbes.com.

Amy, Jeff. 2021. "Georgia Official: Trump Call to 'Find' Votes Was a Threat." *Associated Press*, November 1, 2021. https://apnews.com.

Anderson, Elijah. 1999. *Code of the Street: Decency, Violence, and the Moral Life of the Inner City*. New York: Norton.

Andone, Dankin. 2021. "A Timeline of the Killing of Ahmaud Arbery and the Case against 3 Men Accused of His Murder." *CNN*, November 12, 2021. www.cnn.com.

Arias, Elizabeth, Betzaida Tejada-Vera, Kenneth Kochanek, and Farida Ahmad. 2022. *Provisional Life Expectancy Estimates for 2021*. Hyattsville, MD: Vital Statistics Rapid Release.

Ashby, Matthew P. 2020. "Initial Evidence on the Relationship between the Coronavirus Pandemic and Crime in the United States." *Crime Science* 9 (6). https://doi.org/10.1186/s40163-020-00117-6.

Asher, Jeff, and Rob Arthur. 2022. "The Data Are Pointing to One Major Driver of America's Murder Spike." *The Atlantic*, January 10, 2022. www.theatlantic.com.

Ayres, Ian, and John J. Donohue Jr. 2003. "Shooting Down the More Guns, Less Crime Hypothesis." Faculty Scholarship Series Paper 1241. Yale Law School. http://digitalcommons.law.yale.edu.

Bailey, William C. 1998. "Deterrence, Brutalization, and the Death Penalty: Another Examination of Oklahoma's Return to Capital Punishment." *Criminology* 36 (4): 711–734.

Batton, Candice, and Gary F. Jensen. 2002. "Decommodification and Homicide Rates in the 20th-Century United States." *Homicide Studies* 6 (1): 6–38.

Baumer, Eric, Kelsey Cundiff, and Liying Luo. 2021. "The Contemporary Transformation of American Youth: An Analysis of Change in the Prevalence of Delinquency, 1991–2015." *Criminology* 59 (1): 109–136.
Baumer, Eric, Janet L. Lauritsen, Richard Rosenfeld, and Richard Wright. 1998. "The Influence of Crack Cocaine on Robbery, Burglary, and Homicide Rates: A Cross-City, Longitudinal Analysis." *Journal of Research in Crime and Delinquency* 35 (3): 316–340.
Baumer, Eric, María Vélez, and Richard Rosenfeld. 2018. "Bringing Crime Trends Back into Criminology: A Critical Assessment of the Literature and Blueprint for Future Inquiry." *Annual Review of Criminology* 1:39–61.
Baumer, Eric, and Kevin T. Wolff. 2014. "Evaluating Contemporary Crime Drop(s) in America, New York City, and Many Other Places." *Justice Quarterly* 31 (1): 5–38.
Becker, Gary S. 1968. "Crime and Punishment: An Economic Approach." *Journal of Political Economy* 76 (2): 169–217.
Becker, Howard S. 1963. *Outsiders: Studies in the Sociology of Deviance*. New York: Free Press.
Beetham, David. 2013. *The Legitimation of Power*. New York: Springer.
Benjamin, Arlin J., Jr., Sven Kepes, and Brad J. Bushman. 2018. "Effects of Weapons on Aggressive Thoughts, Angry Feelings, Hostile Appraisals, and Aggressive Behavior: A Meta-analytic Review of the Weapons Effect Literature." *Personality and Social Psychology Review* 22 (4): 347–377.
Berg, Mark T. 2019. "Trends in the Lethality of American Violence." *Homicide Studies* 23 (3): 262–284.
Bier, Davis J. 2022. "Fentanyl is Smuggled for U.S. Citizens by U.S. Citizens, Not Asylum Seekers." *Cato at Liberty* (blog), Cato Institute, September 14, 2022. www.cato.org.
Black, Donald. 1983. "Crime as Social Control." *American Sociological Review* 48 (1): 34–45.
Blumstein, Alfred. 1995. "Youth Violence, Guns, and the Illicit-Drug Industry." *Journal of Criminal Law and Criminology* 86 (1): 10–36.
Blumstein, Alfred, Frederick P. Rivara, and Richard Rosenfeld. 2000. "The Rise and Decline of Homicide—and Why." *Annual Review of Public Health* 21:505–541.
Boine, Claire, Michael Siegel, Craig Ross, Eric W. Fleegler, and Ted Alcorn. 2020. "What Is Gun Culture? Cultural Variations and Trends across the United States." *Humanities and Social Sciences Communications* 7 (21). https://doi.org/10.1057/s41599-020-0520-6.
Bowers, William J., and Glenn L. Pierce. 1980. "Deterrence or Brutalization: What Is the Effect of Executions?" *Crime & Delinquency* 26 (4): 453–484.
Brady, Henry E., and Thomas B. Kent. 2022. "Fifty Years of Declining Confidence and Increasing Polarization in Trust in American Institutions." *Daedalus* 151(4): 43–66.
Braga, Anthony A., Lisa M. Barao, Garen J. Wintemute, Steve Valle, and Jaimie Valente. 2022. "Privately Manufactured Firearms, Newly Purchased Firearms, and the Rise of Urban Gun Violence." *Preventative Medicine* 165 (A): 107231. https://doi.org/10.1016/j.ypmed.2022.107231.

Braga, Anthony A., Elizabeth Griffiths, Keller Sheppard, and Stephen Douglas. 2021. "Firearm Instrumentality: Do Guns Make Violent Situations More Lethal?" *Annual Review of Criminology* 4:147–164.

Braga, Anthony A., David M. Kennedy, Elin J. Waring, and Anne Morrison Piehl. 2001. "Problem-Oriented Policing, Deterrence, and Youth Violence: An Evaluation of Boston's Operation Ceasefire." *Journal of Research in Crime and Delinquency* 38 (3): 195–225.

Braga, Anthony A., Andrew V. Papachristos, and David M. Hureau. 2012. "The Effects of Hot Spot Policing on Crime: An Updated Systematic Review and Meta-Analysis." *Justice Quarterly* 31 (4): 633–663.

Braga, Anthony A., Brandon S. Turchan, Andrew V. Papachristos, and David M. Hureau. 2019. "Hot Spots Policing and Crime Reduction: An Update of an Ongoing Systematic Review and Meta-analysis." *Journal of Experimental Criminology* 15:289–311.

Braga, Anthony A., and David L. Weisburd. 2012. "The Effects of Focused Deterrence Strategies on Crime: A Systematic Review and Meta-Analysis of the Empirical Evidence." *Journal of Research in Crime and Delinquency* 49 (3): 323–358.

Brantingham, P. Jeffrey, Jeremy Carter, John McDonald, Chris Melde, and George Mohler. 2021. "Is the Recent Surge in Violence in American Cities Due to Contagion?" *Journal of Criminal Justice* 76 (September–October): 101848.

Brenan, Megan. 2021. "Americans' Trust in Government Remains Low." Gallup, September 30, 2021. https://news.gallup.com.

———. 2022a. "Congressional Approval Sinks to 18% as Democrats Sour Further." Gallup, January 21, 2022. https://news.gallup.com.

———. 2022b. "Record-High 56% in U.S. Perceive Local Crime Has Increased." Gallup, October 28, 2022. https://news.gallup.com.

Brennan Center for Justice. 2022. "Voting Laws Roundup: February 2022." www.brennancenter.org.

Broidy, Lisa M., Jerry K. Daday, Cameron S. Crandall, David P. Sklar, and Peter F. Jost. 2006. "Exploring Demographic, Structural, and Behavioral Overlap among Homicide Offenders and Victims." *Homicide Studies* 10 (3): 155–180.

Brownlee, Chip. 2023. "A Majority of U.S. States Now Have Permitless Carry." *The Trace*, April 3, 2023. www.thetrace.org.

Brunson, Rod K., and Brian A. Wade. 2019. "'Oh Hell No, We Don't Talk to Police.'" *Criminology & Public Policy* 18 (3): 623–648.

Bureau of Economic Analysis. 2022a. "Employment by State." US Department of Commerce. www.bea.gov.

———. 2022b. "GDP by State." US Department of Commerce. www.bea.gov.

Campedelli, Gian Maria, Alberto Aziani, and Serena Favarin. 2021. "Exploring the Immediate Effects of COVID-19 Containment Policies on Crime: An Empirical Analysis of the Short-Term Aftermath in Los Angeles." *American Journal of Criminal Justice* 46:705–727.

Cantor, David, and Kenneth C. Land. 1985. "Unemployment and Crime Rates in the Post–World War II United States: A Theoretical and Empirical Analysis." *American Sociological Review* 50 (3): 317–332.

Capellan, Joel A., Rachel Lautenschlager, and Jason R. Silva. 2020. "Deconstructing the Ferguson Effect: A Multilevel Mediation analysis of Public Scrutiny, De-policing, and Crime." *Journal of Crime and Justice* 43 (2): 125–144.

Carlson, Jennifer. 2015. *Citizen-Protectors: The Everyday Politics of Guns in an Age of Decline.* New York: Oxford University Press.

———. 2023. *Merchants of the Right: Gun Sellers and the Crisis of American Democracy.* Princeton, NJ: Princeton University Press.

Carr, Patrick J., Laura Napolitano, and Jessica Keating. 2007. "We Never Call the Cops and Here Is Why: A Qualitative Examination of Legal Cynicism in Three Philadelphia Neighborhoods." *Criminology* 45 (2): 445–480.

Carson, E. Ann. 2022. "Prisoners in 2021—Statistical Tables." Bureau of Justice Statistics, US Department of Justice. https://bjs.ojp.gov.

Case, Anne, and Angus Deaton. 2015. "Rising Morbidity and Mortality in Midlife among White Non-Hispanic Americans in the 21st Century." *PNAS* 112 (49): 15078–15083.

———. 2020. *Deaths of Despair and the Future of Capitalism.* Princeton, NJ: Princeton University Press.

Cassell, Paul. 2020. "Explaining the Recent Homicide Spikes in U.S. Cities: The 'Minneapolis Effect' and the Decline of Proactive Policing." *Federal Sentencing Reporter* 33 (1–2): 83–127.

CDC Wonder. 2023. "National Center for Health Statistics: Mortality Data on CDC Wonder." Centers for Disease Control. https://wonder.cdc.gov.

Centers for Disease Control. 2011. "Prescription Painkiller Overdoses at Epidemic Levels." www.cdc.gov.

———. 2024. "U.S. Overdose Deaths Decrease in 2023, First Time since 2018." May 15, 2024. www.cdc.gov.

Chauhan, Preeti, Magdalena Cerdá, Steven F. Messner, Melissa Tracy, Kenneth Tardiff, and Sandro Galea. 2011. "Race/Ethnic-Specific Homicide Rates in New York City: Evaluating the Impact of Broken Windows Policing and Crack Cocaine Markets." *Homicide Studies* 15 (3): 268–290.

Cheng, Cheng, and Mark Hoekstra. 2012. "Does Strengthening Self-Defense Law Deter Crime of Escalate Violence? Evidence from Castle Doctrine." National Bureau of Economic Research Working Paper 18134. www.nber.org.

Cheng, Cheng, and Wei Long. 2022. "The Effect of Highly Publicized Police Killing on Policing: Evidence from Large U.S. Cities." *Journal of Public Economics* 206 (February): 104557.

Clarke, Kevin A. 2005. "The Phantom Menace: Omitted Variable Bias in Econometric Research." *Conflict Management and Peace Science* 22 (4): 341–352.

Cline Center for Advanced Social Research. 2022. "It Was an Attempted Coup: The Cline Center's Coup d'État Project Categorized the January 6, 2021 Assault on the US Capitol." https://clinecenter.illinois.edu.

Cohen, Lawrence, and Marcus Felson. 1979. "Social Change and Crime Rate Trends: A Routine Activity Approach." *American Sociological Review* 44 (4): 588–608.

Cook, Philip J. 2018. "Gun Markets." *Annual Review of Criminology* 1:359–377.

Cork, Daniel. 1999. "Examining Space-Time Interaction in City-Level Homicide Data: Crack Markets and the Diffusion of Guns among Youth." *Journal of Quantitative Criminology* 15 (4): 379–406.

Cross, Allison R., Kelsey E. Tom, Danielle Wallace, Rick Trinkner, and Adam D. Fine. 2023. "Did George Floyd's Murder Shape the Public's Felt Obligation to Obey the Police?" *Law and Human Behavior* 47 (4): 510–525.

Dannenbaum, Jed. 1981. "The Origins of Temperance Activism and Militancy among American Women." *Journal of Social History* 15 (2): 235–252.

Darke, Shane. 2010. "The Toxicology of Homicide Offenders and Victims: A Review." *Drug and Alcohol Review* 29 (2): 202–215.

Death Penalty Information Center. 2020. "Murder Rate of Death Penalty States Compared to Non-Death Penalty States." https://deathpenaltyinfo.org.

Decker, Scott H. 1996. "Collective and Normative Features of Gang Violence." *Justice Quarterly* 13 (2): 243–264.

Derenoncourt, Ellora, Chi Hyun Kim, Moritz Kuhn, and Moritz Schularick. 2022. "Wealth of Two Nations: The U.S. Racial Wealth Gap, 1860–2020." National Bureau of Economic Research Working Paper 30101. https://doi.org/10.3386/w30101.

Deuchar, Ross, Seth W. Fallik, and Vaughn J. Crichlow. 2019. "Despondent Officer Narratives and the 'Post-Ferguson' Effect: Exploring Law Enforcement Perspectives and Strategies in a Southern American State." *Policing & Society* 29 (9): 1042–1057.

Donohue, John J., III, and Steven Levitt. 2001. "The Impact of Legalized Abortion on Crime." *Quarterly Journal of Economics* 116 (2): 379–420.

Donohue, John J., III, and Justice Wolfers. 2006. "The Death Penalty: No Evidence for Deterrence." *Economists' Voice* 3 (5): article 3.

Doti, James L. 2021. "Examining the Impact of Socioeconomic Variables on COVID-19 Death Rates at the State Level." *Journal of Bioeconomics* 23:15–53.

Ducharme, Jamie. 2019. "U.S. Suicide Rates Are the Highest They've Been since World War II." *Time*, June 20, 2019. https://time.com.

Duggan, Mark. 2001. "More Guns, More Crime." *Journal of Political Economy* 109 (51): 1086–1114.

Duhart Clarke, Sarah E., Alex H. Kral, and Jon E. Zibbell. 2022. "Consuming Illicit Opioids during a Drug Overdose Epidemic: Illicit Fentanyls, Drug Discernment, and the Radical Transformation of the Illicit Opioid Market." *International Journal of Drug Policy* 99:103467. https://doi.org/10.1016/j.drugpo.2021.103467.

Elinson, Zusha, Dan Frosch, and Joshua Jamerson. 2021. "Cities Reverse Defunding the Police amid Rising Crime." *Wall Street Journal*, May 26, 2021. www.wsj.com.

Engel, Robin S., Michael R. Smith, and Francis T. Cullen. 2012. "Race, Place, and Drug Enforcement." *Criminology & Public Policy* 11 (4): 603–635.

Environmental Protection Agency. 2023. "Biomonitoring—Lead." www.epa.gov.

Equal Justice Initiative. 2019. "Racial Double Standard in Drug Laws Persists Today." https://eji.org.

Fagan, Jeffrey, Deanna Wilkinson, and Garth Davies. 2007. "Social Contagion of Violence." In *The Cambridge Handbook of Violent Behavior*, edited by Daniel Flannery, Alexander T. Vaszonyi, and Irwin D. Waldman, 688–723. Cambridge: Cambridge University Press.

Farrell, Graham, Nick Tilley, and Andromachi Tseloni. 2014. "Why the Crime Drop?" *Crime & Justice* 43:421–490.

Faverio, Michelle. 2022. "More Americans Are Joining the 'Cashless' Economy." Pew Research Center, October 5, 2022. www.pewresearch.org.

FBI (Federal Bureau of Investigation). 2022. "Crime Data Explorer." https://cde.ucr.cjis.gov.

———. 2023. "Firearms Checks (NICS)." www.fbi.gov.

Federal Reserve Bank of St. Louis. 2022a. "Labor Force Participation Rate (CIVPART)." https://fred.stlouisfed.org.

———. 2022b. "Unemployment Rate (UNRATE)." https://fred.stlouisfed.org.

———. 2024. "University of Michigan: Consumer Sentiment (UMCSENT)." https://fred.stlouisfed.org.

Feldmeyer, Ben, Francis T. Cullen, Diana Sun, Teresa C. Kulig, Cecilia Chouhy, and Michael Zidar. 2022. "The Community Determinants of Death: Comparing the Macro-Level Predictors of Overdose, Homicide, and Suicide Deaths, 2000 to 2015." *Socius: Sociological Research for a Dynamic World* 8:1–24.

Felson, Marcus, and Ronald Clarke. 1998. "Opportunity Makes the Thief." *Police Research Series* 98:1–36.

Felson, Richard. 1996. "Big People Hit Little People: Sex Differences in Physical Power and Interpersonal Violence." *Criminology* 34 (3): 433–452.

Felson, Richard, Mark T. Berg, and Meghan L. Rogers. 2014. "Bring a Gun to a Gunfight: Armed Adversaries and Violence across Nations." *Social Science Research* 47:79–90.

Felson, Richard, and Patrick R. Cundiff. 2018. "The Gold Rush and Afterwards: Homicide in San Francisco, 1849–2003." *Aggressive Behavior* 44:601–613.

Fishman, Mark. 1978. "Crime Waves as Ideology." *Social Problems* 25 (5): 531–543.

FiveThirtyEight. 2022. "How Popular Is Joe Biden?" https://projects.fivethirtyeight.com.

Fox, James Alan. 1996. *Trends in Juvenile Violence: A Report to the United States Attorney General on Current and Future Rates of Juvenile Offending*. Washington, DC: Bureau of Justice Statistics.

Fox, James Alan, and Marianne Zawitz. 2007. *Homicide Trends in the United States*. Washington, DC: Bureau of Justice Statistics.

Franklin, Jonathan, and Emma Bowman. 2023. "What We Know about the Killing of Tyre Nichols." *NPR*, January 28, 2023. www.npr.org.

Franklin, Travis W., and Tri Keah S. Henry. 2020. "Racial Disparities in Federal Sentencing Outcomes: Clarifying the Role of Criminal History." *Crime & Delinquency* 66 (1): 3–32.

Friedman, Andy, and Mason Youngblood. 2022. "Nobody Defunded the Police: A Study." *Real News Network*, April 18, 2022. https://therealnews.com.

Fukuyama, Francis. 1989. "The End of History?" *National Interest* 16:3–18.

Gallup. 2022. "Confidence in Institutions." https://news.gallup.com.

Gandelman, Néster, Ignacio Munyo, and Emanuel Schertz. 2023. "Does Paying with Cards Reduce Crime at Stores? Evidence from a Targeted Cash Ban in Uruguay." *Journal of Law & Economics* 66 (1): 1–20.

Garland, David W. 2001. *The Culture of Control: Crime and Social Order in Contemporary Society*. Chicago: University of Chicago Press.

Gass, Nick. 2015. "'Hands Up, Don't Shoot' Ranked as One of Biggest 'Pinocchios' of 2015." *Politico*, December 14, 2015. www.politico.com.

Gaston, Shytierra. 2019. "Producing Race Disparities: A Study of Drug Arrests across Place and Race." *Criminology* 57 (3): 424–451.

Gaston, Shytierra, Jamein P. Cunningham, and Rob Gillezeau. 2019. "A Ferguson Effect, the Drug Epidemic, Both, of Neither? Explaining the 2015 and 2016 U.S. Homicide Rises by Race and Ethnicity." *Homicide Studies* 23 (3): 285–313.

General Social Survey. 2022. "GSS Data Explorer." https://gssdataexplorer.norc.org.

Gibbs, Jack P. 1966. "Crime, Punishment, and Deterrence." *Southwestern Social Science Quarterly* 48 (4): 515–530.

Gilbert, Michael, and Nabarun Dasgupta. 2017. "Silicon to Syringe: Cryptomarkets and Disruptive Innovation in Opioid Supply Chains." *International Journal of Drug Policy* 46:160–167.

Goldstein, Paul J. 1985. "The Drugs/Violence Nexus: A Tripartite Conceptual Framework." *Journal of Drug Issues* 15 (4): 493–506.

Goldstein, Paul J., Henry H. Brownstein, Patrick J. Ryan, and Patricia A. Bellucci. 1989. "Crack and Homicide in New York City, 1988: A Conceptually Based Event Analysis." *Contemporary Drug Problems* 16 (4): 651–688.

Gottfredson, Michael, and Travis Hirschi. 1990. *A General Theory of Crime*. Stanford, CA: Stanford University Press.

Graham, Amanda, Murat Haner, Melissa M. Sloan, Francis T. Cullen, Teresa C. Kulig, and Cheryl L. Jonson. 2020. "Race and Worrying about Police Brutality: The Hidden Injuries of Minority Status in America." *Victims & Offenders* 15 (5): 549–573.

Green, Ben, Thibaut Horel, and Andrew V. Papachristos. 2017. "Modeling Contagion through Social Networks to Explain and Predict Gunshot Violence in Chicago, 2006 to 2014." *JAMA Internal Medicine* 177 (3): 326–333.

Grinshteyn, Erin, and David Hemenway. 2016. "Violent Death Rates: The U.S. Compared with Other High-Income OECD Countries, 2010." *American Journal of Medicine* 129 (3): 266–273.

Gross, Neil, and Marcus Mann. 2017. "Is There a 'Ferguson Effect'? Google Searches, Concern about Police Violence and Crime in U.S. Cities, 2014–2016." *Socius* 3:1–17.

Hackney, Sheldon. 1969. "Southern Violence." *American Historical Review* 74 (3): 906–925.

Hauser, Will, and Gary Kleck. 2013. "Guns and Fear: A One-Way Street?" *Crime & Delinquency* 59 (2): 271–291.

Hawkins, Deion S. 2022. "'After Philando, I Had to Take a Sick Day to Recover': Psychological Distress, Trauma and Police Brutality in the Black Community." *Health Communication* 37 (9): 1113–1122.

Hepburn, Lisa M., and David Hemenway. 2004. "Firearm Availability and Homicide: A Review of the Literature." *Aggression and Violent Behavior* 9 (4): 417–440.

Hill, Evan, Ainara Tiefenhäler, Christiaan Triedbert, Drew Jordan, Haley Willis, and Robin Stein. 2020. "How George Floyd Was Killed in Police Custody." *New York Times*, May 31, 2020. www.nytimes.com.

Hobbes, Thomas. (1651) 1999. *Leviathan*. University of Oregon. https://scholarsbank.uoregon.edu.

Hockin, Sara, Meghan L. Rogers, and William A. Pridemore. 2018. "Population-Level Alcohol Consumption and National Homicide Rates." *European Journal of Criminology* 15 (2): 235–252.

Hoffman, Kelly M., Sophie Trawalter, Jordan R. Axt, and M. Norman Oliver. 2016. "Racial Bias in Pain Assessment and Treatment Recommendations, and False Beliefs about Biological Differences between Blacks and Whites." *Proceedings of the National Academy of Sciences of the United States* 113 (16): 4296–4301.

Hummer, Robert A. Daniel A. Powers, Starling G. Pullum, Ginger L. Grossman, and W. Parker Frisbie. 2007. "Paradox Found (Again): Infant Mortality among the Mexican-Origin Population in the United States." *Demography* 44 (3): 441–457.

Hutchinson, Bill. 2021. "'It's Just Crazy': 12 Major Cities Hit All-Time Homicide Records." *ABC News*, December 8, 2021. https://abcnews.go.com.

Impelli, Matthew. 2020. "54 Percent of Americans Think Burning Down Minneapolis Police Precinct Was Justified after George Floyd's Death." *Newsweek*, June 3, 2020. www.newsweek.com.

Ingraham, Christopher. 2020. "U.S. Spends Twice as Much on Law and Order as It Does on Cash Welfare, Data Show." *Washington Post*, June 4, 2020. www.washingtonpost.com.

International IDEA. 2021. *The Global State of Democracy 2021: Building Resilience in a Pandemic Era*. Strömsborg, Sweden: International IDEA. www.idea.int.

Jackson, Dylan B., Rebecca L. Fix, and Alexander Testa. 2024. "Sleep Problems among Black Youth Exposed to Police Violence on Digital Media." *Journal of Pediatrics*, March 29, 2024. https://doi.org/10.1016/j.jpeds.2024.114036.

Jacques, Scott, Richard Wright, and Andrea Allen. 2014. "Drug Dealers, Retaliation, and Deterrence." *International Journal on Drug Policy* 25 (4): 656–662.

Jalonick, Mary Clare, Michael Balsamo, and Eric Tucker. 2020. "Barr Defends Aggressive Federal Response Protests." *Associated Press*, July 28, 2020. https://apnews.com.

Jensen, Gary F. 2000. "Prohibition, Alcohol, and Murder: Untangling Countervailing Mechanisms." *Homicide Studies* 4 (1): 18–36.

Jiobu, Robert M., Timothy J. Curry. 2001. "Lack of Confidence in the Federal Government and the Ownership of Firearms." *Social Science Quarterly* 82 (1): 77–88.

Johnson, Nicole J., and Caterina G. Roman. 2022. "Community Correlates of Change: A Mixed-Effects Assessment of Shooting Dynamics during COVID-19." *PLoS One* 17 (2): e0263777. https://doi.org/10.1371/journal.pone.0263777.

Jones, Jeffrey M. 2021. "In U.S., Black Confidence in Police Recovers from 2020 Low." Gallup. https://news.gallup.com.

Jurik, Nancy C., and Russ Winn. 1990. "Gender and Homicide: A Comparison of Men and Women Who Kill." *Violence and Victims* 5 (4): 227–242.

Kannan, Viji Diane, and Peter Veazie. 2023. "U.S. Trends in Social Isolation, Social Engagement, and Companionship-Nationally and by Age, Sex, Race/Ethnicity, Family Income, and Work Hours, 2003–2020." *SSM—Population Health* 21(March): 101331.

Kellermann, Arthur L., and James A. Mercy. 1992. "Men, Women, and Murder: Gender-Specific Difference in Rates of Fatal Violence and Victimization." *Journal of Trauma: Injury, Infection, and Critical Care* 33 (1): 1–5.

Kelling, George, and William J. Bratton. 1998. "Declining Crime Rates: Insiders' Views of the New York City Story." *Journal of Criminal Law & Criminology* 88 (4): 1217–1232.

Kelling, George, Tony Pate, Duane Dieckman, and Charles Brown. 1974. *The Kansas City Preventative Patrol Experiment: A Summary Report*. Washington, DC: Police Foundation.

Kelling, George, and James Q. Wilson. 1982. "Broken Windows: The Police and Neighborhood Safety." *Atlantic Monthly* 249 (3): 29–38.

Kim, Dae-Young. 2022. "The Impact of COVID-19 on Gun Violence across Census Tracts in NYC." *Homicide Studies* 26 (4): 379–402.

———. 2024. "Did De-policing Contribute to the 2020 Homicide Spikes?" *Police Practice and Research* 25 (3): 343–357. https://doi.org/10.1080/15614263.2023.2235056.

Kim, Dae-Young, and Scott W. Phillips. 2021. "When COVID-19 and Guns Meet: A Rise in Shootings." *Journal of Criminal Justice* 73 (March–April): 101783. https://doi.org/10.1016/j.jcrimjus.2021.101783.

Kim, Jessica J., and Kenneth C. Wilbur. 2022. "Proxies for Legal Firearm Prevalence." *Quantitative Marketing & Economics* 20:239–273.

Kleck, Gary. 2015. "The Impact of Gun Ownership on Crime Rates: A Methodological Review of the Evidence." *Journal of Criminal Justice* 43 (1): 40–48.

Kleck, Gary, and J. C. Barnes. 2014. "Do More Police Lead to More Crime Deterrence?" *Crime & Delinquency* 60 (5): 716–738.

Kochanek, Kenneth, Robert Anderson, and Elizabeth Arias. 2020. "Changes in Life Expectancy at Birth, 2010–2018." National Center for Health Statistics, Hyattsville, MD.

Kochel, Tammy R., David B. Wilson, and Stephen D. Mastrofski. 2011. "Effect of Suspect Race on Officers' Arrest Decisions." *Criminology* 49 (2): 473–512.

Koper, Christopher S., and Evan Mayo-Wilson. 2006. "Police Crackdowns on Illegal Gun Carrying: A Systematic Review of Their Impact on Gun Crime." *Journal of Experimental Criminology* 2 (2): 227–261.

Kornfield, Maryl, and Mariana Alfaro. 2022. "1 in 3 Americans Say Violence against Government Can be Justified, Citing Fears of Political Schism, Pandemic." *Washington Post*, January 1, 2022. www.washingtonpost.com.

Kovandzic, Tomislav V., Mark E. Schaffer, Lynne M. Vieraitis, Erin A. Orrick, and Alex R. Piquero. 2016. "Police, Crime and the Problem of Weak Instruments: Revisiting the 'More Police, Less Crime; Thesis." *Journal of Quantitative Criminology* 32 (1): 133–158.

Krivo, Lauren J., and Ruth D. Peterson. 1996. "Extremely Disadvantaged Neighborhoods and Urban Crime." *Social Forces* 75 (2): 619–648.

Kuhns, Joseph B., M. Lyn Exum, Tammatha A. Clodfelter, and Martha Cecilia Bottia. 2014. "The Prevalence of Alcohol-Involved Homicide Offending: A Meta-analytic Review." *Homicide Studies* 18 (3): 251–270.

Lacombe, Matthew, Matthew Simonson, Jon Green, and James Druckman. 2022. "Social Disruption, Gun Buying, and Anti-system Beliefs." *Perspectives on Politics*, December 6, 2022. https://doi.org/10.1017/S1537592722003322.

LaFree, Gary. 1998. *Losing Legitimacy: Street Crime and the Decline of Social Institutions in America*. Boulder, CO: Westview.

LaFree, Gary, and Kriss A. Drass. 1997. "African American Collective Action and Crime, 1955–1991." *Social Forces* 75 (3): 835–854.

Land, Kenneth C., Patricia L. McCall, and Lawrence E. Cohen. 1990. "Structural Covariates of Homicide Rates: Are There Any Invariances across Time and Social Space?" *American Journal of Sociology* 95 (4): 922–963.

Landesco, John. 1932. "Prohibition and Crime." *Annals of the American Academy of Political and Social Science* 163 (1): 120–129.

Lane, Tyler J. 2022. "Police-Involved Deaths and the Impact on Homicide Rates in the Post-Ferguson Era: A Study of 44 U.S. Cities." *Journal of Interpersonal Violence* 37 (19–20): NP17517–NP17539.

LaPlant, Kristina M., Keith E. Lee Jr., and James L. LaPlant. 2021. "Christmas Trees, Presidents, and Mass Shootings: Explaining Gun Purchases in the South and Non-South." *Social Science Quarterly* 102 (1): 387–406.

Larson, Ryan P., N. Jeanie Santaularia, and Christopher Uggen. 2023. "Temporal and Spatial Shifts in Gun Violence, before and after a Historic Police Killing in Minneapolis." *Spatial and Spatio-Temporal Epidemiology* 47:100602. https://doi.org/10.1016/j.sste.2023.100602.

Lauritsen, Janet L., and Theodore S. Lentz. 2019. "National and Local Trends in Serious Violence, Firearm Victimization, and Homicide." *Homicide Studies* 23 (3): 243–261.

Lee, YongJei, John E. Eck, and Nicholas Corsaro. 2016. "Conclusions from the History into the Effects of Police Force Size on Crime—1968 through 2013: A Historical Systemic Review." *Journal of Experimental Criminology* 12:431–451.

Levenson, Eric. 2021. "How Minneapolis Police First Described the Murder of George Floyd, and What We Know Now." *CNN*, April 21, 2021. www.cnn.com.

Levitt, Steven D. 2002. "Using Electoral Cycles in Police Hiring to Estimate the Effects of Police on Crime: Reply." *American Economic Review* 92 (4): 1244–1250.

———. 2004. "Understanding Why Crime Fell in the 1990s: Four Factors That Explain the Decline and Six That Do Not." *Journal of Economic Perspectives* 18 (1): 163–190.

Lin, Ming-Jen. 2009. "More Police, Less Crime: Evidence from U.S. State Data." *International Review of Law and Economics* 29 (2): 73–80.

Lopez, Ernesto, and Richard Rosenfeld. 2021. "Crime, Quarantine, and the U.S. Coronavirus Pandemic." *Criminology & Public Policy* 20 (3): 401–422.

Lott, John, Jr. 2010. *More Guns, Less Crime: Understanding Crime and Gun Control Laws*. 3rd ed. Chicago: University of Chicago Press.

Mac Donald, Heather. 2016. *The War on Cops: How the New Attack on Law and Order Makes Everyone Less Safe*. New York: Encounter Books.

MacDonald, John, George Mohler, and P. Jeffrey Brantingham. 2022. "Association between Race, Shooting Hot Spots, and the Surge in Gun Violence during the COVID-19 Pandemic in Philadelphia, New York and Los Angeles." *Preventative Medicine* 165:107241. https://doi.org/10.1016/j.ypmed.2022.107241.

Maras, Marie-Helen, Kenji Logie, Jana Arsovska, Adam S. Wandt, and Bryce Barthuly. 2023. "Decoding Hidden Darknet Networks: What We Learned about the Illicit Fentanyl Trade on AlphaBay." *Journal of Forensic Sciences* 68:1451–1469.

Massey, Douglas, and Nancy Denton. 1993. *American Apartheid: Segregation and the Making of the Underclass*. Cambridge, MA: Harvard University Press.

McDowall, David. 2019. "The 2015 and 2016 U.S. Homicide Rate Increases in Context." *Homicide Studies* 23 (3): 225–242.

McEnvoy, Jemima. 2020. "At Least 13 Cities Are Defunding Their Police Departments." *Forbes*, August 13, 2020. www.forbes.com.

McGranahan, David, and Timothy Parker. 2021. *The Opioid Epidemic: A Geography in Two Phases*. ERR-287. US Department of Agriculture, Economic Research Service.

McKay, Rich. 2015. "University Police Officer Cleared in Alabama's Student's Death." *Reuters*, September 16, 2015. www.reuters.com.

McLean, Katherine. 2016. "'There's Nothing Here': Deindustrialization as Risk Environment for Overdose." *International Journal on Drug Policy* 29:19–26.

Meldrum, Ryan C., Amelia Mindthoff, Jacqueline R. Evans, and Alex R. Piquero. 2023. "Experimental Evidence That Alcohol Intoxication Diminishes the Inhibitory Effect of Self-Control on Reactive Aggression." *Journal of Experimental Criminology*, January 7, 2023. https://doi.org/10.1007/s11292-022-09549-3.

Messner, Steven F., Sandro Galea, Kenneth J. Tardiff, Melissa Tracy, Angela Bucciarelli, Tinka M. Piper, Victoria Frye, and David Vlahov. 2007. "Policing, Drugs, and the Homicide Decline in New York City in the 1990s." *Criminology* 45 (2): 385–414.

Messner, Steven F., Lawrence E. Raffalovich, and Gretchen M. Sutton. 2010. "Poverty, Infant Mortality, and Homicide Rates in Cross-National Perspective: Assessments of Criterion and Construct Validity." *Criminology* 48 (2): 509–537.

Miller, Amelia R., Carmit Segal, and Melissa K. Spencer. 2022. "Effects of COVID-19 Shutdowns on Domestic Violence in U.S. Cities." National Bureau of Economic Research Working Paper 29429. www.nber.org.

Miron, Jeffrey A., and Jeffrey Zwiebel. 1991. "Alcohol Consumption during Prohibition." *American Economic Review* 81:242–247.

Mishel, Lawrence, Elise Gould, and Josh Bivens. 2015. "Wage Stagnation in Nine Charts." Economic Policy Institute. https://files.epi.org.

Mohler, George, Andrea L. Bertozzi, Jeremy Carter, Martin B. Short, Daniel Sledge, George E. Tita, Craig D. Uchida, and P. Jeffrey Brantingham. 2020. "Impact of Social Distance during COVID-19 Pandemic on Crime in Los Angeles and Indianapolis." *Journal of Criminal Justice* 68 (May–June): 101692. https://doi.org/10.1016/j.jcrimjus.2020.101692.

Molina, D. Kimberley, and Veronica M. Hargrove. 2017. "Can Intoxication Status Be Used as a Prediction Tool for Manner of Death? A Comparison of the Intoxication Status in Violent Suicides and Homicides." *American Journal of Forensic Medicine and Pathology* 38 (1): 69–78.

Morgan, Stephen L., and Joel A. Pally. 2016. *Ferguson, Gray, and Davis: An Analysis of Recorded Crime Incidents and Arrests in Baltimore City, March 2010 through December 2015.* Baltimore: 21st Century Cities Initiative at Johns Hopkins University. http://socweb.soc.jhu.edu/faculty/morgan/papers/MorganPally2016.pdf.

Morris, Camie. 2015. "An International Study on Public Confidence in Police." *Police Practice and Research* 16 (5): 416–430.

Murray, Gregg, and Kim Davies. 2022. "Assessing the Effects of COVID-19-Related Stay-at-Home Orders on Homicide Rates in Selected U. S. Cities." *Homicide Studies* 26 (4): 419–444.

Murray, Mark. 2022. "'Downhill,' 'Divisive': Americans Sour on Nation's Direction in New NBC News Poll." *NBC News*, January 23, 2022. www.nbcnews.com.

Naimi, Timothy S., Ziming Xuan, Susanna E. Cooper, Sharon M. Coleman, Scott E. Hadland, Monica H. Swahn, and Timothy C. Heeren. 2016. "Alcohol Involvement in Homicide Victimization in the United States." *Alcoholism: Clinical and Experimental Research* 40 (12): 2614–2621.

National Center for Health Statistics. 2023. "Provisional Drug Overdose Death Counts." Centers for Disease Control and Prevention. www.cdc.gov.

National Institute on Drug Abuse. 2022. "Drug Overdose Death Rates." https://nida.nih.gov.

Neil, Roland, and Robert J. Sampson. 2021. "The Birth Lottery of History: Arrest over the Life Course of Multiple Cohorts Coming of Age, 1995–2018." *American Journal of Sociology* 126 (5): 1127–1178.

Nevin, Rick. 2000. "How Lead Exposure Relates to Temporal Changes in IQ, Violent Crime, and Unwed Pregnancy." *Environmental Research* 83 (1): 1–22.

NIAAA (National Institute on Alcohol Abuse and Alcoholism). 2023. "Underage Drinking in the United States (Ages 12 to 20)." www.niaaa.nih.gov.

Nivette, Amy E. 2014. "Legitimacy and Crime: Theorizing the Role of the State in Cross-National Criminological Theory." *Theoretical Criminology* 18 (1): 93–111.

Nivette, Amy E., and Manuel Eisner. 2013. "Do Legitimate Polities Have Fewer Homicides? A Cross-National Analysis." *Homicide Studies* 17 (1): 3–26.

Nivette, Amy E., Renee Zahnow, Raul Aguilar, Andri Ahven, Shai Amram, Barak Ariel, María José Arosemena Burbano, Roberta Astolfi, Dirk Baier, Hyung-Min Bark, et al. 2021. "A Global Analysis of the Impact of COVID-19 Stay-at-Home Restrictions on Crime." *Nature Human Behavior* 5:868–877.

Nix, Justin, Jessica Huff, Scott Wolfe, David Pyrooz, and Scott Mourtgos. 2024. "When Police Pull Back: Neighborhood-Level Effects of De-policing on Violent and Property Crime; A Research Note." *Criminology*, February 9, 2024. https://doi.org/10.1111/1745-9125.12363.

O'Brien, Robert, and Jean Stockard. 2009. "Can Cohort Replacement Explain Changes in the Relationship between Age and Homicide Offending?" *Journal of Quantitative Criminology* 25 (1): 79–101.

Olson, Maren E., Douglas Diekema, Barbara A. Elliott, and Colleen M. Renier. 2010. "Impact of Income and Income Inequality on Infant Health Outcomes in the United States." *Pediatrics* 126 (6): 1165–1173.

Ousey, Graham C., and Matthew R. Lee. 2007. "Homicide Trends and Illicit Drug Markets: Exploring Differences across Time." *Justice Quarterly* 24 (1): 48–79.

Papachristos, Andrew V. 2009. "Murder by Structure: Dominance Relations and the Social Structure of Gang Homicide." *American Journal of Sociology* 115 (1): 74–128.

Papachristos, Andrew V., Christopher Wildeman, and Elizabeth Roberto. 2015. "Tragic, but Not Random: The Social Contagion of Nonfatal Gunshot Injuries." *Social Science & Medicine* 125 (January): 139–150.

Parker, Robert Nash. 1995. *Alcohol and Homicide: A Deadly Combination of Two American Traditions*. Albany: State University of New York Press.

Peralta, Eyder. 2015. "Timeline: What We Know about the Freddie Gray Arrest." *NPR*, May 1, 2015. www.npr.org.

Pereira, Ivan, and Meredith Deliso. 2023. "What Was the SCORPION Unit, the Now-Deactivated Police Task Force at the Center of Tyre Nichols' Death?" *ABC News*, January 28, 2023. https://abcnews.go.com.

Peters, David J., Shannon M. Monnat, Andrew L. Hochstetler, and Mark T. Berg. 2020. "The Opioid Hydra: Understanding Overdose Mortality Epidemics and Syndemics across the Rural-Urban Continuum." *Rural Sociology* 85 (3): 589–622.

Pew Research Center. 2023. "Public Trust in Government: 1958–2023." September 19, 2023. www.pewresearch.org.

Pierson, Emma, Camelia Simoiu, Jan Overgoor, Sam Corbett-Davies, Daniel Jenson, Amy Shoemaker, Vignesh Ramachandran, Pheobe Barghouty, Cheryl Phillips, Ravi Shroff, and Sharad Goel. 2020. "A Large-Scale Analysis of Racial Disparities in Police Stops across the United States." *Nature Human Behavior* 4:736–745.

Piquero, Alex R., Wesley G. Jennings, Erin Jemison, Catherine Kaukinen, and Felicia Marie Knaul. 2021. "Domestic Violence during the COVID-19 Pandemic—Evidence from a Systematic Review and Meta-analysis." *Journal of Criminal Justice* 74 (May–June): 101806. https://doi.org/10.1016/j.jcrimjus.2021.101806.

Piza, Eric, and Nathan Connealy. 2022. "The Effect of the Seattle Police-Free CHOP Zone on Crime: A Microsynthetic Control Evaluation." *Criminology & Public Policy* 21:35–58.

Politico. 2022. "Morning Consult + Politico: National Tracking Poll." www.politico.com.

Pratt, Travis C., and Francis T. Cullen. 2005. "Assessing Macro-Level Predictors and Theories of Crime: A Meta-analysis." *Crime and Justice* 32:373–450.

Pridemore, William A. 2008. "A Methodological Addition to the Cross-National Empirical Literature on Social Structure and Homicide: A First Test of the Poverty-Homicide Thesis." *Criminology* 46 (1): 133–154.

Putnam, Robert D. 2000. *Bowling Alone: The Collapse and Revival of American Community*. New York: Touchstone Books.

Pyrooz, David, Scott Decker, Scott Wolfe, John Shjarback. 2016. "Was There a Ferguson Effect on Crime Rates in Large U.S. Cities?" *Journal of Criminal Justice* 46:1–8.

Rand. 2021. "Gun Ownership in America." www.rand.org.

Ratcliff, Shawn. 2022. "Presidential Firepower: The Effect of the Presidential Party on Gun Ownership, 1980–2018." *Social Science Quarterly* 103 (3): 737–751.

Rogers, Meghan L. 2024. "Was There a Universal Homicide Increase in 2014 to 2016 and 2019 to 2020?" *Journal of Contemporary Criminal Justice* 40 (1): 197–217.

Roman, Marcel, Klara Fredriksson, Chris Cassella, Derek Epp, and Hannah Walker. 2023. "The George Floyd Effect: How Protests and Public Scrutiny Changed Police Behavior." www.marcelroman.com.

Romer, Daniel, Patrick E. Jamieson, Kathleen H. Jamieson. 2006. "Are News Reports of Suicide Contagious? A Stringent Test in Six U.S. Cities." *Journal of Communication* 56 (2): 253–270.

Rosenfeld, Richard. 2005. "Firearms Research and the Crime Drop." *Criminology & Public Policy* 4 (4): 799–806.

———. 2009. "Crime Is the Problem: Homicide, Acquisitive Crime, and Economic Conditions." *Quantitative Criminology* 25 (3): 287–306.

———. 2014. "Crime and the Great Recession: Introduction to the Special Issue." *Journal of Contemporary Criminal Justice* 30 (1): 4–6.

———. 2018. "Studying Crime Trends: Normal Science and Exogenous Shocks." *Criminology* 56 (1): 5–26.

———. 2020. "Is De-policing the Cause of the Spike in Urban Violence? Comment on Cassell." *Federal Sentencing Reporter* 33:142–143.

Rosenfeld, Richard, Thomas Abt, and Ernesto Lopez. 2021. *Pandemic, Social Unrest, and Crime in U.S. Cities: 2020 Year-End Update.* Washington, DC: Council on Criminal Justice.

Rosenfeld, Richard, and Robert Fornango. 2007. "The Impact of Economic Conditions on Robbery and Property Crime: The Role of Consumer Sentiment." *Criminology* 45 (4): 735–769.

———. 2017. "The Relationship between Crime and Stop, Question, and Frisk Rates in New York City Neighborhoods." *Justice Quarterly* 34 (6): 931–951.

Rosenfeld, Richard, Robert Fornango, and Andres F. Rengifo. 2007. "The Impact of Order-Maintenance Policing on New York City Homicide and Robbery Rates: 1988–2001." *Criminology* 45 (2): 355–383.

Rosenfeld, Richard, and James Alan Fox. 2019. "Anatomy of the Homicide Rise." *Homicide Studies* 23 (3): 202–224.

Rosenfeld, Richard, Shytierra Gaston, Howard Spivak, and Seri Irazola. 2017. "Assessing and Responding to the Recent Homicide Rise in the United States." National Institute of Justice, Washington, DC. www.ojp.gov.

Rosenfeld, Richard, and Ernesto Lopez. 2021. *Pandemic, Social Unrest, and Crime in U.S. Cities.* Washington, DC: Council on Criminal Justice.

Rosenfeld, Richard, Randolph Roth, and Joel Wallman. 2021. "Homicide and the Opioid Epidemic: A Longitudinal Analysis." *Homicide Studies* 27 (3): 321–337.

Rosenfeld, Richard, Matt Vogel, and Timothy McCuddy. 2019. "Crime and Inflation in U.S. Cities." *Journal of Quantitative Criminology* 35:195–210.

Rosenfeld, Richard, and Joel Wallman. 2019. "Did De-policing Cause the Increase in Homicide Rates?" *Criminology & Public Policy* 18 (1): 51–75.

Rostron, Allen. 2018. "The Dickey Amendment on Federal Funding for Research on Gun Violence: A Legal Dissection." *American Journal of Public Health* 108 (7): 865–867.

Roth, Randolph. 2009. *American Homicide.* Cambridge, MA: Harvard University Press.

Sacco, Vincent. 2005. *When Crime Waves.* Thousand Oaks, CA: Sage.

Saez, Emmanuel, and Gabriel Zucman. 2020. "The Rise of Income and Wealth Inequality in America: Evidence from Distributional Macroeconomic Accounts." *Journal of Economic Perspectives* 34 (4): 3–26.

Sampson, Robert R., and Dawn J. Bartusch. 1998. "Legal Cynicism and (Subcultural?) Tolerance of Deviance: The Neighborhood Context of Racial Differences." *Law & Society Review* 32 (4): 777–804.

Sampson, Robert R., Stephen W. Raudenbush, and Felton Earls. 1997. "Neighborhoods and Violent Crime: A Multilevel Study of Collective Efficacy." *Science* 277 (5328): 918–924.

Schleimer, Julia P., Christoper D. McCort, Aaron B. Shev, Veronica A. Pear, Elizabeth Tomsich, Alaina De Biasi, Shani Buggs, Hannah S. Laqueur, and Garen J. Wintemute. 2021. "Firearm Purchasing and Firearm Violence during the Coronavirus Pandemic in the United States: A Cross-Sectional Study." *Injury Epidemiology* 8 (43). https://doi.org/10.1186/s40621-021-00339-5.

Schleimer, Julia P., Veronica A. Pear, Christopher D. McCourt, Aaron B. Shev, Alaina De Biasi, Elizabeth Tomsich, Shani Buggs, Hannah S. Laqueur, and Garen J. Wintemute. 2022. "Unemployment and Crime in U.S. Cities during the Coronavirus Pandemic." *Journal of Urban Health* 99:82–91.

Schöley, Jonas, José Manuel Aburto, Ilya Kashnitsky, Maxi S. Kniffka, Luyin Zhang, Hannaliis Jaadla, Jennifer D. Dowd, and Ridhi Kashyap. 2022. "Life Expectancy Changes since COVID-19." *Nature Human Behavior* 6:1649–1659.

Seligman, Lara. 2020. "Trump Denounces Mail-In Voting and Again Casts Doubt on the Election Outcome." *Politico*, September 30, 2020. www.politico.com.

Sharkey, Patrick. 2018. *The Uneasy Peace: The Great Crime Decline, the Renewal of City Life, and the Next War on Violence*. New York: Norton.

Sharkey, Patrick, Gerard Torrats-Espinosa, and Delaram Takyar. 2017. "Community and the Crime Decline: The Causal Effect of Local Nonprofits on Violent Crime." *American Sociological Review* 82 (6): 1214–1240.

Shepherd, Joanna M. 2005. "Deterrence versus Brutalization: Capital Punishment's Differing Impact among States." *Michigan Law Review* 104 (2): 203–256.

Sherman, Lawrence W., and David Weisburd. 1995. "General Deterrent Effects of Police Patrol in Crime 'Hot Spots': A Randomized, Controlled Trial." *Justice Quarterly* 12 (4): 625–648.

Shjarback, John, David Pyrooz, Scott Wolfe, and Scott Decker. 2017. "De-policing and Crime in the Wake of Ferguson: Racialized Changes in the Quantity and Quality of Policing Among Missouri Police Departments." *Journal of Criminal Justice* 50:42–52.

Shrider, Emily A., and John Creamer. 2023. "Poverty in the United States: 2022." US Census Bureau. Washington, DC: US Government Publishing Office.

Siegel, Michael, Craig S. Ross, and Charles King III. 2013. "The Relationship between Gun Ownership and Firearm Homicide Rates in the United States, 1981–2010." *American Journal of Public Health* 103 (11): 2098–2105.

Sisak, Michael R. 2023. "Trump's House GOP Allies Take Fight to Manhattan DA's Turf." *Associated Press*, April 17, 2023. https://apnews.com.

Slater, Megan E., and Hillel R. Alpert. 2023. *Surveillance Report #120: Apparent per Capita Alcohol Consumption: National, State, and Regional Trends, 1977–2021*. Sterling, VA: US Department of Health and Human Services.

———. 2024. *Surveillance Report #121: Apparent per Capita Alcohol Consumption: National, State, and Regional Trends, 1977–2022*. Ashburn, VA: US Department of Health and Human Services.

Sohn, Heeju. 2017. "Racial and Ethnic Disparities in Health Insurance Coverage: Dynamics of Gaining and Losing Coverage over the Life-Course." *Population Research and Policy Review* 36 (2): 181–201.

Spelman, William. 2000. "What Recent Studies Do (and Don't) Tell Us about Imprisonment and Crime." *Crime and Justice* 27:419–494.

Spencer, Merianne R., Arialdi M. Miniño, and Margaret Warner. 2022. "Drug Overdose Deaths in the United States, 2001–2021." NCHS Data Brief, no. 457. National Center for Health Statistics, Hyattsville, MD.

Stansfield, Richard, Daniel Semenza, Jie Xu, and Elizabeth Griffiths. 2023. "Licensed Firearm Dealers, Legal Compliance, and Local Homicide: A Case Study." *Criminology & Public Policy* 22 (2): 323–345.

Stemen, Don, and Andres F. Rengifo. 2011. "Policies and Imprisonment: The Impact of Structured Sentencing and Determinate Sentencing on State Incarceration Rates, 1978–2004." *Justice Quarterly* 28 (1): 174–201.

Stickle, Ben, and Marcus Felson. 2020. "Crime Rates in a Pandemic: The Largest Criminological Experiment in History." *American Journal of Criminal Justice* 45:525–536.

Sullivan, Christopher M., and Zachary P. O'Keeffe. 2017. "Evidence That Curtailing Proactive Policing Can Reduce Major Crime." *Nature Human Behavior* 1:730–737.

Sweet, Sarah, Gabriel Alexander, and Russell Alexander. 2020. "The Death of Freddie Gray and Its Impact on Homicides in Baltimore and Maryland." *Journal of Forensic Sciences* 65 (5): 1539–1547.

Tannenbaum, Frank. 1938. *Crime and the Community*. New York: Columbia University Press.

Tcherni, Maria, Andrew L. B. Davies, Giza Lopez, and Alan Lizotte. 2016. "The Dark Figure of Online Property Crime: Is Cyberspace Hiding a Crime Wave?" *Justice Quarterly* 33 (5): 890–911.

Tcherni-Buzzeo, Maria. 2019. "The 'Great American Crime Decline': Possible Explanations." In *Handbook on Crime and Deviance*, 2nd ed., edited by Marvin D. Krohn, Nicole Hendrix, Gina Penly Hall, and Alan J. Lizotte, 309–335. New York: Springer.

Thompson, Franque. 2021. "Seattle City Council Approves 2022 Budget with No Cuts to SPD." Fox 13 Seattle, November 2021, 2021. www.fox13seattle.com.

Towers, Sherry, and Michael White. 2017. "The 'Ferguson Effect,' or Too Many Guns? Exploring Violent Crime in Chicago." *Significance* 14 (2): 26–29.

Tuttle, James. 2024. "The End of the Age-Crime Curve? A Historical Comparison of Male Arrest Rates in the United States, 1985–2019." *British Journal of Criminology* 64 (3): 638–655.

Tyler, Tom R. 1990. *Why People Obey the Law*. New Haven, CT: Yale University Press.

———. 2003. "Procedural Justice, Legitimacy, and the Effective Rule of Law." *Crime & Justice* 30:283–357.

Tyler, Tom R., and Cheryl J. Wakslak. 2004. "Profiling and Police Legitimacy: Procedural Justice, Attributions of Motive, and Acceptance of Police Authority." *Criminology* 42 (2): 253–282.

Udall, Tom, and Jim McGovern. 2020. "Trump and Barr Use a Loophole to Deploy the National Guard to U.S. Cities. It's Time to Close It." *NBC News*, August 7, 2020. www.nbcnews.com.

US Bureau of Labor Statistics. 2024. "12-Month Change, Consumer Price Index, Selected Categories." www.bls.gov.

US Census Bureau. 2022. "American Community Survey (ACS)." www.census.gov.

US Department of Justice. 2015. *Investigation of the Ferguson Police Department*. Washington, DC: US Government Printing Office.

———. 2020. "Justice Department Announced Global Resolution of Criminal and Civil Investigations with Opioid Manufacturer Purdue Pharma and Civil Settlement with Members of the Sackler Family." Press release. October 21, 2020. www.justice.gov.

———. 2022. "Federal Jury Finds Three Men Guilty of Hate Crimes in Connection with the Pursuit and Killing of Ahmaud Arbery." Press release. February 22, 2022. www.justice.gov.

Vann, Matthew, and Erik Ortiz. 2017. "Walter Scott Shooting: Michael Slager, Ex-Officer, Sentenced to 20 Years in Prison." *NBC News*, December 9, 2017. www.nbcnews.com.

Van Zee, Art. 2009. "The Promotion and Marketing of OxyContin: Commercial Triumph, Public Health Tragedy." *American Journal of Public Health* 99 (2): 221–227.

Venkataramani, Atheendar S., Elizabeth F. Bair, and Rourke L. O'Brien. 2020. "Association between Automotive Assembly Plant Closures and Opioid Overdose Mortality in the United States: A Difference-in-Difference Analysis." *JAMA Internal Medicine* 180 (2): 254–262.

Venkatesh, Sudhir. 2008. *Gang Leader for a Day: A Rogue Sociologist Takes to the Streets*. New York: Penguin Books.

Vera Group Institute of Justice. 2020. "What Policing Costs: A Look at Spending in America's Biggest Cities." www.vera.org.

Villaume, Sarah C., Shanting Chen, and Emma K. Adam. 2023. "Age Disparities in Prevalence of Anxiety and Depression among U.S. Adults during the COVID-19 Pandemic." *JAMA Network Open* 6 (11): e2345073. https://doi.org/10.1001/jamanetworkopen.2023.45073.

Wade, Magic. 2023. "'Not as Bad as the '90s'? Firearm Violence in Small, Mid-Size, and Large U.S. Cities, 2015–2021." *Homicide Studies*, April 25, 2023. https://doi.org/10.1177/10887679231163287.

Warren, Patricia Y. 2011. "Perceptions of Police Disrespect during Vehicle Stops: A Race-Based Analysis." *Crime & Delinquency* 57 (3): 356–376.

Weber, Max. 1968. *Economy and Society: An Outline of Interpretive Sociology*. Edited by Guenther Roth and Claus Wittich. New York: Bedminster.

Weisburd, David, David Wilson, Kevin Petersen, and Cody Telep. 2023. "Dose Police Patrol in Large Areas Prevent Crime? Revisiting the Kansas City Preventative Patrol Experiment." *Criminology & Public Policy* 22 (3): 543–560.
Wentzlof, Chloe A., John H. Boman IV, Cori Pryor, and Paul Hemez. 2021. "'Kicking the Can Down the Street': Social Policy, Intimate Partner Violence, and Homicide during the Opioid Crisis." *Substance Use & Misuse* 56 (4): 539–545.
Werb, Dan, Greg Rowell, Gordon Guyatt, Thomas Kerr, Julio Montaner, and Evan Wood. 2011. "Effect of Drug Law Enforcement on Drug Market Violence: A Systematic Review." *International Journal on Drug Policy* 22 (2): 87–94.
Wiebe, Douglas J. 2003. "Homicide and Suicide Risks Associated with Firearms in the Home: A National Case-Control Study." *Annals of Emergency Medicine* 41 (6): 771–782.
Wiebe, Douglas J., Robert T. Krafty, Christoper S. Koper, Michael L. Nance, Michael R. Elliot, and Charles C. Branas. 2009. "Homicide and Geographic Access to Gun Dealers in the United States." *BMC Public Health* 9 (199). https://doi.org/10.1186/1471-2458-9-199.
Wieczorek, William F., John W. Welte, and Ernest L. Abel. 1990. "Alcohol, Drugs and Murder: A Study of Convicted Homicide Offenders." *Journal of Criminal Justice* 18 (3): 217–227.
Wilkinson, Richard, and Kate Pickett. 2011. *The Spirit Level: Why Greater Equality Makes Societies Stronger*. New York: Bloomsbury.
Williams, Sheri. 2021. "Stream of Sadness: You Black Women's Racial Trauma, Police Brutality and Social Media." *Feminist Media Studies* 21 (8): 1270–1284.
Wilson, James. 1975. *Thinking about Crime*. New York: Basic Books.
Wilson, Nigel. 2021. "Millennials and Housing, Part 3: How Wage Stagnation Has Flipped the Housing Equation." *Forbes*, December 18, 2021. www.forbes.com.
Wolfgang, Martin F. 1957. "Victim Precipitated Criminal Homicide." *Journal of Criminal Law and Criminology* 48 (1): 1–11.
———. 1958. *Patterns in Criminal Homicide*. Philadelphia: University of Pennsylvania Press.
World Bank. 2022. "Life Expectancy at Birth, Total (Years)." https://data.worldbank.org.
Wright, Richard, Erdal Tekin, Volkan Topalli, Chandler McClellan, Timothy Dickinson, and Richard Rosenfeld. 2017. "Less Cash, Less Crime: Evidence from the Electronic Benefit Transfer Program." *Journal of Law & Economics* 60 (2): 361–383.
Yim, Ha-Neul, Jordan Riddell, and Andrew Wheeler. 2020. "Is the Recent Increase in National Homicide Abnormal? Testing the Application of Fan Charts in Monitoring National Homicide Trends over Time." *Journal of Criminal Justice* 66:101656.
Young, Robert L., David McDowall, and Colin Loftin. 1987. "Collective Security and the Ownership of Firearms for Protection." *Criminology* 25 (1): 47–62.
Zanona, Melanie. 2020. "'Abusive, Dictatorial, Tyrannical': Republicans Ramp Up Attacks on Lockdown." *Politico*, May 11, 2020. www.politico.com.
Zimring, Franklin. 2007. *The Great American Crime Decline*. New York: Oxford University Press.

INDEX

acquisitive crimes, 13–15, 54, 168–69, 171
aggravated assault, 4–6, 19, 22, 58, 91, 118, 120–22, 125, 127, 129, 132–33, 139, 141, 143–44, 149–54, 157, 164, 166, 171, 181n6
Albuquerque, NM, 2, 140, 175n1, 179n1
alcohol, x, 9, 16–19, 43, 45, 49–59, 53, 62, 67, 100, 118–20, 122, 125–33, 135, 147, 157–58, 163, 167–68, 170, 172; beer wars, 69; death related to, 17, 38-40, 39, 45, 50, 54-59, 57, 76, 140, 168, 176nn1–2, 178n2
American decline, ix–x, 17–18, 18, 20, 43, 45, 58, 75, 133, 157, 167; as "societal decline," 17, 50, 76, 167
amphetamines, 62, 67
anger, 49, 105, 108–10, 113, 115, 117
Antifa, 25, 144
anxiety, 49, 140
Arbery, Ahmaud, 113–14
assassination, of Martin Luther King Jr., 135
Atlanta, GA, 137
Austin, TX, 2, 27, 175n1, 179n1
Austin, Trevis, 105–6

Baltimore, MD, 112–13, 115, 137–39, 158, 172, 179n1
Baton Rouge, LA, 2, 136–38, 175n1, 179n1
beer wars, 69
Biden, Joe, 82, 89
Bitcoin, 49
Black Lives Matter, x, 25, 88–89, 104, 144
Boston, MA, 175n1, 179n1; Operation ceasefire, 34

Bridgeport, CT, 140, 175n1, 179n1
broken windows policing, 25
Brown, Michael, 9, 104–6, 112
brutality, police, x, 4, 9, 11, 16, 19, 21, 40–41, 99–101, 103, 106–12, 115–17, 158
brutalization effect, 18–19, 101, 109–10, 112, 113–17, 155–56, 158, 171–72
Buffalo, NY, 140, 175n1, 179n1
burglary, 4–6, 13–15, 22, 53, 118, 120–22, 124, 127, 129–30, 132–33, 139, 141, 143–44, 149, 151–54, 157, 162, 164, 168–69, 171

Canada, 48
capital punishment, death penalty or, 30, 101, 109, 116
Castile, Philando, 110, 115
Chauvin, Derek, 10, 114
Chicago, IL, 24, 70, 112, 138, 166, 179n1
China, 70
Cincinnati, OH, 138, 140, 175n1, 179n1
Cirrhosis of the liver, 48, 52, 178n2
civil rights movement, 1960s, x, 19, 115, 135
CHOP (Capitol Hill Occupation Protest) zone, 23
Cleveland, OH, 112, 137–38, 175n1, 179n1
Collar, Gilbert, 105–6
collective consciousness, 1, 3
Colorado, 7
Columbus, OH, 2, 179n1
Congress, U.S., 78, 82, 136
consumer sentiment, 12–13
contagion: of violence, 70, 165–67; of suicide, 111
college degree, 48, 63–64, 146, 148–51, 153

203

Constitution, U.S.; First Amendment, 89; Second Amendment, 78, 88; Fourth Amendment, 104; Fourteenth Amendment, 104; Eighteenth Amendment, 51
COVID-19, 17–18, 27, 36–40, 72, 88, 125, 147–50, 153, 162; as "pandemic," x, 23, 38, 40, 44, 47–48, 89, 113–14, 126, 139–43, 159, 166
coup d'état, 18, 83, 89
crack cocaine epidemic, 12, 53, 70–71, 75
crime: acquisitive, 13–15, 54, 168–69, 171; cybercrime, 169–70; media coverage of, 2–3, 16, 85, 90, 160
crime trends, 5, divergence of, 4–5, 14–15, 21, 107, 120, 132–33, 171; of the 1990s, ix, 2–3, 5–8, 12, 14, 14–16, 19, 25, 33–34, 52–53, 67, 70, 75, 92, 97, 136–38; 157, 160–61, 163–64, 169–70; of 2015, ix-x, 1–7, 9–11, 15–16, 20–23, 25, 34–35, 37, 42, 50, 54, 71–72, 95, 99–100, 113, 115, 117, 119, 142, 157–58, 168, 170–72; of 2020, ix-x, 2–7, 9–11, 13, 16, 21–23, 25–29, 34–40, 42, 59, 72, 95, 99–100, 113–17, 119, 121–22, 125, 133–45, 147–55, 158, 162, 166, 171
crime wave, 1–3, 5, 11–12, 22, 24–25, 160, 162, 166, 170
criminal justice system, 19, 84, 86–88, 97, 102, 106, 158
criminal motivation 1, 108, 161, 165, 170
criminal opportunity, 12, 68–69, 108, 139–40, 164
"criminological gravity," 11, 54, 157, 168–69
Cuba, 48
cybercrime (crimes committed online), 169–70

Dayton, OH, 137–39, 175n1, 179n1
death penalty, capital punishment or, 30, 101, 109, 116
deaths of despair, 17, 45–46, 50, 55–56, 59, 63–64, 66, 72

defunding the police, 10, 21, 24, 26–27, 29, 42, 88
deindustrialization; as "manufacturing plant loss," 63: as "rust-belt," 46
Delaware, 7
democracy, 44, 82–83
Democrats, 25, 84–85, 89
Denver, CO, 23, 36, 175n1, 179n1
de-policing, 10–11, 20, 22–23, 32, 34–36, 38, 40–42, 99, 101, 103, 107–8, 114, 133, 135, 142–55, 158, 162, 171, 181n6
depression, 17, 47, 49, 58
deterrence, 21, 24, 30, 32, 34, 41–42, 99, 101, 132
Dickey amendment, 80
disaggregated trends, 55–56, 59, 65–66, 65, 71–73, 95, 160, 177n2
disorder, 1
divergence of homicide and property crime trends, 4–5, 14–15, 21, 107, 120, 132–33, 171; as "decoupling," 53
doctors, 61, 66
domestic violence, 51, 141
drug(s): abuse and overdose, x, 9, 16–19, 38–39, 39, 45, 49–50, 53, 55–56, 58–68, 65, 71–76, 74, 118–20, 122, 125–29, 130–35, 140, 147, 157–59, 163–64, 167–68, 170, 172, 176n1, 176n2, 177n1 179n5; amphetamines, 62, 67; crack cocaine epidemic, 12, 53, 70–71, 75; markets and exchange, 18, 53, 61–63, 68–72, 75–77, 100, 119–20, 122, 140, 158, 164–65, 167–68; opioid epidemic, x, 18, 59–67, 71–72, 157; OxyContin, 60–61, 66; "pill mills," 62. *See also* alcohol

ecology of danger, 112, 166
Eighteenth Amendment, US Constitution, 51
employment: in physically demanding jobs, 63; in retail, 124–25, 164
environmental lead exposure, 15–16, 161, 163

exogenous shock, 16, 23, 40, 100, 120, 126, 142, 158, 172

fear, 1, 9, 31, 81, 85, 97, 108–12, 115, 117, 160, 162
Fentanyl, x, 50, 64, 70, 75–76, 168
Ferguson, MO, 9, 104–5; "effect," 16, 20–21, 34–35
firearm, x, 16–19, 23, 34, 38, 75–80, 84–98, 95, 100, 107, 114, 118–20, 122–23, 125–33, 135, 140, 147, 150–51, 158, 165, 167–68, 172, 177nn1–2, 179n5; background checks and, 96; distrust and, 86, 87; homicide rate 1980-2016 and, 93; mass shooting, 85, 90–91, 177n1; restrictions, 16, 79, 85, 90, 161
First Amendment, US Constitution, 89
Floyd, George, 10, 23, 26, 36–37, 40, 88, 107, 110, 113–15, 142, 154, 158
Fourteenth Amendment, U.S. Constitution, 104
Fourth Amendment, U.S. Constitution, 104

gangs, 34, 69–71
Gen Z, 170
General Strain Theory, 49
Germany, 48
government trust, x, 17–19, 78–79, 82–86, 86, 88, 90, 97, 102–3, 157–58
Grand Rapids, MI, 140, 175n1, 179n1
Gray, Freddie, 112–13
Great Depression, 45
Great Recession, 45

harm reduction, 61
homicide, ix-xi, 2–30, 8, 34–42, 44–45, 50–59, 62–64, 67–79, 82, 90–103, 107–9, 111–13, 115–23, 125, 127–44, 147–72, 175n1, 176n1, 176n2, 177n1, 178nn1–2, 179n5, 181nn5–6; epidemic, 18; offenders, 50–52, 56–57, 59, 67, 165, 172; victims, 37, 50–51, 56–59, 57, 67–68, 72–74, 91, 94, 165, 167; victimization rate, 36, 37, 38-39, 56-57, 57, 72, 73, 74, 94, 95, 176n2, 177n2
hopelessness, 48–49, 58, 64, 67, 171
hot spot policing, 32–33
housing costs, 44, 46, 171

imprisonment trends, 30, 128, 132, 171
incapacitation, 124, 133
Indianapolis, IN, 2, 140, 175n1, 179n1
inequality, 45–46, 123, 154–55, 165–66
inflation, 12–13
institutional trust, x, 19, 78, 86–88, 157
instrumentality hypothesis, 91, 93, 97, 165
Iowa, 7

Jackson, MS, 136, 138, 175n1, 179n1
"just say no," 61

Kansas City, MO, 22, 137–38, 175n1, 179n1
Kansas City Preventative Patrol Experiment, 21–23, 30, 32–34
Kentucky, 7; Louisville, 2, 175n1, 179n1
King, Martin Luther, Jr., 135

larceny, 13, 22, 157
legalization of abortion, 161, 163
legitimacy, 80–82, 102–4; "crisis," 18–19, 41, 76, 78, 82–84, 90, 97–103, 106–8, 116–17, 135, 142–45, 152, 154–55, 158
life expectancy decline, 17, 46, 48
"lockdown" orders, 144; as "social distancing" orders, 140; as "stay-at-home" orders; 89, 139–41
Los Angeles, CA, 24, 140, 159, 166, 175n1, 179n1
Louisiana, 136–37; New Orleans, 137–38, 175n1, 179n1; Shreveport, 137–38, 175n1, 179n1
Louisville, KY, 2, 175n1, 179n1

malaise, 17–18, 44–46, 49, 58, 62, 67, 170
mass shooting, 85, 90–91, 177n1

McDonald, Laquan, 112
media coverage of crime, 2–3, 16, 85, 90, 160
Memphis, TN, 2, 138, 175n1, 179n1; SCORPION unit, 41
middle-aged, 48, 56, 60, 157
Midwest (region), 4, 7–8, 11, 55–56, 72, 136–38, 147–50, 153, 158
Milwaukee, WI, 2, 24, 138, 140, 175n1, 179n1
Minneapolis, MN, 10, 26–27, 37, 88, 110, 113–16, 158, 175n1, 179n1; "effect," 16, 35. *See also* Floyd, George
Mississippi. *See* Jackson, MS
Missouri, 7, 135, 137; Ferguson, MO, 9, 35, 104–5; St. Louis, 2, 9, 136–38, 179n1
monopoly of violence, held by the state, 81
Montana, 7; Billings, 24, 179n1
motor-vehicle theft, 13, 113, 141–42, 168
"murder capital:" St. Louis as, 2; Washington, DC as, 137

National Guard, 88
New Mexico, 7
New Orleans, LA, 137–38, 175n1, 179n1
New York City, 2, 6, 23–25, 33–36, 70, 136–37, 140, 159, 166, 179n1
NIBRS, transition to, 27, 130, 137, 175n1
Nicaragua, 48
normal science, 12, 100, 120, 172
North Dakota, 7
Northeast (region), 55–56

Obama, Barack, 84
Ohio, 7; Cleveland, 112, 137–38, 175n1, 179n1; Columbus, 2, 179n1; Dayton, 137–39, 175n1, 179n1; Toledo, 2, 175n1, 179n1
Operation ceasefire, Boston, 34
opioid epidemic, x, 18, 59–67, 71–72, 157
OxyContin, 60–61, 66

Panama, 48
Pennsylvania, 7; Philadelphia, 2, 51, 72, 137, 159, 166, 175n1
"pill mills," 62
police: brutality, x, 4, 9, 11, 16, 19, 21, 40–41, 99–101, 103, 106–12, 115–17, 158; budgets, 24–29, 31, 42; defunding, 10, 21, 24, 26–27, 29, 42, 88; force size, 31–32; trust in 11, 19, 40–41, 84, 86–89, 97, 99–100, 102–8, 117, 142, 155, 158; violence, 41, 108
policing, 4, 9–11, 16, 20–26, 29–36, 38, 40–42, 99, 106–7, 114, 142, 145, 151, 155, 158–59, 171; broken windows policing, 25; hot spot policing, 32–33. *See also* de-policing
political partisanship, 18, 47, 82–85
Portland, OR, 2, 140, 175n1, 179n1
poverty, 47, 64, 71, 73, 123, 128, 130–33, 146, 151, 171, 181n2
presidential election: of 2008, 84–85; of 2012, 84–85; of 2016, 3; of 2020, 83, 89–90
progressive prosecutors, 25,
Prohibition, 51–52, 69
protests, x, 4, 9–11, 16, 18–19, 21, 23, 25–26, 34–38, 40–41, 88–89, 98–104, 106–8, 110, 112, 114–17, 133–34, 142–46, 148–49, 151–55, 158
Proud Boys, 144
psychosocial well-being, x, 17–18, 43, 45, 76, 158

racialized: interpretation, 106; pattern of violence, 74, 113; police violence, 41, 108; trauma, 111
racial inequality, injustice, and/or discrimination, 9, 40–41, 66, 73–74, 104–5, 110, 113–14, 116, 151, 154–55, 166
religion, 46, 84
Republicans, 84–85, 89, 136

Richmond, VA, 137–38, 175n1, 179n1
robbery, 4–6, 13, 22, 53, 113, 118, 120–22, 124, 127, 129, 132–33, 139, 141, 143–44, 149–54, 157, 162, 164–65, 168–69, 171, 181n6
Rochester, NY, 2, 175n1, 179n1
routine activities theory, 12, 124, 129, 133, 139, 164
Rice, Tamir, 112

San Bernadino, CA, 138, 179n1
SCORPION unit, 41
Scott, Walter, 110, 112
Seattle, WA, 23–24, 27, 35, 140, 175n1, 179n1; CHOP zone, 23
Second Amendment, U.S. Constitution, 78, 88
security hypothesis, 12, 164
segregation, 73, 151, 166
self-control, restraint or, 12, 50–51, 163
"self-help," unilateral violence or, 61, 68, 100, 103, 107
shoplifting, retail theft and/or, 1, 3
Shreveport, LA, 137–38, 175n1, 179n1
simultaneity bias, 29, 31–32, 124
social atomization, 46–47
social class, 17, 44–47, 60, 63, 171
social disorganization, 64, 71, 131–32
social disruption, 141, 143
social isolation, 17
social welfare spending, 24
South (region), 8, 56, 85, 136–38, 147
South Carolina, 7, 112
South Dakota, 7
St. Louis, MO, 2, 9, 136–38, 179n1
St. Paul, MN, 2, 175n1, 179n1
"Stateless" location, 61, 68
stationarity of data, 178n4
stress, 47–49, 58
suburbs, 60, 71, 73, 94
suicide, 17, 48–50, 55–56, 58, 67, 73, 76, 111, 122, 176n1, 177n1

theft: motor-vehicle, 13, 113, 141–42, 168; shoplifting and retail, 1, 3. *See also* burglary; robbery
Toledo, OH, 2, 175n1, 179n1
trauma, 108, 111, 115
"trickle-down" economics, 47
Trump, Donald, 44, 82–83, 89–90
trust, 87; in criminal justice system, 19, 84, 86–88, 97, 102, 106, 158; in government, x, 17–19, 78–79, 82–86, 86, 88, 90, 97, 102–3, 157–58; in institutions, x, 19, 78, 86–88, 157; in police, 11, 19, 40–41, 84, 86–89, 97, 99–100, 102–8, 117, 142, 155, 158
Tucson, AZ, 2, 175n1, 179n1

unemployment, 124–25, 127, 131, 141, 147
unilateral violence, 61, 68, 100, 103, 107
United Kingdom, 48
urban, 60, 64, 71, 73, 94, 135

vaccines, 48
victims, homicide, 50–51, 56–59, 67–68, 72–74, 91, 94, 165, 167
victimization rate, homicide, 36, 37, 38–39, 56–57, 57, 72, 73, 74, 94, 95, 176n2, 177n2
Vietnam, 48
violence; contagion of, 70, 165–67; domestic, 51, 141; monopoly of, 81; pattern of, 74, 113; police, 41, 108; unilateral, 61, 68, 100, 103, 107

wage stagnation, 45–47
Washington, DC, 88, 120, 137–38, 175n1, 179n1
West (region), 56, 138
Wilson, Darren, 9
Wisconsin, 7; Milwaukee, 2, 24, 138, 140, 175n1, 179n1

youth offending trends, x, 15, 34, 53–54, 70, 75, 157, 162, 169–70

ABOUT THE AUTHOR

JAMES TUTTLE is Assistant Professor in the Department of Sociology and Criminology at the University of Montana. He was awarded his PhD in sociology from North Carolina State University, where he was recognized for his outstanding dissertation by the College of Humanities and Social Sciences in 2018. His research has been previously published in several academic journals, including *Justice Quarterly*, *British Journal of Criminology*, *Homicide Studies*, and the *Journal of School Violence*.

www.ingramcontent.com/pod-product-compliance
Lightning Source LLC
Chambersburg PA
CBHW031149020426
42333CB00013B/576